The White Bonhoeffer

The White Bonhoeffer

A Postcolonial Pilgrimage

Tim Judson

scm press

© Tim Judson 2025
Published in 2025 by SCM Press
Editorial office
3rd Floor, Invicta House,
110 Golden Lane,
London EC1Y OTG, UK

www.scmpress.co.uk

SCM Press is an imprint of
Hymns Ancient & Modern Ltd (a registered charity)

Hymns Ancient & Modern® is a registered trademark of
Hymns Ancient & Modern Ltd
13A Hellesdon Park Road, Norwich,
Norfolk NR6 5DR, UK

All rights reserved. No part of this publication may be reproduced,
stored in a retrieval system, or transmitted,
in any form or by any means, electronic, mechanical,
photocopying or otherwise, without the prior permission of
the publisher, SCM Press.

The author has asserted his right under the Copyright, Designs and
Patents Act 1988 to be identified as the Author of this Work

Scripture quotations are from New Revised Standard Version Bible:
Anglicized Edition, copyright © 1989, 1995 National Council of the
Churches of Christ in the United States of America. Used by permission.
All rights reserved worldwide.

British Library Cataloguing in Publication data

A catalogue record for this book is available
from the British Library

ISBN: 978-0-334-06536-4

EU GPSR Authorised Representative
LOGOS EUROPE, 9 rue Nicolas Poussin, 17000, LA ROCHELLE, France
E-mail: Contact@logoseurope.eu

Typeset by Regent Typesetting

Contents

Foreword by Professor Anthony Reddie	vii
Abbreviations	x
Introduction	xi

Part 1 Themes and Theology

1 Christ and Scripture	3
2 Creation and Space	18
3 Context and Sin	32
4 Communion and Salvation	46
5 Creed and Story	61

Part 2 Works and Witness

6 Dissertations and Lectures on Christology	83
7 Creation and Fall	95
8 Discipleship	108
9 Life Together and Prayerbook of the Bible	120
10 Ethics	133
11 Letters and Papers from Prison	145
Conclusion	157
Bibliography	164
Index	175

Foreword

Anthony Reddie

There is no doubt that Dietrich Bonhoeffer has become something of a religious and cultural icon. Not many scholars have an international congress named after them. Not many academic theologians can claim to be a hero to young people. When I was an undergraduate student in the mid to late 1980s, I remember hearing about Bonhoeffer from my peers undertaking the BA honours in theology (I was undertaking my studies in church history). Within the student chaplaincy and the work of the Student Christian Movement (SCM), talk of Bonhoeffer was rife. He was spoken of as if he were a contemporary theological and ethical rock star, on a par with Nelson Mandela, then imprisoned on Robben Island. He was no longer a relatively conservative German Lutheran pastor. Having shared in some activities with the contemporary SCM, I can attest to the fact that Dietrich Bonhoeffer remains a hero. Such has become the mythologized nature of Bonhoeffer's persona; it is now difficult to determine where the real man ends and the myth begins.

Prior to the emergence of this wonderful text, the author and I co-organized an international conference on Bonhoeffer at Regent's Park College, in the University of Oxford, where we both work. What was striking about the conference was meeting the great Reggie Williams. Williams was one of our keynote speakers. His brilliant book, *Bonhoeffer's Black Jesus* (Williams, 2014) is perhaps the most striking debunking of the mythology that has grown around this seemingly mystical figure. In my many conversations with Tim Judson, following the publication of my SCM text on James Cone (Reddie, 2022), I spoke of the importance of theologians engaging with Whiteness. James Cone once argued that 'Theology's Great Sin was its silence in the face of White supremacy' (Reddie, 2004, pp. 139–52). We both noted how Bonhoeffer was one of the few White theologians for whom James Cone had an unequivocal high regard. And yet, Tim and I both realized, along with Reggie Williams, that Bonhoeffer 'didn't quite get there' in terms of repudiating his White privilege.

Given the iconic status held by Dietrich Bonhoeffer as a theological anti-racist hero, I have long thought that what was needed was a robust study that will wrestle with Bonhoeffer in terms of his Whiteness. David Clough's penetrating critique of Barthians being somewhat more problematic than Barth, in terms of their lack of commitment to being anti-oppressive in their theological ethics (Clough, 2023), could be levelled at the cadre of Bonhoeffer fans as it pertains to anti-racism or, indeed, critiquing Whiteness. I have lost count at the number of White people who have claimed to be big fans of Dietrich Bonhoeffer and yet their ethics and praxis seemed at variance with the very factors or concerns for which he died. This has always evoked a sense of cynicism in me. Not cynicism at Bonhoeffer, but cynicism at the White people who claimed to be his fans. The key problem when engaging with these so-called fans was their lack of awareness of their own White privilege and the implications of that as they engaged with Bonhoeffer, another White person imbued with a sense of entitlement. But while Bonhoeffer began to wrestle with the implications of his Whiteness, realizing the consequences of it forced him to be in solidarity with others who were being racialized, it was not uncommon to see no such awareness in his so-called fans. Clearly, Bonhoeffer fans often lack the moral clarity of the man himself. The critical challenge has often been one of deconstructing Whiteness. In what ways was Bonhoeffer himself constrained by his own White privilege? How can the contemporary challenges around deconstructing Whiteness learn from and respond to the ethical journey outlined by Bonhoeffer himself?

The joy of Tim Judson's book lies in the courage to reflect on and name those perspectives that have hitherto long gone unmentioned and unexplored. The joy of reading this book is to see the growth and exploration in the author himself. Black theologians have long argued that all theology is some form of autobiography. James Cone was perhaps the first and the greatest exponent of writing from within the prism of his own experience. Namely, that all theology emerges from existential concerns and contexts. The problem with much White academic theology is that the authors rarely acknowledge their existential concerns and contexts. The relationship between the theologian and their constructive talk about and of God is often opaque. Many White theologians write assuming that their work is ubiquitous and universal. The impact of lived experience is rarely explored and hardly even recognized.

All of the aforementioned are factors that are, thankfully, absent in this hugely important book. As Judson outlines in this fine text, he is on a pilgrimage. We see the evidence of this pilgrimage unfold in front of us. Judson explores how his lived experience, his encounter with God, self and others in the world, not only informs his theology but frames his engagement with Bonhoeffer. *The White Bonhoeffer* is a bold and imaginative reflection on this iconic figure. But it is more than that. It is an invitation, especially for White readers, to engage on a pilgrimage with the author. At the time of writing this Foreword, Britain has been engulfed by a series of race riots. Angry White people have descended on mosques or hotels housing asylum seekers and have terrorized visible ethnic minorities, people who are not White. This has been shocking. It has reminded us of the toxic nature of Whiteness. On 30 April, a 14-year-old Black boy was attacked and killed by a White man with a sword in London. His death did not give rise to riots across the country. Conversely, the horrific death of three young White children by a Black assailant did. Whiteness needs to be deconstructed.

The witness of Dietrich Bonhoeffer is that Whiteness can be rethought. A privileged White man can follow Jesus' teachings in Matthew 16.34, namely, to deny self, to take up the cross (meaning being in solidarity with all those who are crucified on contemporary crosses of hatred and anger) and to follow Jesus. Bonhoeffer demonstrated what it means to live for others. What does it mean to be in solidarity with others, people being marginalized and oppressed, to be alongside and in support of minorities being scapegoated, blamed and attacked, both psychologically and physically?

Most of all, this is a hopeful book. It is book that reminds us of the redemptive powers of the Christian faith and the challenges and the joys of following Jesus. Tim Judson has done a great service to the Christian theological community. This is the direction in which Christian theology should go. It charts a hopeful direction for Christian theology. It is a book that deserves to be read and recognized. Now is the time for many others to join Tim Judson on his pilgrimage.

Anthony Reddie
Professor of Black Theology
Regent's Park College, University of Oxford

Abbreviations

DBWE Bonhoeffer, Dietrich, 1996–2014, *Dietrich Bonhoeffer Works*, ed. Victoria J. Barnett, Wayne Whitson Floyd Jr, and Barbara Wojhoski, 17 volumes, Minneapolis: Fortress.

LL92 Bonhoeffer, Dietrich, 1995, *Love Letters from Cell 92: The Correspondence between Dietrich Bonhoeffer and Maria von Wedemeyer 1943–45*, ed. Ruth-Alice von Bismarck and Ulrich Kabitz, trans. John Brownjohn, Nashville: Abingdon.

Notes on quotations

Unless otherwise indicated, or quoted by another author, all biblical citations are from the 1995, *New Revised Standard Version, Anglicized Edition*, Oxford: Oxford University Press.

Unless otherwise indicated, quotes that are fully or partly italicized pertain to the original authors.

Introduction

It was the beginning of April, during the Easter holidays 2024. My family were staying with my wife's parents in their idyllic Kentish village. The journey was always long to get there, but well worth it. We currently live in Honiton, Devon, where I had recently stepped down from being pastor of the Baptist church to focus more on my academic work. Despite laying down pastoral ministry in the new year, I nevertheless felt the same anticipation of a rest with my in-laws, a chance to goof around with my kids, and to hopefully get a chance for an evening with my wife, Becca. Her parents were happy to put the boys down one night so that we could go for a walk in the countryside and a drink at the local pub.

We set off in the early evening. Becca and I enjoyed a nice cool breeze as we rambled through fields, along tracks and over country lanes. The orange sun was just setting and we were talking about goodness knows what. More than anything, it was simply enough to be with one another in an unhurried and uninterrupted manner. We were grateful.

We entered a forest path that went around a golf course and, just as it was getting darker, we were intrigued to hear some noises ahead. As we approached, the noises turned into voices, which became unwelcome shouts. From what it sounded like, the group consisted of some young males shouting racist remarks at a considerable and constant rate. They came into sight, and there were probably more than ten of them. They were mostly dressed in black, and almost all of them had their faces covered, so that only their eyes were showing. However, it was clear enough to see that these young men (or boys) were White-skinned. I apologize for quoting their words verbatim, but the starkness of their chanting still rings in my memory: 'You fat fucking nigger! You stupid nigger! Fucking fat nigger!' This invaded the space as we approached, enveloping the bird song and sound of swaying trees so that our attention was suddenly arrested by them alone.

I walked slightly ahead of Becca as we got nearer to the group, recognizing in that moment that it was a narrow path and there was no way around them. As we walked past them, one of the group (not wearing a mask) expressed his seemingly sincere apologies, 'So sorry, mate, I'm sorry about this', while continuing to walk with his crew. The expletives continued until they passed us. In a moment of, frankly, fear and anger, I turned back and exclaimed, 'Guys, seriously, what the hell?!' The apologetic guy apologized again while his companions appeared to direct their vocabulary towards me now. They did not stop walking or talking in this way but continued to hurl the abuse, now at me it would seem.

We briefly went to the pub for a drink, and the barman we spoke to said he had heard them pass. Becca was quite distressed, shocked that people can be like that. When we got back to her parents' house, my father-in-law quite rightly suggested I needed to report this to the police, which I did. They followed up with an investigation, though as far as I know, nothing has come of it.

Racism takes different forms. When many of us hear the word, we might naturally imagine situations like the one I have described above, where the rhetoric is loaded and stark, and therefore easy to identify. This incident was clearly a racist one, and I was awake in the night reflecting on how horrendous it would have been for one of my Black-skinned friends to be walking with me that evening. I am not Black. My skin is very pale in comparison to most people. I am what you would describe as Caucasian but, regardless, this incident and the language of 'nigger' is devastatingly offensive in its explicit, racist associations. Still, if I had been disturbed, how much worse, how much more horrific would it have been for those who are subject to these insults precisely because of their skin colour?

But there are other types of racism. Or, to use more nuanced language, there are types of *racialized behaviour* that happen all the time around us, and even within us, within me. This is not a book that can explore this specifically, though I raise it because I think it might help those of us White folks who say we are not racist like the gang I encountered, but who might find a certain awkwardness or predisposed prejudice or posture towards those who are not White like us.

When George Floyd was murdered on 25 May 2020, the global constraint instigated as a response to Covid-19 arguably served as a melting pot for the global reaction felt by many communities. There are many things this incident prompted, but one of the things is that White Christian communities in the UK began to become more open to the subject of race. I spoke with a Baptist minister who recalls having a church meeting where a White congregant expressed shock upon hearing that a Black brother was regularly stopped by the police. This would be unsurprising to many Black or Brown folks, but some of us in our well-meaning naivety (or piety) simply do not see these things happening. I have written elsewhere on my own journey of waking up to the reality of life that is experienced by those who inhabit a different skin to myself. We cannot reduce people's experience into lazy generalities, nor should we dare assume to know how others feel (Marsh, 2023, pp. 193–207). What we can and should do is learn at the behest of Black and Brown sisters and brothers, neighbours and enemies, who we are as those who are White. To be White is not necessarily to be normal, though I have had the privilege of living most of my life with this undergirding and unconscious assumption.

I say all of this to make a point that much of my heritage as a disciple of Jesus has been grounded in a White Western paradigm. Despite what some may think, I do not believe this paradigm should be, nor can it be, totally disregarded. There are gifts to be gleaned from within the chaff of our tradition, but we cannot fully assess that from within our own horizons. It is with well-meaning hubris that Christian theology in the West has often sought to observe and understand God and the world objectively. Indeed, some theologians talk about the Triune God as though they have the ability to carry out some sort of divine ethnography, having greater insight into the Godhead than even God does! I joke, but all jokes have an aspect of seriousness behind them.

Aidan Kavanagh offers the helpful analogy of a tour guide trying to explain an Indian rain dance: 'our intellectual ecology pushes us to accept more readily the tourists' than the Indians' sort of knowing. Learned papers on the rain dance astonish no one more than Indians' (Kavanagh, 1992, p. 10). Kavanagh is making a case for the performative nature of liturgy, arguing that participating in liturgical action means more than observing it. I agree, but his analogy is also helpful for approaching the subject of race. I am not sure about you, but if you are a White reader, you might also have something inside you that wants to, or even believes you can, understand race. There are urban myths of highly educated White theologians offering to produce magisterial systematic theologies on the subject in order to help non-Whites in their struggle. This posture exposes the epistemological imperialism within us, and the reality that we know things on a very different plane to many others around the world. That is not to say we should stop thinking, stop seeking understanding. However, the way we approach knowing, understanding, and how that relates to our practice of the Christian (or human) life requires greater humility on our part. One of the ways I believe we need to do this is to appraise our heritage, to do so in dialogue with our traditions, renouncing the inclination for epistemological mastery, and instead, embracing the limits of our horizons in our thinking and our practice. Over the course of this book, I will share lessons I am learning and mistakes I have made at times in terms of how I sometimes act in ways that are inadvertently racialized, both in terms of making assumptions of what is 'normal' and also making assumptions of those who are 'non-White'.

Bonhoeffer, race and the beginning of pilgrimage

I have hopefully couched something of the hope behind this book. I discovered Dietrich Bonhoeffer properly in my third year of training at Bristol Baptist College. I was aware of him. He had written the popular Christian classic, *The Cost of Discipleship* (also known as *Discipleship*, *DBWE* 4). I also knew him as an inspiring figure who stood up to Hitler and the Nazis and died as a result. In my first year of college, I spotted the *Dietrich Bonhoeffer Works* on a library shelf and wondered in my charismatic evangelical arrogance as to whether he *really* knew Jesus. It was only a few years later that I would begin a pilgrimage that would involve Bonhoeffer, and through which I would learn on many levels how to live by faith rather than by sight (2 Cor. 5.7).

I came to Bonhoeffer via two seemingly different avenues: Karl Barth and Black theology. I took a module for my MA course on Karl Barth and, while I struggled to understand everything in that course, I became gripped with the Swiss theologian's passion for the living-ness of God's word, revealed ultimately and fully in Jesus Christ, as witnessed to in the Scriptures and proclaimed in the church. This was liberating for me as I had struggled with an approach to the Bible that seemed fairly legalistic and closed at times. But I also wanted to revere the Scriptures and to learn how to read them faithfully, with openness to the Holy Spirit in a manner that was not arbitrary or dangerous. Barth helped me with this, and the more I read him, the more he seemed to be pushing me towards Dietrich Bonhoeffer.

It was through meeting Anthony Reddie in my second year of college that I experienced what some refer to as a 'second conversion' experience. I had long been passionate about issues of justice and had lived alongside the poor before getting married and moving to Bristol for my studies. I had travelled to Uganda and Rwanda, Israel/Palestine, as well as Thailand, which had given me a sense deep down that faith in Jesus is profoundly different (almost unrecognizable at times) in other non-Western contexts. Yet, I had not appreciated that my perception was through a lens that had been formed as a matrix of sensibilities and stories that would funnel my very perception and engender a sense of superiority within me. Meeting Anthony Reddie, learning from his radical horizons as a Black liberation theologian, I began a journey of appreciating the presumptions in my imagination, my mind, my morals and my body. The desire to serve others, especially the poor, was well meaning, but carried a dynamic that was closed from the possibility of my own transformation and blessing, positing myself as being Christ to others. I can now consciously recognize when, to my shame, I make judgements about people based on the colour of their skin, treating them in a way that offers patronage while imagining deep down that I am better than them. In reality, I have discovered through Black theology and experience that there is a Jesus in the Scriptures who confronts me on a level far deeper than I would have discovered myself. God is the God of the oppressed, and in Christ we are called to repent of the ways we share in the judgement and oppression of others, even when our intentions are well meaning.

I was remarking a while back on how pleased I was for Anthony Reddie to be made a full professor at the University of Oxford, how I considered this to be a 'triumph' for justice. An older and more Oxfordshire-formed student remarked that it was hardly a triumph, but merely a 'natural progression' in a world where 'people from these other countries are become more educated'. I get their thinking and their logic. However, while his parents immigrated from Jamaica as part of the famous Windrush generation, Anthony and his siblings were born in Yorkshire and are British citizens. There are also assumptions here regarding what it means to be 'educated' and what confers 'education' upon people. Furthermore, this student was, in my mind at least, not willing to recognize the racialized and racist institution that is Oxford. I am a Baptist, and Oxford carries deep Anglican roots, but I can walk into libraries and colleges without anyone batting an eyelid; yet this is not the same for everyone. One can become a professor at Oxford for far less as a man, from certain stock, or private school educated, but more than all of these, being Black offers a far bigger obstacle.

James Cone, the father of Black theology, refers to Dietrich Bonhoeffer as a standout exemplar of Christian faith and obedience, noting his immersion in the Black life, experience and spirituality of African Americans, in contrast to those who preferred to act like tour guides or tourists (Cone, 2013, pp. 41–2). This was not mere virtue signalling. I believe Bonhoeffer sensed something in the Black church that, while not being the be all and end all, represented something of the Christ he anticipated needing in his life. If we can overlook the now problematic language, he would later reflect that 'This personal acquaintance with Negroes was one of the most important and gratifying events of my stay in America' (*DBWE* 10, p. 315).

So my pilgrimage with Bonhoeffer has been one that began with an attentiveness to the subject of race, and a particular draw towards Black and, later, womanist theology. I am an evangelical Christian, who values the shoulders I stand on, but who also considers those shoulders to be crooked and broken in places. Why is it that evangelical Christians who value the Bible have been so disregarding of the subject of race, racism and racialization? I suppose I am writing this book out of a concern to recognize my evangelical moorings, and to recognize also how those very moorings, which I have found comforting at times, represent a Christianity that has served slavery, segregation, discrimination and White supremacy.

Bonhoeffer has been a close companion along the way, as someone whose life was similar to mine. He was born into a privileged middle-class home, raised in a nice part of his country, well educated, sporty, musical, academically bright. He was all these things on a level far beyond me, but I find in him a kindred spirit, someone who was wrestling with the question of who Jesus Christ is in a world that served him well, but which excluded and exterminated others. He was male and he was White, and while his context was different from mine, he was asking some similar questions, as a fellow pilgrim along the way. The book is not an introduction to Bonhoeffer in the conventional sense. It is more a reading through Bonhoeffer's corpus that asks questions about race. Reggie Williams, an esteemed Black theologian and Bonhoeffer scholar, once commented on how bizarre it was that Bonhoeffer's main struggle in his lifetime concerned the racialized maltreatment of Jews, but so little work on his life and thought directly touches on that subject. Hopefully this book contributes in a small way to redressing that oversight.

This book is a *postcolonial* pilgrimage. The Pasifika theologian and Methodist minister Jione Havea highlights a move that is being encouraged by the World Council of Churches, which entails a shift in language from *mission* to *pilgrimage* (Havea, 2016). Havea explains that the missionary impulse of the Western church has caused significant harm to people of other nations through facilitating the occupation of foreign land and the damage to the self-understanding of indigenous people groups, in the name of (White) Jesus. Even today, certain people live in colonized places, and there is a legacy we need to reckon with as White Western Christians regarding this. There is not the space to offer an all-encompassing history and commentary on colonialism, but I think Havea raises an important issue for us to contemplate. Anthony Reddie defines postcolonialism as 'a critical, intellectual and methodological approach to deconstructing and unmaking the surreptitious, hegemonic power

INTRODUCTION

of colonialism, which arises from the toxic residue of empire' (Reddie, 2019, p. 45). Reddie goes on to suggest that the missional Christianity of Western imperialism 'has exerted a form of cultural dissonance on the colonized mind of the Black Christian subject in the United Kingdom, to such an extent that many are unable to incorporate their own material realities and existential needs alongside that of their faith' (Reddie, 2019, p. 45). That may not have been the intention behind the piety of zealous, sacrificial missionaries, and yet the inclination to give our White forebears the benefit of the doubt needs to be acknowledged as something of a privilege conferred upon them, which is certainly not the lot of non-Whites. The much-celebrated David Livingstone of London Missionary Society is known for encapsulating 'Christianity, commerce, and civilization' in his vision of the British empire's missionary project (Snyman, 2023, pp. 279–80). While some of our heritage carries traces of the prince of peace, there is much that needs to be interrogated, such as marrying the faith with state power and privilege, which has irrevocably changed the way Christianity is viewed by many beyond the Western world. For many global communities, to be a Christian is primarily to be a White Westerner, not first and foremost a disciple of Jesus Christ, the Jewish messiah who graciously enfolds Gentiles into the people of God. Thus this book seeks to retrace familiar ground with Bonhoeffer in the hope that we might learn where we need to redress or repent of aspects of who we are as White Christians. People from a Global Majority Heritage will also be invited to host our journey along the way, highlighting to Bonhoeffer, myself and the reader where things may have been missed, overlooked or traversed too brazenly. Without this, the risk of someone like me doing postcolonial work would mean I get nowhere new or renewing.

It is quite common for people in the West to reason that 'the end justifies the means' and yet I do not think we witness such a perspective in the life and ministry of Jesus. I sometimes say to my students that if Jesus had been an idiot on the way to the cross, then whatever happened on the cross would have been a waste of time. The means and ways by which we seek to share the 'good news' of Jesus is critical; indeed, this is the heart of pilgrimage. The journey is transformative. So part of this book will hopefully explore some of the factors that perpetuate the methodological, theological and ethical disconnects and distortions within White Western Christianity, seeking more integrity between the means and goal of Christian discipleship. I believe that Jesus Christ is God's ultimate Word to the whole world, spoken in Jewish flesh for all nations to witness, but I am increasingly wary of prescribing what that looks like in particular spaces and people groups, particularly as someone who has lived so much of my life with prevailing norms that have refracted Jesus of Nazareth through my White Western impulses. Hence, this book will shelve the language of mission (of *us* going to *them*) and explore the language of pilgrimage as a posture that offers a potential way forward.

This book is a pilgrimage in a few ways. First, as I have said above, it is a generous and critical appraisal of Bonhoeffer's life and thought as it relates to the subject of race as well as occupied space.

Second, the book is a pilgrimage through Bonhoeffer's work that is limited. When I go on a hike, I spot different things along the way. The weather changes, the landscape alters through the seasons, and each time it is a different experience. I do not think this book is remotely exhaustive in its endeavour; it represents one journey through, which could be done by a different person who would observe and analyse Bonhoeffer differently. Therefore, as a pilgrimage, I hope this book creates space for others to breathe freely, to dialogue with Bonhoeffer as a fellow companion along the way.

This book is also a pilgrimage in the sense that it is not for everyone. Havea makes the point that the practice of pilgrimage is not one that is prevalent in his country of Tonga, yet he notes the way the language frames an imaginative horizon for many others such as people like me. I love going on physical pilgrimage. Since I was ordained as a Baptist minister, I have taken days out at times to walk and have it out with God. I've also been taking a week every year or so to slowly work my way from Land's End to John O'Groats, bit by bit, spiritually embodying my lifelong pilgrimage of discipleship. Most of it has been on my own, but I have had companions for short parts. One of them was a close friend, Nathan, who is a fellow adventurer, and who is also Black. He has been a dear friend and I have learnt so much from him, but hiking with him made me realize how easily I can tread the paths I chose without a second thought, while many encounters along the way resulted in interactions that were markedly racialized. People made comments about his skin colour or his hair which were mostly well-meaning but clumsily presumptuous and highly racialized. Yet no one picks up on my being White. This deserves further analysis but the point I want to make here is that not everyone has the same experience on pilgrimage as me, and not everyone can or should make this pilgrimage. I have been on the journey for a while now and it has been transformative. I still struggle to make sense of it sometimes, and at my worst I feel like giving up because it is hard, but having others to journey alongside me is a reminder that this pilgrimage is real, and some people have no choice but to keep going.

In 1934, Bonhoeffer was trying to discern whether to return to Germany

INTRODUCTION

from his stint in London, or whether to spend time with Gandhi in India. He was shocked to observe how the German universities acquiesced in support of the Nazi regime. Writing to Erwin Sutz, he opined,

> The next generation of pastors, these days, ought to be trained entirely in church-monastic schools, where the pure doctrine, the Sermon on the Mount, and worship are taken seriously – which for all three of these things is simply not the case at the university and under the present circumstances is impossible. (*DBWE* 13, p. 217)

Bonhoeffer's engagement with monasticism is already explored by others (e.g. Gardiner, 2018; and De Gruchy, 2021). A common practice for monastic communities is to undertake pilgrimage, to go into the wilderness and seek God, open to the Spirit's leading in ways that are sometimes surprising and sometimes precarious. I think this is a helpful metaphor for how readers could approach this book, especially those who are White and Western like myself.

The structure of the book

Each chapter begins with an analogy or anecdote that contextualizes what is to come, and I interact with Bonhoeffer as a key dialogue partner. It is like going on a pilgrimage with him through his own journey, noting what is helpful and asking questions or offering critiques where it seems he may have reached his limits or even, at times, having gone the wrong way. Each chapter then concludes with either a biographical note about Bonhoeffer himself or an incident in my own life.

Part 1, Themes and Theology, presents a thematic exploration of some key themes in Bonhoeffer's thinking. Chapters 1–5 are not really a summary of his thought, but a sharp focus on the ideas that carry some import for a critical discussion about race. Chapter 1 begins where Bonhoeffer would want us to start. It would not be a book that had integrity if we insisted on beginning somewhere else, though it will become apparent that beginning with Christ and Scripture could mean beginning somewhere that is approaching these themes from a different place. For Bonhoeffer, though, Jesus Christ is the foundation of everything (Feil, 1985, pp. 59–98). Here, we see how Bonhoeffer's unwavering focus on Jesus Christ as the Word of God, witnessed in the Bible, takes shape in the form of a community that embodies the word made flesh, paying particular attention to his experience in the African American church.

Chapter 2 builds on the particular experience Bonhoeffer had by assessing his doctrine of creation, and how created space constitutes who we are as human beings, that is, in our particularity, without which we fail to pay attention to the particular experiences and sufferings of others. In this chapter, I point to the helpful work of Willie James Jennings in particular.

Chapter 3 develops Bonhoeffer's notion of sin as 'the heart turned in upon itself', which is exhibited by a closing oneself off from God and others in the world through epistemological introspection, that is, the dual evil of self-mastery and the mastery of others. Here, the work of David Olusoga illuminates the way sin has been reduced to serve the religious, political and moral sensibilities of the White Western world, thus perpetuating injustice towards others and conferring blessing on European Christendom.

Chapter 4 delves deeper into Bonhoeffer's doctrine of sin by exploring how sinful certain approaches to salvation have been. The overriding emphasis in his thinking is that Christians are not those who are saved from the world in and of itself, but rather are saved and set free to live *for* and *with* the world that God has reconciled in Christ. While questions of life after death are considered, Bonhoeffer's main focus is to articulate the importance of participating in the new humanity that people are enfolded into through Christ. Salvation is not something that relates to God in abstraction, but always in relation to the neighbour and the world as a whole.

Chapter 5 seeks to address the difficulty in much of our White Western thinking with regard to universal truths about God and Christ. To reframe something I said earlier, I believe God has spoken ultimately in Jesus Christ, and yet God took form in the penultimate time and space of worldly life. This is a conflict that prompts significant struggle in how we navigate the concrete issues of our time. Here, through dialogue with Howard Thurman, I show how Bonhoeffer was straining to make sense of the penultimate in ways that were perhaps at times more anxious about 'order' in society than freedom in Christ.

Part 2, Works and Witness, moves on from the broad themes of Bonhoeffer's thinking and carries our postcolonial pilgrimage through his main publications. Chapter 6 picks out the key motifs in his two early dissertations, *Sanctorum Communio* (*DBWE* 1) and *Act and Being* (*DBWE* 2), and his unpublished but hugely illuminating 'Lectures on Christology' (*DBWE* 12, pp. 299–360). This chapter is quite dense, so the reader may prefer to come back to it if they need to. Here I show the intrinsically social and ecclesial nature of being a Christian for Bonhoeffer, which carries huge implications for social life, not just in the church but in the world. How he envisages this is worth bearing in mind for those who may be anxious to 'solve' the problems of race.

Chapter 7 engages with *Creation and Fall* (*DBWE* 3), building on the work of Chapter 2 in terms of his doctrine of creation, but reflecting on his exegesis of Genesis 1—3 in light of the coercion and imposition of race historically and presently. I attend to what it means to be human in Bonhoeffer's mind, and what it means to be un-human, which looks remarkably similar to the postures and reactions from some White folks when confronted by the subject of race.

Chapter 8 examines *Discipleship* (*DBWE* 4), and seeks to fill out some of the incompleteness within this well-known classic that Bonhoeffer himself sensed would need to be done. Having unpacked his understanding of the ultimate and penultimate in earlier chapters, I pick up some of the tricky passages in the Sermon on the Mount where Bonhoeffer retrospectively suggests there needs to be some development in order to take the penultimate seriously.

Chapter 9 takes a look at both *Life Together* and *Prayerbook of the Bible* (*DBWE* 5). Here, we explore Bonhoeffer's Christologically mediated spirituality. First, the chapter considers how he understands the reality of community in Christ in contrast to other notions of community that are based on ideological like-mindedness, lofty ('visionary') dreaming or 'love' in a self-absorbed and ultimately introspective sense. Second, we explore Bonhoeffer's idiosyncratic theology of prayer through the psalms, considering how this might reorient people away from individualistic piety towards sharing in Christ's life of prayer which involves praying *for* and *with* others, disrupting the presumptions with which White Western horizons commonly appropriate this ancient Jewish prayerbook.

Chapter 10 covers *Ethics* (*DBWE* 6), which was published posthumously and, as far as we know, had been left unfinished. Still, it offers one of Bonhoeffer's most mature lines of thought, having written these essays in the very midst of the most difficult days in Nazi Germany. The scope is vast, and so this chapter is more a survey of key themes that bear thinking about to show the theological importance of attending to race in a humble, non-violent way.

Chapter 11 draws upon the creative musings that are recorded in Bonhoeffer's *Letters and Papers from Prison* (*DBWE* 8). Here, I offer some reflections on his plumb-line Christological ideas, which he explores in fascinating and somewhat unhindered ways in these theological writings. Through engaging with certain feminist and womanist writers, I gesture at how even the most fundamental motifs in his thinking require some contextualization and nuance, lest they assume a horizon and experience that is synonymous with his own, at the expense of those who live life 'from below'. I note the impact of Kelly Brown Douglas especially, whose work and physical presence during an encounter had a profound impact on me personally as I continue to discern who Christ is today.

The reader will notice that I have not included Bonhoeffer's *Fiction from Tegel Prison* (*DBWE* 7). This is a worthwhile read, but in my own studies I found myself drawing on it less than the other publications. This work comprises a play, novel and story, all of which are unfinished. It is not irrelevant to this book, but the other works took precedence from my perspective.

Finally, in the Conclusion I offer some reflections regarding some of the ongoing questions I have as a White Christian who is entangled in the history and heritage of White Western colonialism, gazing with blurry, dim eyes (1 Cor. 13.12) for where Jesus is leading me, and perhaps, so I am not alone, leading others too.

It strikes me that when a person goes on pilgrimage, the place they arrive at is somewhere that is already inhabited by others. Some of the lessons I have learnt through reading Bonhoeffer are lessons that others have not had to learn themselves. Furthermore, the experience and theological thinking of some key Black friends has been illuminating for me, and I feel as if I have been heading to a place that they have not needed to make the journey towards, as they get it already. That is not to say I have nothing to offer them, but that my own pilgrimage has been kenotic at times, realizing not just in theory but in practice through relationship that I carry significant ignorance regarding who I am, who God is, and what this world is as well.

Already, I have used words like White and Black. I am not able to address fully at this stage what I mean by these terms, because we need to explore it. I would say that I am 'white' in terms of describing my body purely aesthetically as pale-skinned, in contrast to someone who may be described visually as black or brown. However, I am also 'White' (capital 'W') in the sense that I inhabit a body that, whether I acknowledge it or not, carries a certain socio-political freight to it, something bestowed and embraced from within a predominantly Western paradigm that developed through modernity regarding what it means to be human. For a brief introduction to this, you may want to read my short work, which is merely touching the surface of this ideological horizon that has for a long time led me to qualify people who are not like me as 'non-White' while seeing myself as 'normal' or even 'neutral' (Judson, 2024). Better still, you could read and engage with the work and experience of those who have for too long been designated as 'other' or not 'normal' and potentially less human, whose witness has arrested my heart and mind. I will expand a bit on what I mean by all of this as the book unfolds, but it was worth qualifying early on that I am generally adopting the advice offered by Kwame Anthony Appiah who capitalizes 'Black' and 'White' as a way of acknowledging the terms as those that are historically created racial identity markers. I thereby capitalize White to recognize its import as a social construct, and to acknowledge that there is nothing biologically or anthropologically substantive about racial categories (Appiah, 2020).

You will also notice that from the outset, I often write in the first person plural, talking about 'us' and 'we' as I imagine (and hope) numerous White folks will read this book. I am referring to you (Whites) when I use these pronouns, hoping you might reflect alongside me as someone who may imagine the world through a similar lens to mine. You may have never considered your being White as a thing worth considering. You may be wary of this language. You may be intrigued, and may know far more than me about the subject matter. Regardless, let us be fellow pilgrims and companions.

Of course, I also hope Black, Brown and other 'colours' of people will read this book. Those who have experienced the marginalization and dehumanization of not 'fitting' the White script and the White vision of human morality and being, I hope this book honours you as I attempt to recognize the subjectivity and supposed neutrality of Whiteness that has often gone unrecognized and uninterrogated in the church and theological academy.

One of my mentors, John Colwell, once said with a hint of humour, 'The older I get, the more I realize I don't really know anything, and the only comfort I get is that everyone around me probably doesn't know anything either.' John has written a lot about God, about the Bible, the Christian life and other such matters. I take his comment with a hint of humour (as he would intend), recognizing that everything I say here is ultimately just words. We see in Jesus that, somehow, the Word of God became human flesh. There has been a long struggle through history for Black and Brown people to be treated as human. In theory, I am sure that many of us would claim this is true. Sadly, the practice in our churches, our theological institutions, our societal structures, and our own hearts, is that this reality is not enfleshed. I hope that this book will encourage people to read Bonhoeffer for themselves. But moreover, I hope this book will encourage White folks, White Christians and White theologians like myself to consider the possibility that we cannot evade the voices of those who represent a challenge to our oftentimes White Western perspectives. To evade these voices, to avoid these bodies, risks evading Christ himself, not just in theory but in practice.

PART I

Themes and Theology

I

Christ and Scripture

In 1936, when Bonhoeffer was nearly 30 and leading a seminary in Finkenwalde for Confessing Church pastors, he wrote the following words to his friend, Elisabeth Zinn, concerning the change that had apparently taken place in his life:

> I [previously] threw myself into my work in an extremely un-Christian and not at all humble fashion. A rather crazy element of ambition, which some people noticed in me, made my life difficult and withdrew from me the love and trust of those around me. At that time, I was terribly alone and left to myself. It was quite bad. But then something different came, something that has changed and transformed my life to this very day. For the first time, I came to the Bible. That, too, is an awful thing to say. I had often preached, I had seen a great deal of the church, had spoken and written about it – and yet I was not yet a Christian but rather in an utterly wild and uncontrolled fashion my own master. I do know that at the time I turned the cause of Jesus Christ into an advantage for myself, for my crazy vanity. I pray to God that will never happen again. Nor had I ever prayed, or had done so only very rarely. Despite this isolation, I was quite happy with myself. The Bible, especially the Sermon on the Mount, freed me from all this. Since then everything has changed. (*DBWE* 14, p. 134)

The above reveals something of the centrality of the Bible for Bonhoeffer, which grew over time, after he had already been familiar with the Scriptures, as well as preached them! Towards the end of his life, he read the Bible regularly, meditated on passages, wrote poetry based on biblical figures (such as Moses and Jonah), and developed his theological ideas with an imagination that was immersed in the Scriptures (Kuske, 1976, pp. 132–59). He wrote of 'going through weeks without reading much of the Bible' but anticipated that 'after a time I'll be ravenous again' (*DBWE* 8, p. 326). Overall, his time in prison was steeped in the Bible, and notably the Old Testament (*DBWE* 8, p. 181). Personal discipline certainly enabled a regular reading of the Scriptures, but Bonhoeffer also believed that he truly needed the Scriptures in his life.

Given the strong emphasis he places on the Scriptures and their interpretation, it is intriguing that this aspect of Bonhoeffer's thinking has only come to the fore in more recent years. At the time of writing this book, some very helpful texts have been published that explore Bonhoeffer's 'bibliology' (Banman, 2021), his approach to reading the Scriptures as a church community (Taylor, 2020), his method of interpretation in the backdrop of 1930s Germany (Ross, 2023), and his commitment to being a pastoral theologian of the word of God (Olivieri, 2023). Rather than use limited space in this chapter to say what others have already said, my purpose here is to trace some of the key aspects of Bonhoeffer's understanding of Christ and the Scriptures. I also want to explore how he outworked his thinking, which will yield some interesting insights regarding both his espoused and operant approaches to the Bible, and how this aspect of his thinking is critical for understanding his view of Jesus Christ.

Christ, the Bible and the 'Word of God'

Philip Ziegler identifies Bonhoeffer as a 'theologian of the Word of God' (Ziegler, 2013, p. 19). This means that Bonhoeffer's project is founded on the revelation of God's own word spoken in Christ, 'understood as a divine performative address which judges, forgives and commands' (Ziegler, 2013, p. 19). Such a perspective regarding the word of God necessarily requires attending to the Bible 'as a unique creaturely medium of the Word', and so rather than being gnostic or otherworldly, 'such a theology affirms the concreteness and contemporaneity of God's promise and claim' (Ziegler, 2013, p. 19). Ziegler helpfully gestures at how Bonhoeffer approaches the Bible as a unique, material means through which Christ himself addresses the world ever anew as God's self-revealing Word. This means that 'as a whole and in all its parts, it [the Bible] is nothing other than this witness of Christ, Christ's life, death and resurrection' (*DBWE* 14, p. 424). The implication of such a view of the Bible is, as Michael Mawson summarizes, that 'the Bible discloses and directs us to God in and as Jesus Christ' (Mawson, 2019, p. 126).

From the beginning of his career, Bonhoeffer claimed that one cannot talk about God without Scripture (*DBWE* 9, p. 289). His perspective and understanding developed over time, but from the beginning, he appeared to value the Bible, at least in theory. We recall the quote at the beginning of this chapter, which highlights that some of us read the Bible and may take it seriously, but at some point it becomes a living encounter with God's self-revelation in Jesus Christ.

For Bonhoeffer, church liturgy in general, but specifically preaching, depends on the written word of God, because 'The biblical witness itself and alone is the content of our witness' (*DBWE* 14, p. 535; *DBWE* 12, pp. 367–77). Bonhoeffer upheld Scripture simultaneously alongside the centrality of Christ for understanding the freedom of the church (Ziegler, 2013, pp. 35–46). This means that the Bible witnesses, or, rather, the Bible is God's self-witness (having bound himself to it by the Holy Spirit) to *the* Word of God in Jesus Christ. It is therefore inconceivable to consider Christ or the church apart from the Scriptures. Biblical study, meditation and reading to discern the call of Christ in a life of communal discipleship are fundamental for faithfulness in the Christian life. Some claim that Bonhoeffer is weak on referring to the Holy Spirit here, but I would disagree, as would David Emerton in his recent monograph (2020). I would suggest that it is precisely because of the work of the Holy Spirit that Bonhoeffer holds to a view of the Bible that considers it to be God's *dynamic* word that cannot be imprisoned within human knowledge, and so cannot be read merely as a blueprint. A blueprint requires no mediation, and without the Holy Spirit the Bible is just words on a page that can be manipulated according to all manner of ideological means. That is not the Word of God. Wolf Krötke explains that Bonhoeffer believed God's Holy Spirit made the word of Scripture God's own Word. 'Exegesis therefore has the task of allowing the Spirit of the Scriptures to move us' (Krötke, 2019, p. 181). This redresses how people read the Bible and what they think they are doing when they read or study it. 'Bonhoeffer did not deny the validity of historical-critical-exegesis ... But it had limited significance for him. It could uncover only the human dimension of the biblical witness' (Krötke, 2019, p. 181; see also *DBWE* 12, p. 386). Understanding the context of a passage was important for Bonhoeffer, but it was not the ultimate purpose of reading the Bible. Someone could show all the dexterity of modern biblical studies but never actually obey God's word. These tools, which are prevalent today, serve the reader in approaching the Scriptures as a unique material document through which God ultimately (and graciously) speaks anew in the here and now, with the call of Christ to trust and obey. As the book of Christ and of the church, the Old and New Testaments confront and challenge all universal truths or ethical norms, disrupting the sensibilities that we may otherwise hold up against the living God (*DBWE* 14, pp. 420–1). Putting it another way, someone could read the Bible as a religious text without believing that

God is actively addressing the reader or hearer here and now. Bonhoeffer felt that much of the modern methods of interpretation had got in the way. Bonhoeffer once said to Willhelm Rott:

> The professors accuse me of being unscholarly, because of my biblical work on the Old Testament (in the light of the Church Struggle); but they forget that there was genuine exegesis before the new fields of research, the historico-critical and the comparative approach, existed. (Rott, in Zimmerman, 1973, p. 133)

To summarize, Bonhoeffer claims that the Bible is the word of God in the sense that God has 'bound the divine self to the mediating word' (*DBWE* 2, p. 141). God speaks God's own word through the Bible because God freely chooses to mediate God self in this way. I stress again that this does not mean individuals can approach the Bible with the intention of extrapolating this or that 'truth' from it like a guidebook. Such a view of Scripture reduces it, and reduces God's word (and God) to something that can be grasped by us. This is the mistake made by Job's friends, who regurgitate timeless truths which ring hollow in the contingency of real life for the suffering and faithful Job. The point for Bonhoeffer is that God's living and Spirit-breathing word grasps at us through the mediated means of the Scriptures and we dare not prescribe in human terms how we think that looks, seems or feels. The Bible is God's word strictly in this mediated sense. Without God speaking God's word through the Bible freely and by the gracious power of the Holy Spirit, the Bible is not the word of God, but a book or ancient religious text.

Bonhoeffer, the Bible and the Black Christ

During a year of study in America (1930–31), Bonhoeffer felt that his only experience of genuine preaching of the word of God was in the African American church. Reggie L. Williams informs us that 'Bonhoeffer arrived in New York one year after the stock market crash that initiated the worldwide Great Depression. He disembarked onto American shores to meet scenes of hunger and despair that resembled postwar Germany' (Williams, 2021, p. 16). Alongside famine and economic difficulty, Bonhoeffer also encountered a form of theology that he felt was vapid, and which belittled his own background in dogmatics (Williams, 2021, p. 17). He had been fortunate enough to receive a Sloane Fellowship for one year as a resident scholar at Union Theological Seminary, New

York. His report at the end of the year wrote about 'students in practical theology seminars asking whether one really must preach about Christ' (Williams, 2021, p. 17). Bonhoeffer felt that much of the content taught at Union – which was founded upon modern American liberalism – was 'woefully inadequate at best or at worst heretical' (Williams, 2021, p. 17).

Williams tells us: 'The white churches that Bonhoeffer visited were plagued with the same theological problems that he found in the classroom at Union' (Williams, 2021, p. 18). Bonhoeffer himself writes:

> In New York, they preach about virtually everything; only one thing is not addressed, or is addressed so rarely that I have as yet been unable to hear it, namely, the gospel of Jesus Christ, the cross, sin and forgiveness, death and life ... So what stands in place of the Christian message? An ethical and social idealism borne by a faith in progress that – who knows how – claims the right to call itself 'Christian'. (*DBWE* 10, p. 313)

Bonhoeffer goes on to suggest that the White churches are not really churches but social corporations (*DBWE* 10, p. 313). He concludes: 'they have forgotten what the real point is' (*DBWE* 10, p. 314), before qualifying: 'the church of the outcasts of America stands fairly untouched, indeed, avoided by the white church: the Negro church' (*DBWE* 10, p. 314). He then discusses his immersion and active involvement in the life and experience of the Black church, 'observing white America from this rather hidden perspective' (*DBWE* 10, p. 314). At Abyssinian Baptist Church in Harlem, Bonhoeffer taught Sunday school, conducted a Bible study group for women and helped during a weekday church school, as well as visiting the homes of congregants. 'This personal acquaintance with Negroes was one of the most important and gratifying events of my stay in America' (*DBWE* 10, p. 315). But Bonhoeffer did not just turn up at Abyssinian on a whim or by some accident. It was through his acquaintance with an African American peer at Union, Albert Franklin Fisher, that Bonhoeffer was enabled to encounter a Christ who did not reflect his own sensibilities. In contrast to his other friends at the seminary – such as Paul Lehmann, Erwin Sutz and Jean Lasserre, with whom Bonhoeffer had a lot in common – Fisher was Black, he did not speak German, and he was born into a world that considered him to be subhuman. In contrast to Bonhoeffer's White, upper-middle-class horizons, Fisher had been born in the segregated American South, where racism was explicit and life-threatening for Blacks, often in the name of Jesus.

Fisher's family experience of Christianity in America indicated that navigating the poles of fundamentalism and liberal modernity were not the only challenges facing the gospel in America. Most liberal whites failed to see white supremacy as a matter for Christian attention, and as a consequence they ignored the constant dangers of daily life in America for black people. But avoiding racism was not a choice for African American Christians. (Williams, 2021, p. 21)

Williams argues that 'At Abyssinian with Fisher, Bonhoeffer found Christ existing as community where historically marginalized and oppressed black people knew Jesus as cosufferer and the gospel spoke authoritatively into all areas of life' (Williams, 2021, p. 26). Being a Christian was not an idea or an ascent to some propositional attitudes for the Black church; it was a light of hope and courage bleeding through the darkness cast by White supremacy, which had been preached in the name of Jesus using the Bible as its justification. Bonhoeffer sensed something disrupting his rational and cerebral German sensibilities as he worshipped alongside his Black brothers and sisters, for whom the gospel was the power to liberate them from despair amid constant dehumanization and brutality. Christ was no idea; Christ is real. As a result of his time at Abyssinian Baptist Church, Bonhoeffer was *formed* just as much as he was *informed*, rubbing shoulders alongside believers with whom he had very little in common. His understanding of 'Christ' changed, emerged, took on flesh within a community that were themselves the incarnate and enfleshed presence of Christ in the world. In his report, Bonhoeffer wrote that 'I heard the gospel preached in the Negro churches' (*DBWE* 10, p. 315). He continued:

> Here one really could still hear someone talk in a Christian sense about sin and grace and the love of God and ultimate hope, albeit in a form different from that to which we are accustomed. In contrast to the often lecturelike character of the 'white' sermon, the 'black Christ' is preached with captivating passion and vividness. Anyone who has heard and understood the Negro spirituals knows about the strange mixture of reserved melancholy and eruptive joy in the soul of the Negro. The Negro churches are proletarian churches, perhaps the only ones in all America. (*DBWE* 10, p. 315)

Without being too categorical, Bonhoeffer did not visit every White and every Black church in America. We would therefore do well not to jump on this reflection from 1931 as an absolute judgement on all White or

Black churches both then and now. Bonhoeffer caveats his description of the Black church in America by describing it as 'one small church group to which most of what has been said [about the White church] applies only to a small extent' (*DBWE* 10, p. 314). Therefore, he perhaps reserves any criticisms he may have regarding Black congregations due to his damning assessment of White churches. If anything, this highlights that Bonhoeffer was a critical character at this time. That said, his encounter with the Black Christ was undoubtedly transformative. This body of people confessed an allegiance to Christ that reconfigured much of Bonhoeffer's 'mental grid' (Williams, 2021, p. 79) as a White theologian from Germany. Reinhart Staats reflects that Bonhoeffer simply 'did not become aware of the gospel's opposition to racism until he was personally confronted with the "situation of negroes" in America' (Staats, *DBWE* 10, p. 609).

Bonhoeffer's experience within the Black church, under the biblical and contextual preaching of Adam Clayton Powell Sr (Williams, 2021, pp. 86–101), pressed him towards a belief that the Bible was neither an interesting academic nor an inspiring devotional text. He came to realize that the Bible was dangerous. On the one hand, it could be wielded to oppress and demonize others because of their skin colour or cultural differences. On the other hand, its own power as God's life-giving word could be relativized and deadened. More positively, the Bible became the word of God *who* incarnates through a community of proclamation, a community who are attentive to God's own self-witness in Jesus. This is the humiliation of the God of the gospel, something that Bonhoeffer develops later in his 'Lectures on Christology' (*DBWE* 12, pp. 299–360). Black Christians are welcome in the church of the word. Also, for Bonhoeffer, Black congregations were the only authentic community of Christ because, according to him, they took the gospel of Jesus in the Bible seriously. It was in the Black church that Christ confronted Bonhoeffer with his call to discipleship in the world, a call that would eventually cost him his life. The Black Jesus whom he witnessed most profoundly in the Black church refused to allow him to annex God to a religious, intellectual or super-spiritual dimension. Christ became too real for that.

Christologically grounding the Bible

After he returned to Germany, Bonhoeffer took what he had learnt through this embodied experience, seeking to ground his biblical imagination, or, rather, to have his biblical imagination grounded by opening himself to Christ's call in the reality of life. This occurred through a dynamic reading of the Scriptures that did not try to extrapolate timeless truths or abstract dogmas, but which believed the Bible was the word of God for the contemporary context.

This is not dissimilar to the way many Black theologians have found an affinity with the Exodus narratives as a prophetic witness to God's work of liberation for Black people. Kelly Brown Douglas argues: 'Identifying particularly with the Israelite slaves, black slaves often sang songs about the exodus event, which expressed certainty that God would deliver them as God delivered the Israelites' (Douglas, 2019, p. 23). During the Civil Rights Movement, Martin Luther King Jr regularly likened African Americans to the Israelites. At times, 'King compared his followers to the Israelite slaves who left Egypt, but with an important difference: his followers didn't have to travel to find the land of milk and honey; they were already there' (Eig, 2023, p. 435).

Coming to the Bible with an openness to be confronted by the living, Spirit-breathing, incarnating word of God meant that Bonhoeffer began to approach the Scriptures with an almost childlike posture, one that refused to constrain God intellectually or experientially within a mere book. To paraphrase Karl Barth, Bonhoeffer believed that he did not grasp at the Bible, but the Bible grasped at him (Barth, 1995, p. 110). Bonhoeffer had seen the evil caused when human beings wielded the Bible in their own power. In 1932, during an address at the International Youth Conference in Gland, he tried to articulate his concern over the misuse of the Bible. His words express a lament over the domestication and religious constraining of the word of God within human piety and ideology:

> [H]as it not become terribly clear, again and again, in all that we have discussed with one another here, that we are no longer obedient to the Bible? We prefer our own thoughts to those of the Bible. We no longer read the Bible seriously. We read it no longer against ourselves but only for ourselves. (*DBWE* 11, 377–78)

Bonhoeffer was concerned that the Bible was not upheld properly as the unique medium through which Christ confronts his people, calling them to a new life of discipleship in the world here and now. Bonhoeffer considered the Bible to be the word of God grasping at humanity as Christ's ultimate address in the here and now, disrupting their gaze and thrusting them into a choice of repentance or self-enclosure. The Bible is not a proof text for one's present lifestyle, nor a rule book, nor a fanciful fetish of spiritual sayings. Bonhoeffer claims the Bible is the way God self-witnesses God's reconciliation in Jesus. Much of this understanding was sharpened and grounded within the Black church, a community that took sin, mercy, justice, kindness, love, life and death, basically, Jesus Christ, seriously. That is why, for him, we can only know the living and present Jesus Christ as he is revealed in the Scriptures, but, critically, the Scriptures themselves point to Christ as the one who is the ultimate source, mediator and goal of the Scriptures. The Scriptures are not Christ himself. Christ, *the* Word of God, grasps humanity through the words of Scripture, its reading and reception, in Christian community. Strictly speaking therefore, the Bible is not the sole authority for the Christian faith per se, but Jesus Christ is, as the one revealed dynamically by the Holy Spirit in the Holy Scriptures. He is the one for whom the Scriptures ultimately exist, and without whom even the most zealous religious reader of the Bible will miss him. There is a semantically subtle but theologically significant difference here. The Bible could be drawn upon, and has been drawn upon, to give a remit for disastrous things, not least the barbaric enslavement of African people, and subsequent deformations of their personhood. However, the Christological grounding of the Scriptures orients the point of departure through which we read the Bible, a hermeneutic that recognizes Jesus' presence, Jesus' character and historical continuity over and against even our reading of the text at times, not just in our interpretation, but in the very means and ways by which we navigate what it really is to read the Scriptures as God's living word.

There are risks associated with Bonhoeffer's approach to the Bible. There is a possibility of diminishing the particular history and context of passages, especially in the Old Testament, if read through the blinkered lens of 'Christ' as a static goal we need to somehow arrive at. The funny story goes that a child is asked in Sunday school if they can think of something black and white that lives in the Antarctic and eats fish, to which the child replies, 'I know the answer must be Jesus but it sounds a lot like a penguin!' Unfortunately, some 'Christological' readings can veer towards this clunky and clumsy approach to the Scriptures, which also carries greater dangers such as disregarding the Jewish wisdom that could be lost by neglecting the particularity of Israel's narrative in texts. This also happens in the New Testament, and some great work has been done by folks to help Christians read their New Testament more holistically (one Jewish scholar I would recommend is Amy-Jill Levine, 2015; 2020). More recently, Stephen R. Haynes has critiqued Bonhoeffer for occasions where he has allegedly plundered the Old Testament for ways of 'Christologizing' biblical texts (Haynes, 2006, pp. 97–8).

This was a tendency for Bonhoeffer at times. However, he also made significant moves to uphold the whole of the Scriptures, especially foregrounding the Old Testament as a *Jewish* text that points to Jesus for Christians. Given his context of Nazi Germany, where Christ was initially being reduced to an Arian macho man, one can appreciate the emphasis he continually wanted to make regarding the Jewishness of Jesus. His 'daily and detailed reading of the Psalms' in his seminary 'represented a refusal to bow to Nazi pressures to abandon the Old Testament' (Reynolds, 2016, p. 108). His time in prison prompted an even deeper love for the Old Testament, a love that was not looking for 'Christ' under every verse. For example, in a letter to his best friend Eberhard Bethge he reflects on Song of Solomon (or Song of Songs), stating, 'you really can't imagine a hotter, more sensual, and glowing love than the one spoken of here' (*DBWE* 8, p. 394). In encouraging Eberhard to embrace his longing for Renate (Eberhard's wife), Bonhoeffer writes, 'It's really good that this is in the Bible, contradicting all those who think being a Christian is about tempering one's passions' (*DBWE* 8, p. 394). Later, he reflects, 'I would in fact read it as a song about earthly love, and that is probably the best "Christological" interpretation' (*DBWE* 8, p. 410). Here we read the reflections of someone who believes so strongly that Christ is the origin, mediator and goal of all things (cf. Col. 1.16–17) that he approaches the Bible without having to make everything crudely 'Jesus-centred' and, for him, this is how to read the Bible in a truly Christological way.

Jesus Christ speaks through the Bible today

Part 2 of this book examines Bonhoeffer's main works, some of which engage extensively with the Bible. For now, though, it is worth highlighting a few of the concrete ways in which Bonhoeffer carried and was carried by the Scriptures, amid the ebbs and flows of his own life. I particularly want to note some of the ways that he approached the Bible using this Christological method I have described above.

Much of Bonhoeffer's Christological bibliology is found in his sermons. While he was wary of reducing Christ and the Scriptures to experience alone, he was bold in demonstrating that experience is enfolded into the Word of God in Christ. On 3 December 1933, he preached a sermon in London on Luke 21.28: 'Now when these things begin to take place, look up and raise your heads, because your redemption is drawing near.' He began by citing some recent mining disasters in Wales and Derbyshire. 'You all know about accidents in mines. In the last few weeks we have had to read over and over in the papers about such an accident' (*DBWE* 13, p. 337). Unabashedly, he imagines with the congregation how overwhelming it would be to be in 'the moment that even the bravest miner has dreaded all his life' (*DBWE* 13, p. 337). Without being pithy, he then relates this experience to Advent as he describes the desperate longing for rescue that is felt deep within creation:

> He can't see anything at all, but he can hear the voices of his helpers ... Rescue is at hand, only one more step and he will be free ... this is God coming near to humankind, the coming of salvation ... look up and raise your heads because your redemption is drawing near. (*DBWE* 13, p. 338)

Anecdotes such as these do not dominate Bonhoeffer's sermons, but they immediately open the Scriptures, or, rather, they open the congregation to God's word in the Scriptures.

On 9 November 1938, the Nazis initiated a campaign that arguably marked the start of the Holocaust. Known as *Kristallnacht* (the night of the broken glass), this day received its name from the looting, burning, vandalism and destruction of Jewish shops and synagogues. It is estimated that around 100 Jews were murdered, tens of thousands taken to concentration camps, and 267 synagogues were destroyed. Bonhoeffer was with a group of ordinands when this happened, and was already becoming involved in the plans for a *coup d'état* (Schlingensiepen, 2010, p. 216). In his Bible for private prayer and meditation, Bonhoeffer underlined Psalm 74.86, 'they burned all the meeting places of God in the land', and next to the verse he wrote, '9.11.38' (Bethge, 2000, p. 607). He also wrote to his seminarians and encouraged them to pray and reflect on Psalm 74, noting the contemporary resonances of this passage with the present situation (*DBWE* 15, p. 84). What is interesting about this incident is that Bonhoeffer does not read the Bible for himself as such. Rather, he observes an act of evil and violence through the imaginative horizons that have developed within himself, to the extent that his routine Bible reading and praying of the psalms read this passage as a confrontation calling him to pray and act for his Jewish neighbours.

One of the most astonishing examples of where we observe the dynamic impact of Christ in the Scriptures for Bonhoeffer is from a diary that he kept during his second visit to America in 1939. At this point in his life, people his age were being conscripted to fuel the Nazi war machine, which he did not consider an option due to his commitment to peace. However, refusing military service would also be complex, due to the suspicion and difficulty it would cause many others in the Confessing Church by association. 'Bonhoeffer's proposed yearlong sabbatical to New York seemed to him, at least, to offer him some space, if not reprieve, from his dilemmas and doubts' (Fabrycky, 2020, p. 97). This trip was organized with good intentions and much prayer in communion with others, but his journey to America increased a sense of anxiety in himself as he travelled from the fraught situation in Germany to the comparative safety of New York.

What struck me as I began to write this chapter is how much Bonhoeffer recognizes his own predicament enfolded into the biblical narrative. In his American diary, he notes down the Watchwords from the Moravian Daily Texts (*Die Losungen*), adding his reflections underneath (*DBWE* 15, pp. 217ff.). Laura Fabrycky (2020, p. 97) explains that Watchwords 'were, and are, daily Scripture meditations published every year by the Moravian Brethren, a Protestant group that traces its religious heritage to a pre-reformation movement of pietists who were committed to Scripture, prayer, and evangelism'. It was after reading Fabrycky's observations that I noticed the dynamic, vulnerable and intense way that Bonhoeffer read the Bible. In a sense, this could be overlooked by merely assessing his Christology and theology of Scripture without any accompanying biography. He reflects on his arrival in New York in relation to Acts 15.40, which reads: 'But Paul chose Silas and set out, the brothers commending him to the grace of the Lord.' Bonhoeffer writes: 'Arrival in New York. To know in these first hours that brothers have commended us to the grace of the Lord was decisive' (*DBWE* 15, p. 220). Later on: 'Almost two weeks have passed now without my knowing anything from over there [Germany]. That is hardly bearable' (*DBWE* 15, p. 222). He then immediately quotes the text for that day: 'It is good that one should wait quietly for the salvation of the Lord' (Lam. 3.26).

This dialogue between his stressful estrangement from Germany and the inspiration from the Daily Texts continues, with Bonhoeffer appearing to sense God's word tangibly through the verses he reads. On 18 June, he writes: 'How good the Daily Texts for today are' (*DBWE* 15, p. 225). He senses a concrete resonance with his situation and the biblical texts he is given for the day.

On 15 June, he wrote in his diary, 'Since yesterday evening my thoughts cannot get away from Germany' (*DBWE* 15, p. 222). He struggled being in America and not in Germany, which was made harder by those around him who were convinced he should indeed be in New York, 'as if prayers had been heard' (*DBWE* 15, p. 228). He refers to the Daily Text again (Mal. 3.3), which likens God to a refiner and purifier who will refine and purify his people. Bonhoeffer writes: 'I no longer know how things stand with myself. But God knows, and in the end all actions and deeds will be clear and pure' (*DBWE* 15, p. 229).

On 26 June, a moment comes, to which everything else appears to have been building. One can almost anticipate Bonhoeffer reaching a point of decision and resolution that he would not stay in America, but would return to Germany:

> Today I happened to read from 2 Tim. 4.21 'come before the winter' – Paul's plea to Timothy. Timothy is to share the suffering of the apostle and not be ashamed. 'Come before the winter' – otherwise it might be too late. That is haunting me the whole day ... God acts not only through pious impulses but also through such vital stirrings as well. 'Come before the winter' – it is not a misuse of the Scripture if I allow this to be said *to me*. If God gives me the grace for that. (*DBWE* 15, p. 232)

Up to this point in his diary, Bonhoeffer was clearly struggling with his decision to leave Germany and go to America, despite the many assurances he received from others that it was the 'right' thing. In the end, his anxiety and inner turmoil was consoled only through what he believed was a word from Christ to him directly at the end of June, to 'Come before Winter' as the above excerpt shows. This was a moment of clarity for him, as subsequent diary entries show: 'I must leave at the first possible date' (*DBWE* 15, p. 233). 'I have decided to leave with Karl Friedrich on the eighth ... That was a major decision' (*DBWE* 15, p. 234). He refers to the Daily Texts again in subsequent entries, writing on 3 July, 'I must watch myself, that I don't become neglectful in reading the Bible and in prayer' (*DBWE* 15, p. 236).

Laura Fabrycky warns us, quite rightly in my view, not to make this overly dramatic or to romanticize the situation (Fabrycky, 2020, p. 99). Bonhoeffer had lived with these daily texts for a long time and had persevered with the Bible as his companion along the way in a manner that was extremely ordinary for the most part as he prayerfully meditated on the word of God. I think this moment was unusual. However, he felt confident enough to believe Christ was speaking to him here. Interestingly, he did not look back on his shortened visit to America with any regret:

> I am glad to have been over there, and glad to be on my way home again ... Probably this visit will have a great effect on me ... Since I have been on the ship, the internal tension about the future has stopped. I

can think about the abbreviated time in America without reproach. (*DBWE* 15, pp. 237–8)

Conclusion

When you read almost any scholarly material on Bonhoeffer, it becomes clear that his understanding of Jesus Christ cannot be separated from the Bible, and his approach to the Bible cannot ignore the centrality of Jesus Christ. He claims that God's revealed Word in Jesus Christ is the ultimate reality that defines all other reality, and this includes how we approach and respond to the Scriptures. We cannot constrain or confine God within the Bible in and of itself. However, God has indeed chosen to speak his word anew through the Bible, through this ancient and sometimes enigmatic text. Christ is always present in the encounter where people are willing to open themselves to his confrontation and comfort as Lord of all.

This means that we dare to read the Bible as those who do not claim to have a full grasp of it, nor of the God that the Bible witnesses to. The word of God, spoken ultimately in Jesus Christ, witnessed to in the Scriptures, refuses to be enslaved to the ideas, frameworks and synthesized arguments of human religiosity. The very sincerity and piety of wanting to be faithful to God can sometimes deceive us into seeking control over God, reducing the gospel to something we can wield, albeit with good intentions. We will see in the following chapters that Bonhoeffer was keen not to limit God to the Bible, though recognize that God has graciously chosen to speak through the Bible in ways that challenge our preconceived ideas about God.

In this book, we will explore some of the ways in which folks like myself have carried assumptions about how to read the Bible or how to understand Christian faith, in a desire to remain faithful to orthodoxy or evangelicalism. I myself am an evangelical Christian, and I treasure the Scriptures. From within that tradition, I am becoming increasingly aware of the ways that my tradition has been blind to the assumptions made, equating the Bible with the word of God, which refuses any openness to the Holy Spirit bringing this text alive in any new way. When I say 'new' I mean potentially different readings of the Scriptures, but also ways that renew and that confront us anew in ways we are hitherto asleep to. For White Western Christians and churches, this is of paramount importance. Today we are confronted by a global perspective that prompts us to reconsider much of our tradition and heritage. If we do not consider the blind spots and mistakes we make in our interpretation, we will struggle to discern the gifts we should treasure and bring with us. I think we should take the Bible seriously, really seriously, and I think we should take it seriously the way God does, because the Bible is not God, it is the word of God in as much as it is a witness to God's own self-revealed Word spoken in Christ. God speaks to us today, a reality that is staggering in terms of its grace and wonder and implications. As we read the text of the Bible, we witness the prophets' and apostles' witness to the God who truly speaks, and who has spoken finally and fully in the flesh:

> Long ago God spoke to our ancestors in many and various ways by the prophets, but in these last days he has spoken to us by a Son, whom he appointed heir of all things, through whom he also created the worlds. He is the reflection of God's glory and the exact imprint of God's very being, and he sustains all things by his powerful word. (Heb. 1.1–3)

Having studied Bonhoeffer for a number of years now, I have come to believe that God is more real than I have believed God is. God will not be constrained by my presumptions, nor my doctrines. Christian doctrine at its best recognizes the limitations of human language and ideas to understand God. The person and work of Jesus Christ is God's own Word to us, God's coming to us, because we cannot articulate God for ourselves. And yet, Christ is with us as the one who is not going to be constrained or controlled by us. Even death could not hold him. While it might not always be as dramatic as we might sometimes desire, the Bible is the means through which God reveals his Word to us each day anew, in the ordinary and extraordinary parts of life in the created world. It may be sobering to note that when Bonhoeffer sensed God speaking to him so directly and dramatically through the Bible, it resulted in an act that cost him his life. 'Whenever Christ calls us, his call leads us to death' (*DBWE* 4, p. 87).

2

Creation and Space

My parents live in a town called Bewdley, which is just on the River Severn in Worcestershire. We moved there when I was 15 as my dad (who helped to provide the information below) took up the role as pastor of the Baptist church. Bewdley was quite well known for being a town that flooded regularly. Water would fall on the surrounding area, eventually flowing as groundwater into the Severn, but there would sometimes be significant surface run-off due to saturated fields. When the Severn winds near to Bewdley, it has already travelled a long way from its original source in the Cambrian mountains of mid-Wales. Rain in Wales, Shropshire and other areas (not just in Worcestershire where Bewdley is situated) finds its way through numerous tributaries into the river at a rate that would sometimes be too high for the banks to cope. The year 2000 marked the wettest October in 270 years, which resulted in river levels reaching an unprecedented height. 'The resulting deluge engulfed not only Bewdley but other towns and villages across the Severn Vale, damaging 10,000 homes and businesses at 700 locations' (Laville, 2024). The prime minister at the time, Tony Blair, came to visit us in his wellington boots and promised urgent action, which resulted in an £11 million flood defence system which would be installed along the banks of the river. Whenever I think about Bewdley, I think about the 'triumph' of human engineering that held back the floods there.

In contrast, most people do not think of Bewdley when there is talk about flooding. In Carlton Turner's book, *Caribbean Contextual Theology* (2024), he gives an account of flooding that demonstrates a very different horizon, experience and response to flooding. We live in the same created world, yet the memories, resources and challenges for his Bahaman land are starkly different from those of my parents' community in Bewdley. Both are formed imaginatively within those particular places. Turner notes that 'Between 2000 and 2019 there were 548 floods, 330 storms, 75 earthquakes and 74 droughts, 66 landslides, 50 instances of extreme temperature, and 38 volcanic events' (Turner, 2024, p. 163). He challenges the presumption by many White Western (especially North

American) nations who equate the travails of Caribbean existence with demonic evil, or who overlook the philanthropic disempowerment of Caribbean people (Turner, 2024, pp. 166–70). Turner argues that colonial expansion (with its intrinisic racial superiority), Western commerce and wealth extraction 'must be abandoned for a deeper, embodied, ecological kind of thinking or theology' (Turner, 2024, p. 175). The way we perceive different people and places will vary based on the horizons within which we are placed and positioned. That is the point of this chapter, to encourage us not to base our understanding merely in our heads, but in our bodies, and the created place within which our bodies live.

Invaded space

Selina Stone talks about the way that Africa was previously described as the 'dark continent' in a colonial motif, not just in reference to the darker pigments in people's skin but because 'Africa was a mysterious place with many unknown elements in terms of geography, climate, culture, religions, languages and history' (Stone, 2024, p. 8). Presumption and an inadvertent ignorance on the part of White Western colonials refracted their gaze of the 'heathen' towards an objective judgement that African people were inferior, unenlightened and 'unchristian'. This was far more comprehensive than skin colour. Part of the fallacious vision behind White Europeans was the way they interpreted how non-Europeans 'used' land. Rather than subduing it into private property for the sake of maximum production and profit, land was treated differently by non-Europeans, with a restraint that was strange for the White settlers. For colonial imaginations, there was so much 'potential' for getting more out of the land.

This was not just in Africa, but everywhere in the world that British (and other White European) colonials settled. Two *Pākehā* (White New Zealanders), Andrew Picard and A. D. Clark-Howard, have carried out some archival work regarding the history of Aotearoa (New Zealand). They demonstrate that White settlers assumed they could fully 'understand and interpret indigenous peoples and cultures' (Picard and Clark-Howard, 2022, p. 78). Furthermore, 'Within the theological cosmology of the missionaries, there was no room for shared conversation, learning, or growth' due to a categorical equating of Maori life with the demonic (Picard and Clark-Howard, 2022, p. 80). White colonials conceived humankind's relation to the land through the prism of White Western capitalism, fuelled significantly by their readings of Genesis 1.28.

The theo-logic went as follows: land that was uncultivated is 'available' and 'should' be claimed by the Crown as 'waste land' to serve the population back home. Maori people had allegedly failed to 'subdue' the land in accordance with the biblical creation mandate, so Christian settlers needed to do this, as well as 'Christianize' the Maori people. Yet, in the short-sightedness of White Western piety, 'Depriving Māori of their waste lands and forcing them to become agriculturalists [among other things] overlooked the fact that they also used the lands for hunting' (Picard and Clark-Howard, 2022, p. 83). If they had been open to the perspectives of Maori people, Western settlers would have learnt this. The complex diversity of indigenous groups in the Caribbean, Africa and New Zealand further highlights how clumsily the White Western gaze has been in the past, failing to afford agency and determinative integrity to these groups, and homogenizing them as pagans, heathens and anti-Christian others.

Not only was the land's purpose viewed differently by indigenous peoples; it also constituted the identity of its people. The settlement and expansion of Western civilization into what became the Americas, Africa, as well as other nations, marked what Willie James Jennings calls the 'colonial moment' (Jennings, 2010, pp. 24, 83). Indigenous people, tribes and families had dwelt in these lands for generations. They loved, hated, worked, played, fought, reconciled and learnt together within the contours of the landscape, as well as the ebbs and flows of the rivers and tidal currents. The earth grew who they were as those who were part of it. The meshwork of flora and fauna gave more than existence, but meaning and wisdom to the people. In many ways places constituted *who* they were (Jennings, 2010, p. 49). White Christians did not appreciate this fully, blinkered as they were through a lens that precluded their openness to others, all in the name of (the White) Christ, which was repulsed by things that they did not fully understand, and maybe never would.

How we live is shaped by (and in turn, gives shape to) the places within which we live. I am not referring just to the natural world, though this is critically significant. I also mean the infrastructure in our neighbourhoods, the ways that service providers are organized or operative, the particular logics that govern how we distribute resources, education, food, healthcare, even how we imagine what it is to love and be loved. The places within which we breathe (or cannot breathe) yield a particular somatically charged predisposition in us, individually as well as communally, economically and politically. Without attending to this, we lose out on the gifts within our particular places, and we can judge or falsely interpret those who inhabit other spaces (or other bodies in those spaces) according to our epistemological paradigm of a fairly limiting 'right and wrong' dualism.

Selina Stone talks about her experience of growing up in Handsworth, which was considered to be a 'dark' place to live by some. The 'ghetto', as it was referred to, was 'a little rough' at times, 'but it was all I knew, and I loved it' (Stone, 2024, p. 27). Stone's gaze pierces the ignorance of those who may not 'see' what she saw, not least the incredible diversity (Stone, 2024, pp. 27, 28). She also describes the significance lying behind her long days at church within her Black Pentecostal tradition.

> The world of our church communities can be vastly different from what we experience in our day-to-day lives ... Black churches have always provided a special kind of refuge in places such as the UK ... Your face will not be misread in this place, your tone will not be misunderstood ... It is no wonder people never seemed to want to leave. (Stone, 2024, pp. 28–9)

I had never appreciated this dimension to Black church life until reading about it, having imagined other reasons for why, in contrast, my church services often last just over an hour, before people usually go straight home to their more closeted lives. My experience of church is not usually a whole day of feeling liberated to breathe deeply and express the fullness (joy and sorrow) of my life with others, to remember I am loved, to laugh and cry without pretence. Frankly, I really wish it was like that!

Creation 'speaks'

Hopefully what I have said so far at least opens the possibility for a robust consideration of the materiality involved in human creaturely life if we think about a doctrine of creation. Yet, I am also referring to the creation and space of the human imagination, the limits and potential of our minds and our theological vision, which is so often divorced from or seen as incidental in relation to physical places and the cosmologies that narrate our understanding of God, others and the world itself. This inevitably affects how we live in relation to physical places and physical people. This is what Willie James Jennings refers to when he argues that the White Western church suffers from a 'diseased social imagination' (Jennings, 2010, p. 6).

In this chapter, I will show some of the ways that Bonhoeffer was wrestling with the problems he observed in the White Western imagination through his doctrine of creation. There is a sense in which, for many non-White people, 'creation speaks' (Jennings, 2018). This is to say creation has its very own, unique integrity as that which is distinct from God and, precisely because of this, creation 'lives' and acts from within its own (God-given) agency and particular essence. The question arises as to whether creation speaks for White people too, and whether White Western sensibilities (and theology) is aware of this, or whether our aversion to paganism, syncretism or natural theology has made us resistant to the gifts that are offered in humbly embracing the natural world as a voice of integrity regarding our creatureliness. There are some who are doing this work (see, for example, Joerstad, 2021; Middleton, 2022), but it is not pervasive, especially in many streams of the White Western church.

I think it is critical that our discipleship and God-talk in the White Western world concedes to the kaleidoscopic reality that we merely have a particular gaze. Even (and especially) Christians must recover an awareness of our secondary witness, our Gentile existence, to remind us that we are not the primary or sole harbingers of truth, even the gospel truth (Jennings, 2010, p. 258). We must accept that we have this particular gaze, this limited perception, these visceral predispositions; none of these things are necessarily valid for all (Christians or otherwise). God became flesh in a particular place. We are bound to and formed by this earth as those who are *all rooted* in the *different soils* of creation. I think Bonhoeffer was trying to grapple with thoughts like this when responding to the rhetoric of National Socialism. The remainder of this chapter will focus on how Bonhoeffer envisaged the theological significance of creation, and what this might mean for those of us living as White people in a postcolonial era. There are some really helpful ways he interprets the narratives, and there are ways in which he remained colour-blind in his devotion to the project of Western Christianity. We will come to these things below.

Humanity is earthy

'Humankind is derived from a piece of the earth. Its bond with the earth belongs to its essential being' (*DBWE* 3, p. 76). This radical statement asserts the creatureliness of people while also recognizing the constitutive value of the earth itself. Humanity cannot be envisioned apart from its bodily grounding in creation: 'a human being is a human body' (*DBWE* 3, p. 77). Therefore, 'People who reject their bodies reject their existence before God the Creator' (*DBWE* 3, p. 77). His point here is that creaturely life is good, and before sin it was not marred or assailed by any introspective presumptions or confusions regarding what it means to be human. Bonhoeffer does not take this point further, but we could also argue that people who fully reject their bodies and creation itself, reject their existence as well as creation itself before God the creator. Moreover, they reject God the creator and creation itself, for humankind is inseparably bound to creation and creator, without which it is lost. There is nothing inherently anti-God about upholding the materiality of creation, but rather, failing to reckon with materiality is anti-God or, to be specific and pointed, anti-Christian. In relating creation and the natural world to the incarnation, John Colwell asserts that God embraces and affirms 'the entire materiality of creation in all its present messiness ... there is surely something appropriate in celebrating this divine affirmation of materiality' (Colwell, 2007, p. 35). More radically, Colwell argues that redemption must refer to 'the fulfilment, completion, and perfection of the material creation, not its abandonment and replacement. What is passing away is this material world's order (or disorder) rather than its materiality' (Colwell, 2007, p. 37).

We see this in reference to Genesis 1.31: 'God saw everything that he had made, and indeed, it was very good.' Over and against an anthropocentric interpretation of the creation story, creation is deemed very good because God saw *everything* that God had made, 'and indeed, it was very good'. When everything exists alongside everything else, with the God-given distinctions and variations of form, number, agency, poise or whatever, God gazes at creation in its polyphonic complexity (of which humanity is a constitutive but limited part), saying *it* (creation) is very good. In other words, creation is 'deeply pleasing' (my translation) not because of humanity per se, but because the earth as a whole is made beautiful. We might say that creation gives witness through its beauty to the beauty of creator God, though at the same time it is beautiful in and of itself because God has made it that way, whether it knows it or not, and it yields its very own integrity regarding its own material beauty. God does not perceive it to be very good *for* anything; God simply sees that it is very good. In its ineffable variation, creation graciously includes the particularity of humanity within its bosom. If anything, the role of humankind is to live and work within the contours of creation, for people to sing their kaleidoscopically different witnesses to the glory of their creator in step with the earth's song. On the earth, they are called to live as those who are enmeshed in their mutifaceted materiality and sociocultural distinctiveness. To be a person, a people, is to live, move and have our being in the Spirit who constrains and maintains the power of creation through creation.

Bonhoeffer gestures at the notion of human creatures needing to recognize their limitations within the God-given boundaries of creation, but we should take it further, and I will focus on the imagery he initially uses of the tree of life and the tree of the knowledge of good and evil.

In reference to the tree of life, Bonhoeffer writes, 'At the center of the world that has been put at Adam's disposal and over which Adam has been given dominion is not Adam himself but the tree of divine life' (*DBWE* 3, pp. 83–4). This tree (an icon of creation) is at the centre, not humankind itself. The tree of the knowledge of good and evil 'indicates to this human being ... their limit or boundedness, that is, the human being's creatureliness' (*DBWE* 3, p. 85). It is with profound insight that Bonhoeffer concludes: '*The human being's limit is at the center of human existence*' (*DBWE* 3, p. 86). The limit of humanity's essence is also its freedom. But this limit is not on the far horizon, in the discovery of the 'New World' nor in the accumulation and *synthesizing* of knowledge in the Spirit of truth (a Hegelian fallacy). The heart of one's humanness is encountered in the very *place* the human being is enfleshed. That is not to say we should not explore new things. That misses my point. What I mean is that creation itself yields the very material by which human beings re-member themselves within the earth. The tree (creation's gift of freedom) is the constraint upon which human beings encounter themselves precisely as those who live within creaturely limits. These boundaries and limits are not human made and oppressive, but a beautiful, if fragile, gift of substantial grace, without which humankind would have no substance to its being, sinking instead into the void and abyss of nothingness. 'The life that comes from God is at the center' (*DBWE* 3, p. 83). Joel Lawrence summarizes: 'These two trees stand at the center of the garden precisely because both indicate what it is to be human ... Bonhoeffer orients human living outside the self ... human life can only be what God intends when humanity is not the center of its own existence' (Lawrence, 2013, p. 117).

This is precisely why creation and space relates to epistemology. Western thinking has long since divorced epistemology from creation. The self-enclosed knowledge of an isolated individual's mind reduces creation and the significance of place to something we can grasp, rather than it being something that grasps us. Bonhoeffer gestured wonderfully at the way in which creation itself (the tree, and Adam and Eve's freedom for one another respectively) limits humankind. It seems Bonhoeffer did not ground his notion of human freedom as the image of God within the contours and particular place of creation itself. At points in his doctrine, I would argue Bonhoeffer abstracts humanness away from creation itself, when (following much of his thinking) he could instead recognize the agency creation holds for speaking life into *Adam* (man and woman).

Constraining freedom

From the beginning of creation itself, through to the incarnation of Christ within creation, God loves and speaks the divine word over, through and alongside creation as its Creator, Sustainer and Lord. Dianne Rayson explains that 'God keeps and nurtures it. It is under God's dominion' (Rayson, 2021, p. 88). Yet, the dominion that God exercises cannot be equated with the dominion of sinful humanity. That is one of the huge mistakes made in Western Christianity based on common interpretations of Genesis 1.28, and approaches to humanity's relationship with creation are often limited to these few verses in Genesis rather than the rest of Scripture. Bonhoeffer does not make much of this verse in his writing. As I mentioned above, this verse was evoked by many colonial Christians as a justification for claiming dominion over land, turning places into private, productive, profitable spaces. The verse reads as follows:

> God blessed them [humanity], and God said to them, 'Be fruitful and multiply, and fill the earth and subdue it; and have dominion over the fish of the sea and over the birds of the air and over every living thing that moves upon the earth.'

Historically, the language of 'subdue' has been understood in the White Western church in a particular way. That is not to say that other parts of the world have got it spot on, but the way we envision community, society and our vocation as humans will often inform our self-understanding, along with our construal of everything else. The word we translate as 'subdue' (from the Hebrew root, *kavash*) is used elsewhere in the Old Testament in reference to subduing land through military subjugation of places and people (e.g. Num. 32.22, 29; Josh. 18.1; 2 Sam. 8.11; 1 Chron. 22.18). However, it also has connotations with rape (Esth. 7.8; McKeown, 2008, p. 27). A literal reading as many of us may understand it will therefore have no end of theological and ethical problems.

One possibility that bears reflection is the idea that God's command to subdue and exercise dominion over the earth 'does not have to do with exploitation and abuse' but is about 'securing the well-being of every other creature and bringing the promise of each to full fruition' (Brueggemann, 1982, p. 32). After all, those bestowed with the image of God are to act according to God's way, which requires acting not primarily for oneself, nor solely through the exclusive logic of one's own impulses, but for and alongside the very creatures and creative world we inhabit together.

There is an element of constraint emphasized in Bonhoeffer's theological cosmology that is important for ensuring that all creation collectively thrives according to the rhythm of its distinct forms and potentialities (e.g. *DBWE* 3, pp. 43–4, 54, 57, 85–7, 92). For him, living within healthy limitations is to be free, recognizing we are not limitless like God. However, constraint and limits become complex when we examine how the human imposition or transgression of limits sometimes take root. This applies regarding the violation and exploitation of creation, as well as the 'deprivation of physical [and other forms of] freedom' for human beings, which represents 'serious invasions of the right conferred on human beings at creation' (*DBWE* 6, p. 214).

Karl Bonhoeffer (Dietrich's father) instilled an awareness of the dynamic between constraint and freedom within his family. As professor of psychiatry and neurology at the University of Berlin, he valued the rational approach to life that was typical of modern liberalism, and brought his children up 'to respect the opinions of others, to recognize their own limitations and see life in proportion' (Bethge, 2000, p. 16). But his sense of responsibility meant he considered *self*-constraint alongside a sometimes-necessary (if regrettable) constraining of others. In 1938, Karl Bonhoeffer headed a team of fellow psychiatrists who, with the support of some military personnel, planned to overthrow Hitler by arresting him, declaring him insane, and constraining him within the confines of a mental institution (Szasz, 1997, p. 314). This obviously never happened, and I have not been able to discover why exactly. Karl's approach to life would have inevitably formed his son's horizons to an extent. Dietrich would later reflect that '*too little* law and order or *too much* law and order compels the church to speak' (*DBWE* 12, p. 364). He goes on to describe three stages of responsibility for the church in relation to state injustice:

1 The church must question the state's legitimacy to act in certain ways, advocating for those who have no voice in the world, whether inside or outside the church community (*DBWE* 12, p. 365; cf. Gal. 6.10).
2 The church has an 'unconditional obligation toward the victims of any societal order, even if they do not belong to the Christian community' (*DBWE* 12, p. 365). Only caring for Christians (or our own people group) is apostasy (Pangritz, 2019, p. 95).
3 If the church regards the state to be failing in its responsibility, such as disregarding or robbing people of their rights, it must take political action, and 'not just to bind up the wounds of the victims beneath the wheel but to seize the wheel itself' (*DBWE* 12, p. 365). This is an extreme case.

Note the freedom of agency that Bonhoeffer assumes of the church here. His experience frames his particular horizon regarding a Christian response to injustice in general. While his thinking is helpful in many contexts, it is also imbued with the joint privileges of agency and resource which he enjoyed in spades, but which he appears to have overlooked in his paradigm. The church itself has historically enjoyed influence and power in Western spaces, which has inevitably shaped its optic of justice and constraint due to the space and privilege afforded to it. John Colwell wrestles with this predicament:

> Certainly the world, and human society within it, is not yet as God would ultimately have it to be: fallen humanity is characterized by violence, exploitation, tyranny and injustice. Certainly in such a context, if the poor and the vulnerable are to be protected, there is yet place, regrettably, for limited coercive restraint. (Colwell, 2007, p. 90)

Of course, navigating injustice requires recognizing the place held by those who suffer injustice, for them to speak about their perspective on the matter. In addition, these different horizons entail varied dimensions of agency. One person might have freedom to exercise agency for justice, while another may not. Not everyone is the same. And critically, the access and agency we have in creation is, in part at least, what constitutes our very horizons regarding what injustice *is*. Without this appreciation for the creaturely (and limited) nature of life and creation, justice (and other values) can be so easily reduced to principles of 'fairness' that may achieve 'equality' but not 'equity' and merely perpetuate injustice for the poor and marginalized with well-meaning (but ignorant) intentions (Reddie, 2019, pp. 165–6).

Limiting the White imagination

There are some who think Bonhoeffer fell short in his theological vision by presuming too much of his particular gaze. J. Kameron Carter commends a lot of Bonhoeffer's life and work. However, he argues that '[Bonhoeffer's] vision, while well-intended, fails precisely because of how Whiteness generally and White supremacy specifically as a global ordering system goes uninterrogated' (Carter, 2020). There are traces in Bonhoeffer's thought where he equates Jesus Christ, the gospel, the kingdom and justice of God, with the 'unity' of the Western world, or to be specific, with the White, Euro-centric project of Christendom. For example, in his *Ethics* essay 'Ethics as Formation', Bonhoeffer writes that 'the form of Christ is the unity of the Western peoples' (*DBWE* 6, p. 101). In Bonhoeffer's challenge against Hitler's politics of nationalism and Arian (which is a form of White) supremacy, Carter argues that Bonhoeffer's corrective was for the West to embrace a 'benevolent internationalism' (Carter, 2020). Bonhoeffer's vision of what it means to be human is oriented by some ethical presumptions that are Western in nature, and an ethic of Whiteness by virtue of this presumption. In other words, while Bonhoeffer is theologically wrestling against the Arian vision of humanity, and the failure of modern ethics, his category of the 'human being' remains ethically 'over-determined' in his thought and ends up constraining his theological anthropology according to the White Western imagination of what it is to be human (Carter, 2020). This is not apart from, but critically determinative of, his Christology, which could arguably be called a colonial Christology.

> The unity of the West is where the Western peoples have been reconciled in Christ, and they become the vehicles for the reconciliation of all the peoples of the world in Christ ... the oneness that is held together in Christ is borne by the West. (Carter, 2020)

The West carries a certain Christian heritage (Holland, 2020). However, this does not mean that Christianity is Western, nor does it mean that the West is universally or exhaustively 'Christian' in character. Abstracting people away from their culture, land, biology and social space became a tool for asserting a universalized form of 'Christian values' and 'Christian ethics' which Bonhoeffer deployed 'in order to move the issue of difference to a nonessential level' (Ray, 2003, p. 93). Western Christianity dissolved the abiding Jewishness of baptized Jews, perceiving them as no longer Jewish but a 'Christian of Jewish origin' (*DBWE* 12, p. 370). Those who 'converted' to Christianity from Judaism or from any other non-Western place would have their biology, their creaturely history and distinct identity sublated into the oneness of (Western) Christianity. Reggie L. Williams summarizes that in his efforts to validate the humanness of Jews: 'Bonhoeffer remained caught inside the problem he was trying to address' (Williams, 2019, p. 394). This problem was a lack of recognition that creation will always be inhabited by those who will share the earth but occupy a different (creaturely and epistemological) space, and any unity or oneness between people in creation is not based on a universal principle, heritage or Christological humanism. In many senses, the only oneness that truly binds humanity together in creation

(Jews and Gentiles) is the acknowledgement of difference, which yields a kaleidoscopic aesthetic of creation, and engenders the constraint of all whose notions of freedom diminish the life and place of others.

Conclusion

In *The Christian Imagination*, Willie James Jennings chronicles the experience of the Jesuit priest José de Acosta, who arrived in Peru not long after recent conquests of key Incan cities. Acosta's lived experience was different from what he had anticipated, even in terms of the climate (Jennings, 2010, p. 85). However, his encounter of the 'New World' was made tenable for him by envisaging this strange place according to what he could extract of its meaning epistemologically. That enabled him to 'understand' it on his own terms. Jennings explains that 'Acosta's would be a totalizing epistemological gesture that was a harbinger of the kind of Western conceptual hegemony that has come upon the world since the sixteenth century' (Jennings, 2010, p. 87). Like many in the West at this time, Acosta posited himself and his people as the 'elect' bringers of God to 'Gentile' heathens, dismissing the reality that he and others in his nation were also themselves (secondary) *Gentile* believers (Jennings, 2010, pp. 97–8). Theology was safeguarded in the hands (and minds) of the colonial settlers, whose 'discovery' constrained this strange place within the White religious, political and moral gaze. Everything different from Western 'Christianity' was idolatry and counterfeit to faithfulness. Consequently, Acosta, an Aristotelian-Thomist, sought to 'form' the indigenous people through the discipline and *habitus* of (White) 'Christian education'. Whatever was Christian here was deeply intertwined and disfigured by the abstracted association of Christ with Whiteness.

The term Jennings uses to describe the conquest and overturning of life for the Incan people is the Andean word, *pachacuti* ('upheaval', Jennings, 2010, pp. 72–3). Acosta entered the colonial logic of the *pachacuti*, with it having been initiated already by the conquistador Francisco Pizarro. With unrivalled piety, he sought to inhabit and promulgate a Christianity that would for ever 'other' indigenous (or non-Western) people. Jennings' work is a tour de force in narrating the complex and devastating impulses that have left the world for ever changed by Western colonialism, regardless of any good fruit that may have emerged despite the unequivocal evil of this global *pachacuti*. I think every Western Christian should read Jennings' work. The following song does not parallel his breathtaking prose, but owes its inspiration to his lucid storytelling.

THE WHITE BONHOEFFER

Pachacuti

Beneath the painted veneer of peace
A fire burns that will never cease
Ablaze with silence and shackled hands
A great white shadow across our lands
From overseas far away, More of them every day
Are bringing their steel and stealing everything in their way
Raping the land of our people in their path
And we're losing the game before they told us to start

Allichu wayki [Quechua for 'please friend/family'], do not forget me
As the world falls in a pachacuti
Redeem a drip-feeding, false leading, White-wash story bleeding
O Lord awake, allichu wayki

Concocting doctrines of blood and creed
A new messiah to fuel their need
Jesus Christ as a white-fleshed man
Who rules from Rome over tongue and clan
Crossing our people out, faith over any doubt
That God is with them and spreading the word about
And the end they see will justify the means
Of this Andean purging for an Arian dream

Allichu wayki, do not forget me
As the world falls in a pachacuti
Redeem a drip-feeding, false leading, White-wash story bleeding
hate growing only showing worldly chaos overflowing
slave making, body hating, pleasure bound through our breaking
O Lord awake, allichu wayki

Acosta, see how the sting of death
Is felt here now while you still draw breath
By all who fail to be just like you
Your gospel's warped even if it's true
The Quechua scream aloud, and Babylon would be proud
Of capital gains from our land which you shackled and ploughed
Too blind and White to see the pride in your piety
Preaching of freedom while enslaving me

CREATION AND SPACE

Allichu wayki, do not forget me
As the world falls in a pachacuti
Redeem a drip-feeding, false leading, white-wash story bleeding
hate growing only showing worldly chaos overflowing
slave making, body hating, pleasure bound through our breaking
Image bearing our despairing hanging by the shame we're wearing
Ripping off our skin for shipping cotton, gold and tin and Jesus'
weeping over sin is yelling over all the din and screaming
O Lord, awake, allichu wayki

(Penned December 2016)

3

Context and Sin

On 25 May 2020, the 46-year-old Black man, George Floyd, was murdered in Minneapolis by the White police officer, Derek Chauvin. This event occurred following an incident where Floyd had tried to buy some cigarettes with a $20 bill that the store clerk believed to be fake. Chauvin knelt on Floyd's neck for 8 minutes and 46 seconds, as Floyd lay face down and handcuffed on the street. Significantly, two other police officers, Thomas Lane and J. Alexander Kueng, assisted Chauvin in restraining Floyd, while another officer, Tou Thao, prevented bystanders from intervening in the situation.

The risk of repeating a story that has been heard, seen or read about numerous times is that we can sometimes become numb or even indifferent to its horror, much like Jesus' Passion. I am conscious that this is a reflex that can emerge within me. Staying awake to pray and act justly in the face of suffering and evil is difficult. Furthermore, watching and resisting the temptation towards racial slumber is difficult as a White person, not least because we are habitually predisposed towards apathy. We (White folks) may sometimes feel tired or patronized when someone with Black or Brown skin 'plays the race card' and some of us may roll our eyes when the subject is raised 'again!'. Yet James Cone categorically rebukes this reflex: 'Whites should remember that Blacks have the "race" card to play because America [and I would add Britain] dealt it to them. It is not a card that we wanted' (Cone, 2004, p. 148). Regarding the British context, Anthony Reddie notes the more subtle (and possibly more insidious) nature of racism which contrasts that in America. 'In the politely veneered climate of British racism, this form of effortless cultural superiority is not spelt out in the visceral and polemical terms that have characterized the USA' (Reddie, 2009, p. 8). For those of us who may want to challenge racism, we must also be attentive to the anxiety that desires to enact change without being changed ourselves. This is a privilege that White people have, to opt out of the situation when we desire. This 'privilege' is manifested in a 'contractual compassion' which exhibits obedience to love our Black neighbour provided that our neighbour conforms to our White image, and doesn't actually affect our White lives and contexts (Reddie, 2008, pp. 137–56).

Reddie clarifies this from the perspective of being a Black man living in Britain today, who works in both the church and the sphere of academic theology. 'To belong to British society and that of the church, for a Black person, necessitates a denial of one's self' (Reddie, 2006, p. 22). Whiteness (a concept that will require development) enables White people to ignore race, along with the invisible subjectivity of being White, and in contrast Blackness often suffers diminishment and a denial of agency. This diminishment is not just at the hands of Whiteness. In a recent work, Reddie articulates the tragic complexity and insidious pathology of Whiteness upon 'non-White' people, which distorts Black imaginative horizons ontologically. This means Black people imbibe a self-understanding that is engendered by a White gospel, and a White Christian anthropology is self-denigrating for Blacks. 'Christianity has conditioned Black people into internalizing the tropes of empire within their psyche, so they end up, inadvertently, defending the very entities that have oppressed them (Reddie, 2019, p. 7).

One of the things that possibly resulted off the back of Floyd's death was that White contexts (including churches and theological institutions) became confronted by the reality of race and the presumptuous postures and sensibilities of Whiteness that have hitherto been evaded or relativized. Yolanda Pierce suggests that White privilege 'allows [me] to turn the bad news off and walk away' (Pierce, 2016). I wonder whether Floyd's death has resulted in a global protest which has made it impossible for some White contexts to ignore this any longer.

Saying that, some have certainly tried. Arun Arora notes the disdain expressed for Floyd as a 'worthless piece of scum' by some who did not know his context, nor did they know him (Arora, 2023, p. 61). Arora presents a different story of George Floyd from the one projected by those who do not know him. Growing up in Houston, he went from being a promising athlete to entering a history of crime that involved drugs and theft, resulting in his imprisonment. While incarcerated for five years, he 'turned to Jesus Christ' and, upon his release, became committed to changing his ways and following Jesus in his context. His involvement in a local church demonstrated his commitment to spiritual and social change. 'A friend from the church said that George recognized the deep-seated issues in the area and wanted to help be part of the change' (Arora, 2023, p. 61). Arora quotes Floyd himself, who, in a local video, remarked on his concern to end gun violence in the name of Jesus, as someone who knew the reality of life in his neighbourhood:

I've got my shortcomings and my flaws and I ain't better than nobody else. But, man, the shootings that's going on, I don't care what 'hood you're from, where you're at, man. I love you and God loves you. Put them guns down. (Arora, 2023, p. 62)

In 2017, Floyd moved to Minneapolis from Houston as part of a discipleship programme through the church. He 'helped many in his community, becoming part of a church seeking to improve the lives of those in need ... even in death, it seems George Floyd is not free from judgement by those who will never be able to see the image of Christ in him' (Arora, 2023, p. 63). In reading this illuminating perspective on George Floyd, I was reminded of something that Bonhoeffer writes in his most famous book, *Discipleship*. I will quote him at length, as he seems to recognize the image of Christ in folks like Floyd, while offering a sharp rebuke against those who dismiss him as 'scum':

Jesus' community today ought to examine whether at the moment it enters God's presence for prayer and worship many accusing voices rise up between it and God and hinder its prayers. Jesus' community ought to examine whether it has given a sign of Jesus' love, which preserves, supports, and protects lives, to those whom the world has despised and dishonored. Otherwise the most correct form of worship, the most pious prayer, and the bravest confession will not help, but will give witness against it, because it has ceased following Jesus. We are not allowed to separate God from our sister or brother. (*DBWE* 4, p. 123)

For too long, many White churches have separated God from our Black or Brown sister or brother. Indeed, our understanding of salvation, sin, faith and other theological concepts has been abstracted away from any context whatsoever. To a certain extent, there is scope for this. After all, the God we contemplate and worship is more than and different from the creaturely time and space within which we exist; God is present as the one who is invisible, near to us through the divine hiddenness, not paradoxically nor in a manner that is commensurate with creatures, but God is mysteriously compatible with creation without ceasing to be the creator. 'The utter Otherness of God remains in the midst of His Nearness to creation' (Sonderegger, 2015, p. 85). That said – and some dogmaticians may convincingly disagree with me here – any talk about 'God' is *always* operative from within a social, political, historical, economic (and other) context. A particular arrangement of doctrinal claims will emerge in response to challenges of the time (the Nicene Creed being a case in point). Emphases are constituted based on the questions that are contemplated by individuals and people groups in particular places and times. We might say, risking pretentiousness in the process, that 'Jesus Christ alone is perfect theology' (*theos-logos*). What I mean by this is not to reduce God-talk to Christocratic absolutism, but to suggest that attending to God's word spoken in the human flesh of Jesus of Nazareth may yield a posture regarding how we pursue faith seeking understanding in this world that abstracts faith away from context (much as Western Christianity has done with Jesus himself).

Thinking about this makes it surely understandable why numerous Black folks have engaged in Black theology, why many women find their voice in feminist theology (or Black women in womanist theology), and why theological discourse increasingly emerges in a manner that takes context (in its broadest sense) seriously, free from any anxiety of somehow diminishing our God-talk as a result. I believe we can talk about God in a way that nevertheless and significantly gives integrity to the particular contextual meshwork within which we (by God's grace) live and move and have our being. Part of this book is to situate Bonhoeffer as a theologian who is Western and White (as well as Lutheran, German male etc.), operating within that paradigmatic context. This bestows integrity on his life and thought precisely as a theologian operating within a particular frame of reference. In other words, Bonhoeffer has his contextual limits. Therefore, a dynamic recognition of his contextual development is always important for appreciating *what* he says, which is yielded in part by *who* he is, and this is formed in the complex reality of life in the world alongside others. If biographies about Bonhoeffer show us anything, it is that what anyone considers noteworthy varies, as well as the interpretation of what is noted. As such, the picture painted of him varies significantly. Of course, this book is no exception, as I, like anyone else, live within a particular context, so I must be read alongside others, in openness and sociality. This point gestures at the heart of how Bonhoeffer understands his doctrine of sin.

Sin as the 'heart turned in on itself'

Throughout his work, Bonhoeffer adopts and socializes the Reformation suggestion that sin can be described (though not explained) as the *cor curvum in se*, the 'heart turned in upon itself' which he deploys in a way that is both vertical and horizontal. Sin in this way is 'the ontic inversion into the self' (*DBWE* 2, p. 46). Understanding sin this way removes it from moralisms that we can discern in and of ourselves. Part of the problem for Bonhoeffer is that ethics (including 'Christian' ethics) presumes that human beings can know what is good or evil/sinful, which is precisely the issue he wants to address. Human beings do not know the reality and depths of sin until they are confronted by God's revelatory Word in Christ. As with revelation, any self-understanding of sin that is wrought internally in human self-knowledge merely exhibits the self-enclosure of the *cor curvum in se* that has been exposed and judged by God in Christ (*DBWE* 2, p. 81). To say 'this is good' or 'this is bad' is potentially problematic in that sin is far deeper and more serious than merely designating right from wrong. The very act of posturing ourselves to be arbiters of right and wrong is the original, or we might say the 'ultimate', sin. We note Bonhoeffer's interpretation of Genesis 3, that Adam and Eve wanted to abstract the knowledge of good and evil away from the tree (land) which meant away from God, which resulted in them abstracting themselves away from one another, their hearts turning inwards as a result (*DBWE* 3, pp. 115–20). In breaking away from fellowship with God and the freedom their creator bestows within the boundaries of creation and its creatures; in turning away from God's word, they intrinsically turn away from creation and its creatures. There is a simultaneity between the vertical (God–human) and the horizontal (human–human) relation (Bethge, 2000, p. 135). Therefore, 'It is by losing their direct relationship with God that they lose their direct relationship with each other and the community is broken' (Greggs, 2016, p. 86). This is one of the reasons why Bonhoeffer is critical of the preoccupation with one's own individual soul or salvation. He considers such piety to be 'nothing but ultimate egotism in its purest state, spiritualized and disguised and thus all the more dangerous' (*DBWE* 10, p. 533). The individualism behind this view of Christian faith is actually anti-Christian, idolatrous and merely religious escapism (*DBWE* 12, p. 286; cf. Luke 17.33). This is not to say Bonhoeffer does not care for ultimate and eschatological questions or individual people. What matters, however, is that individuals are saved by Christ from their introspective egotism or self-enclosure, to be reconciled to God and creation as well as themselves, by being brought into a new humanity that offers a new (redeemed) individuality so to speak. This is why coaxing people into heaven by trying to convince them how sinful they are is theologically short-sighted, and such an approach remains encaged within the *cor curvum in se* that Bonhoeffer believes we are called to renounce. In prison, he poses a question to Bethge: 'Hasn't the individualistic question of saving our personal souls almost faded away for most of us?' (*DBWE* 8, p. 372). This perspective of the gospel pervades Christian communities, including my own Baptist tradition.

This is why Bonhoeffer was more forthright than others in his challenging the Third Reich and the exclusion of Jewish believers from German congregations. On 15 September 1935 the Nuremberg Laws cancelled citizenship for German Jews and prohibited marriage between Jews and Aryans (*DBWE* 5, p. 183). This had direct implications for Bonhoeffer's family, as his sister, Sabine, had married a Jewish man, Gerhard Leibholz. Moreover, the fate of the church and its witness was at stake. In 'Heritage and Decay', which is an essay from *Ethics*, he claims, 'Driving out the Jew(s) from the West must result in driving out Christ with them, for Jesus Christ was a Jew' (*DBWE* 6, p. 105). If sin is understood on individualistic terms, the way others are treated may be important to an extent – as a missional technique or a means of sanctification perhaps – but will not be critical for one's personal salvation. This is precisely the understanding of sin and salvation that Bonhoeffer challenges in his view of the gospel of Jesus Christ. He would claim that our broken relationship with God (however we might understand that) is intrinsically wrapped up in our broken relationship with others and, indeed, with creation as a whole. He frames this as a vertical (God and humanity) and horizontal (humanity and humanity) issue (Bethge, 2000, p. 135). What he means by this is that turning away, falling away from, losing faith in, or rejecting God (however you may want to put it) not only has implications for our life as people. This brokenness and sinfulness that we are trying to get a sense of is enacted and borne within the arena of creaturely life. Therefore, separating our fall from God from our fallen relationships is not a biblical, Christian concept. Rather, it is a posture driven by the individualism and cheap gospel that we see today, and which Bonhoeffer witnessed in his own time. For Bonhoeffer, excluding Jews was not a moral or ethical issue, but a salvation issue, a real-time falling away from the freedom God established for humanity. Bonhoeffer therefore went so far as to write about this using strong doctrinal language in a 1936 essay, 'On the Question of Church Communion':

> *Extra ecclesiam nulla salus* [outside of the church there is no salvation]. The question of church communion is the question of the community of salvation. The boundaries of the church are the boundaries of salvation. Whoever knowingly separates himself from the Confessing Church in Germany separates himself from salvation ... Those who separate the question of the Confessing Church from the question of their own salvation have not comprehended that the struggle of the Confessing Church is the struggle for their salvation. (*DBWE* 14, p. 675)

For those of us who are used to articulating a faith that is personal, this may seem a little intense and imperialistic of Bonhoeffer. How dare he claim that not being part of the church is a salvation issue! Well, we will come onto the matter of the church more in the next chapter. For now, the point I want to highlight is the strong, doctrinally charged distinction and unreconcilable opposition that Bonhoeffer was making between the Confessing Church (*Bekennende Kirche*) and the Reich Church (*Reichskirche*). The Confessing Church derived its name as a Protestant movement that arose in opposition to the government-sponsored efforts to unify every Protestant church and denomination into the German Evangelical Church, which was pro-Nazi. For the 'German Christians' it was absolutely fine to say that God is real, that they believed in the gospel of salvation and the forgiveness of sins even, while participating or being complicit in the exclusion of Jewish believers from their congregations and shared worship. This is not merely an ethical or moral matter for Bonhoeffer because the very crucible of Christian community is the social context within which the salvation of God in Christ is wrought and given anew. To tamper with this context by choosing who can or cannot be within it is to disfigure the person and work of Christ, and to distort any proclamation of the gospel away from its origin. In other words, Bonhoeffer hated the doctrines of sin that enabled people to reduce Christ to a vending machine of self-serving piety, which conveniently required nothing from people's lives that would cost them.

In *Discipleship*, Bonhoeffer went to town against what he described as 'cheap grace', and the following passage – which is quite long but definitely worth it – offers a profound challenge to those of us for whom sin and salvation have nothing to do with our neighbour, nor anything to do with what we do in this life:

> Cheap grace is the mortal enemy of our church … Cheap grace means grace as bargain-basement goods, cut-rate forgiveness, cut-rate comfort, cut-rate sacrament … It is grace without price, without costs … Cheap grace means grace as doctrine, as principle, as system. It means forgiveness of sins as a general truth; it means God's love as merely a Christian idea of God. Those who affirm it have already had their sins forgiven. The church that teaches this doctrine of grace thereby confers such grace upon itself. The world finds in this church a cheap cover-up for its sins, for which it shows no remorse and from which it has even less desire to be set free. Cheap grace is, thus, denial of God's living word, denial of the incarnation of the word of God. Cheap grace means justification of sin but not of the sinner. Because grace alone

does everything, everything can stay in its old ways. 'Our action is in vain.' The world remains world and we remain sinners 'even in the best of lives.' Thus, the Christian should live the same way the world does ... The Christian better not rage against grace or defile that glorious cheap grace by proclaiming anew a servitude to the letter of the Bible in an attempt to live an obedient life under the commandments of Jesus Christ! ... So the Christian need not follow Christ, since the Christian is comforted by grace! That is cheap grace as justification of sin, but not justification of the contrite sinner who turns away from sin and repents. It is not forgiveness of sin that separates those who sinned from sin. Cheap grace is that grace that we bestow on ourselves.

Cheap grace is preaching forgiveness without repentance; it is baptism without the discipline of community; it is the Lord's Supper without confession of sin; it is absolution without personal confession. Cheap grace is grace without discipleship, grace without the cross, grace without the living, incarnate Jesus Christ. (*DBWE* 4, pp. 43–4)

Bonhoeffer is not disregarding the doctrine of salvation by grace alone. He is a Lutheran after all. However, he perceived a doctrine of grace that had manoeuvred the seriousness of sin into a little pious corner of what we could call pseudo-Lutheranism. The grace of God in Christ does not mean that people can lean on 'forgiveness' or 'sorrow over sin' as a way of evading the new life to which Christ calls them, and to which the Holy Spirit thrusts them. To separate one's eternal 'soul' from one's earthly 'soul' is to reject the God of the Bible, for in Christ we witness the reality of God and the world inseparably bound together (*DBWE* 6, p. 55).

But we miss the point if we think that sin is simply about excluding people from church based on their racial profile. Pragmatically and morally, we may look back and feel horrified that this happened under the watch of 'Christian' people. Indeed, some of us in Britain may look at America and be perplexed at what we witness in terms of the racism that continues there. However, while people in Britain spoke boldly and categorically against slavery in my country, and some philanthropists even offered financial support to the 'Black poor' of Britain in the freezing winter of 1785–86, this was often less than what was offered to those Whites who were also poor. Furthermore, the gratuitous giving offered by some Whites, such as John Julius Angerstein, for example, had come from the backs of their Black slaves in the colonies, content to support the freedom of Blacks on British soil while perpetuating the enslavement of others on plantations (Olusoga, 2021, pp. 161–3). Thus they made themselves richer while appearing virtuous at the same time. It strikes me that some of us (myself included) can be much more receptive to those in front of us, that is, those with whom we rub shoulders on a regular basis. It is easier to reduce a person to an idea if we are not physically confronted by them in time and space. I know various folks who are not White British, who found it very frustrating and patronizing when the Brexit vote happened in 2016 for the UK to leave the European Union. A number of predominantly White and British people seemed surprised that their British Caribbean, Canadian, German or Indian friends felt upset by their desire to leave the EU. The common rhetoric often went along the lines of: 'I don't mean you, but those other people, you know, real foreigners. I think we should protect our country from them.' The big problem with excluding people from the Christian community is that we can reduce individuals and people groups to abstract ideas, which encourages us in our incessant inclination to judge others. While having face-to-face encounters with others is not a foolproof way of avoiding judgement (if only!), the confrontation and struggle to navigate real encounters with real people reduces the likelihood of envisaging them and judging them within our own isolated epistemology. Rubbing shoulders with Jewish believers under word and sacrament was far more important to Bonhoeffer than merely being inclusive or moralistic. It was to come face to face with the human propensity to 'other' others according to the world's rubric of what was good and right and true. For Bonhoeffer, this touches on the very heart and depths and elusive seriousness of sin.

One of our issues in the White Western church is that we sometimes end up with a polemic of whether we talk about sin as a communal, social, structural phenomenon, or whether we talk about sin as an individual, (intra-)personal, moral issue. Bonhoeffer is not interested in joining the discussion as he thinks both are an attempt to reduce our understanding of sin to being something that we can grasp and then potentially manage, explain or utilize for our own ends. Sin is not merely disobeying God's command. People can sin in their obedience. As Matthew Kirkpatrick puts it, 'For Bonhoeffer, the greatest danger is not a rejection of God but an acceptance of God *on our own terms*' (Kirkpatrick, 2024, p. 48). We value the use of reason, not least in theology, but sin is the enthroning of reason in the place of God as the human means of discerning good and evil. In ourselves, our own musings and moral compasses, we think we know what it means to be human, what good and evil are, how to love, who to spend time with, the way we should prioritize responsibilities, and various approaches to right living, even in what we deliberate over as Christian ethics. Bonhoeffer seems to suggest that people in this world are not generally evil by intent, but good intentions 'can grow out of very dark backgrounds in human consciousness and subconsciousness, and that often the worst things happen as a result of "good intentions"' (*DBWE* 6, p. 52). In a London sermon from 1934, Bonhoeffer recalls the familiar phrase, 'The road to hell is paved with good intentions' (*DBWE* 13, p. 347). Sin is not reducible to a lack of desire or rational orientation towards the good, right and true. Rather, sin is the extrapolation of what is good, right and true away from its ultimate origin, mediator and goal in God. Drawing on Augustine and Luther, Bonhoeffer's simple description of sin can be located in the motif of the *cor curvum in se* – the heart turned in upon itself (*DBWE* 2, pp. 46, 80, 89; *DBWE* 10, p. 399; *DBWE* 12, pp. 229–30). Human 'fallenness' is the state of humankind turned inwards, away from God and others, towards the self, which is a perpetual cycle of self-reference, self-verification, self-justification, self-deification, self-isolation, self-division and self-loathing (*DBWE* 3, p. 26). To put it simply, Bonhoeffer identifies sin as the state of being utterly obsessed by and enslaved within the self. This is why individualistic notions of salvation perpetuate the very fallenness that Bonhoeffer believes we are saved from, and why so many people find a gospel message that foregrounds the question of 'heaven or hell' to be vapid and, frankly, not good news at all.

This critique offered by Bonhoeffer demonstrates why so many non-White, non-Western people have struggled with the Christian witness of the White Western church. A myopic focus on everlasting life after death was the very distortion that enabled White slaveholders to 'participate in the business of slavery without denouncing their Christian faith' (Douglas, 2019, p. 3). There is a pious anxiety (or zeal) to save people from an eternal conscious torment in hell, and this is the key driving factor that constitutes and governs the mechanisms and means of much missional Christianity and evangelism. However, this 'gift' that is offered actually betrays the very essence of Christ's person and work, because it operates through and appeals to the heart turned in on itself.

There is more that can be said, but it relates a lot to the next chapter, for it is through the salvific work of Christ existing as community that the depths of sin are exposed and dealt with dynamically; that is to say, Christ confronts and redeems us regarding sin again and again as a reality that is 'ever anew' in time and space (*DBWE* 10, pp. 365–6, 457, 459, 515; *DBWE* 12, pp. 192, 229; *DBWE* 15, p. 477). At this point, you could skip forward to Chapter 7, where we explore 'Creation and Fall'. This is probably the most extensive and grounded (and accessible) place where Bonhoeffer presents a doctrine of sin within his doctrine of creation. You could go there now if you want to, or continue on to the next chapter, where we consider how Bonhoeffer understands the salvific importance of community in Christ as the critical means of rescuing isolated sinners from the heart turned in on itself, the *cor curvum in se*.

Conclusion

Bonhoeffer's personal relationships were affected by the rise of Hitler and National Socialism. He had numerous Jewish friends. In particular, he was very close to Franz Hildebrandt, a Jewish Christian. They were so close that John de Gruchy suggests, 'Had another of Bonhoeffer's close friends (say Franz Hildebrandt) become Bonhoeffer's literary executor and written his biography, in all likelihood we would have a rather different Bonhoeffer today' (De Gruchy, 2005, p. xiii). Eberhard Bethge, who wrote the authoritative (and over 1,000-page!) biography of Bonhoeffer, spent much more time making music with Bonhoeffer when they were together, as they were both musicians. In contrast, according to Bethge's wife Renate (Bonhoeffer's niece), 'when Bonhoeffer and his close friend Franz Hildebrandt met they invariably talked theology' (quoted in De Gruchy, 2005, p. 17). Mark Nation suggests that Hildebrandt's unyielding commitment to non-violence may have offered a different lens for interpreting Bonhoeffer's life, particularly his involvement in the *Abwehr*. As an Anabaptist, Nation asks:

> What difference would it make to our reception of the legacy of Dietrich Bonhoeffer if we quit framing his life and thought in terms of his being executed for his role in the plots to kill Hitler and instead began with the realization that he was executed in Nazi Germany for courageously proclaiming, and seeking to live faithfully in light of, the gospel of Jesus Christ? As a result, he was executed for rescuing Jews, being a conscientious objector to military service, and being perceived as an enemy of the state. (Nation, 2022, p. 23)

Throughout his life, Bonhoeffer sought to live in freedom for God and others, and much of his project is a cry against the human heart's inclination to turn inwards. This even happens within Bonhoeffer studies, where particular horizons are foregrounded, and (so I am told) those with different views can fall out and fall away from one another. I am aware that the subject of race is contentious, and from my own experience some White people are wary of recognizing and validating the perspectives shared by Black and Brown people on the experiences they have had. We are all tempted at times to solidify our perspective as a means of bolstering what we believe to be good and right and true, and while robust dialogue and exchange is important, the means and the ways by which we go about this are critical. Sometimes the way we (Whites) respond to challenges and criticisms by Black and Brown people can be indignant, defensive, bewildered or sorrowful in a self-focused way, perpetuating the state of the heart turned in upon itself. I struggle with this too, yet I think we must be wary of reacting in an introspective way towards others in this discussion, and in relation to others who confront us with challenges pertaining to racialization and race. The problem of sin and, for this book in particular, racism, is that it lures us into isolated spaces, opposing oppressed and oppressor against one another. There are multiple viewpoints regarding how 'non-White' people should posture themselves in this regard, and I do not want to focus on that so much. Instead, I want to speak from my own horizons, as someone who has rarely had to change the tune of my life to fit in with this world. White folks would do well to recognize the challenge we are posed with, to humble ourselves to listen and not to be closed off because of the different starting points or perspectives that are thrown in our direction. Sometimes, we perpetuate sin and human fallenness by reacting against others who we may never fully understand.

I am encouraged that Bonhoeffer was not perfect. Sometimes he is painted as a sinless saint, particularly in popular circles. He would have hated such a designation, but what encourages me is that he was committed to recognizing sin (including his own) and to facing it without any pretence or illusory evasiveness. On 11 April 1933, Gerhard Leibholz's father died. As I have mentioned above, Gerhard was married to Dietrich's twin sister, Sabine, and he was Jewish. Gerhard's father had never been baptized, but the family asked Dietrich to conduct the funeral. Bonhoeffer 'was persuaded to consult his general superintendent', writes Bethge, 'who strongly advised against conducting a funeral service for a Jew at this particular time' (Bethge, 2000, p. 275). Several months later, on 23 November 1933, Bonhoeffer wrote to his brother-in-law expressing his deep regret:

> I am tormented even now by the thought that I didn't do as you asked me as a matter of course. To be frank, I can't think what made me behave as I did. How could I have been so horribly afraid at the time? It must have seemed equally incomprehensible to you both, and yet you said nothing. But it preys on my mind, because it's the kind of thing one can never make up for. So all I can do is ask you to forgive my weakness

then. I know now for certain that I ought to have behaved differently ... I believe that your father, Gert, would probably have lived through even these times with an unwavering and much stronger confidence in the future than most of us have. But it must be wonderful to be at peace, as Hans said at the time ... I'm sorry! (*DBWE* 13, pp. 42–3)

Bonhoeffer could not change what he did (or rather, did not do), but acknowledged it, sought forgiveness, and appears to have moved forward in the light of that experience as one who had repented, who did not want to carry on living evasively and out of the privilege of self-preservation. He discovered that his relationships with others would require renouncing his own security and desire to be right. For some of us, particularly White men, it can be difficult to be criticized for unintentional racialized behaviour. This is partly because we want to be in control of our sin, and in Bonhoeffer's mind that is the deep crux of our sinfulness. I am not saying that all White men are racist in the basic sense, but reacting individualistically in defence of ourselves risks the posturing to turn inwards upon ourselves, thus falling away from those through whom we could have mutual community. As I was writing this chapter, I was reminded of a song I wrote that captures some of this, the depths of the human heart, the confusion we sometimes face, and the presence of a God who meets us in the midst of it.

Brother

We're locked up tight sometimes,
chained down by thoughts we don't understand
Like every honest man
We long to break out but,
there's no way of losing our own enemy
When you're the one you flee
We feel at sea with our evil deeds
and our infant dreams hide our inner demons and
All we need is some room to breathe and
some time to see where the light could be

Oh, my brother, when we fall we may let go
And we would lose ourselves but
don't you know, we're bound by blood and water
and it overflows, bleeding through our darkness

CONTEXT AND SIN

Great secrets we compose,
trying to shine and finding we are only more exposed
whatever light we try to show
We hide our failures,
fearing revealing the impostors we really are
Honest lies and open scars
Oh and we cry, 'Abba, Father' into the great abyss within our soul
Where no holy saint should go
And we need an answer that doesn't leave us dying in this bleak
For I know I am far too weak
Old pithy comebacks from over-trodden tracks
all throwing facts that just attack
While the smoke and the mirrors all hammer and hack
at a starving humanity plagued by a lack of

Oh, my brother, when we fall we may let go
And we would lose ourselves but
don't you know, we're bound by blood and water
and it overflows, bleeding through our darkness

The day plays many tricks,
treats us like fools for being tied within our time
Where no moment is truly mine
The space we move in, mocks the way we cannot make it
to every place that we dream to go
It stops you feeling free you know
But being human, is surely more than,
feeling lost and finding nothing
We're tired of fighting and always losing,
and I need something more than me

Oh, my brother, when we fall we may let go
And we would lose ourselves but
don't you know, we're bound by blood and water
and it overflows, bleeding through our darkness

(Penned July 2017)

4

Communion and Salvation

In April 2023, my wife Becca and I went to Rome to celebrate our ten-year anniversary. Our parents agreed to tag team in relieving us from our crazy, wonderful boys so that we could get a few days alone together. After deliberating over whether we should fly, given the carbon footprint of aeroplanes, we decided to go for it, and had a really special time in the ancient city.

We saw a lot of the old sights, and like a proper Bonhoeffer geek I read his diary entries from when he had visited Rome 99 years earlier than us (in 1924). I found the colosseum particularly mind-blowing, and I learnt that they even had 'water fights' there, having flooded the whole arena to include hippos and boats in the theatrics of antiquity's iconic spectacles.

While in Rome, I attempted to embrace Bonhoeffer's spirit of ecumenism and so we visited St Peter's Basilica, as well as the Vatican. While I do not regret heading to these places, and found them beautiful on many levels, my memory of these places are also tainted with sadness.

First, we entered the Vatican. After passing through the security checks, we came to a spiral path that ascended upwards. Along this winding walkway, there were displays and pictures of boats from all around the world. At the very foot of the ascent, there was a sign explaining the significance of this exhibition. Part of the sign read as follows:

> These [boats] represent the civilizations of Humankind, they are witness to the historical attention, the curiosity and the respect of the Catholic universe toward non-European cultures. They symbolize the destiny of the Church of Rome that is 'Peter's boat' in the journey toward the salvation of all.

Before we had gone anywhere, I was overcome with a kind of gloom. I was maybe wrong to interpret the sign in the way I did, but it appeared to be equating the 'Catholic universe' and its Roman Catholic optic with European culture. For someone who is wrestling through the legacy of colonial Christianity, this was deeply troubling (for reasons I have explored in the previous chapter). Furthermore, the sign also intimated that the 'destiny' of the (White European) Catholic Church is to be the 'vessel' of salvation to the world. There is much to reflect on here, but this posture seems (to this Baptist minister and theologian at least) not only theologically hubristic, but historically inaccurate, given that Christianity did not originate with Europe at all, nor have Europeans (let alone the Catholic Church) ever been the sole or even primary 'vessel' of salvation in the world (Wilmore, 2004, pp. 103–10).

We went through the Vatican, with its White aesthetical vision of Christ and the Christian story, and then found ourselves in St Peter's Basilica. The opulence was quite something to witness, but what was tricky for us was the experience of being excluded from taking communion, or the Lord's Supper, or Eucharist, depending on your tradition. As someone who is used to entering spaces freely and feeling welcome to breathe easily, it was a potent (albeit polite) realization of how it feels to be excluded and dismissed as not Christian enough. I appreciate much about the Roman Catholic Church, not least the theological and social examples of folks such as Oscar Romero and Mother Teresa, as well as the intellectual insights I have learnt from reading Thomas Aquinas. However, it was (and continues to feel) difficult that my wife and I were not accepted at the (Roman Catholic) Lord's table. Would it have been sinful for us to be welcome to share in the sacrament? From my perspective, it felt sinful and institutionally short-sighted to exclude us, though nonconformists like me are well known for our sin and ignorance! That said, if a fellow child of God and disciple of Jesus is not welcome to share bread and wine, to commune with the Lord alongside other saints from other streams of the church, what does that mean theologically? What does this do theologically, and does it have implications regarding salvation and how we understand salvation? On a more practical (but not unrelated) level, how does this relate to our lives in real terms, as well as the witness of our churches and liturgies, our political entanglement in the world, and what it *is* to be a Christian? While I cannot satisfy my questions fully here, this chapter will explore some of Bonhoeffer's thinking in terms of how he understands the Christian community, and how his doctrine of salvation cannot be separated from the church. This is because, for Bonhoeffer, the church in its most essential sense is 'Christ existing as community' (*DBWE* 1, p. 141). We will see that his understanding of salvation is both Christologically ecclesial and ecclesiologically Christological.

Saved from what and for what?

In his 'Lectures on Christology', Bonhoeffer qualifies from the outset that 'Christology is not soteriology' (*DBWE* 12, p. 308). His point here is twofold. First, the *work* of Christ is not the totality of *who* he is, though it of course reveals *who* he is. The problem with identifying Christ's person and work synonymously is that *who* we worship is at risk of being reduced to a mere functionary. Love is indeed a verb, as DC Talk would say. However, love is also a person, not just the actions that person carries out. Therefore, Christ is not just a means to an end; he is the way, the truth and the life, the reality of a new humanity which he achieves for us and mediates to us as the goal of *who* we are. Second, it is dangerous to think that our interpretation of Christ's work gives us a full picture of who he is. 'Even the works of Christ are not unambiguous' (*DBWE* 12, p. 309). A doctrine of salvation is an attempt to narrate the work of God (ultimately revealed) in Christ so that the world may witness *who* God is in relation to the world as its creator, reconciler and redeemer. Mark Knight suggests that Bonhoeffer's theology seeks to avoid such a 'functionalism insofar as the saving work of Christ does not exhaust, but is rather wholly rooted in and shaped by his person' (Knight, 2019, p. 211). To summarize, the work of salvation we witness in Christ reveals *who* he is, but he is *more* than merely his work; for Bonhoeffer, Christ is everything. Christ points us to the Triune God who achieves salvation for the world while not being strictly defined or constituted by the world (see Webster, 2015, p. 143).

This might seem incidental and irrelevant, but imagine for a moment what it would be like if people were not treated merely based on what they do, but on who they are. Imagine if a person's value was constituted by their givenness, the assumption that they were loved and, according to God's word, loveable and capable of love. Of course, love is not a mere state of mind, but the angst within much of our society to prove ourselves (including our love) plagues many of our relationships, and much of our make-up in society, including the church. People are deemed of worth based on what they can do for 'us' or 'me'. This not only reduces human beings to human doings, but also views them through a narrow optic of self-focused acquisition. I want something, or more of something, and a person is useful if they can enable me to achieve that. Furthermore, my assumptions of what I want or need will confer value upon others through my very assumptions of what I want or need. In other words, a person's value is partly based on presumptions of what is good, right and true *for me*. Even the 'gospel' of Jesus Christ suffers from this introspective and self-serving vision of salvation at times. A pious prayer of repentance seems more than adequate as a means of securing oneself against God's merciful judgement and costly grace. Such a perspective on the saving work of Christ is anaemic and anti-gospel precisely because its sole focus is on one's own salvation, rather than the God who saves and those with whom we are saved. This is precisely the sort of 'gospel' and religion that was deployed to assuage any discipleship and responsibility for justice during the transatlantic slave trade, and why the contemporary issue of race is dismissed by so many White people as being 'not a gospel issue' or even disregarded so quickly as 'woke' or 'Marxist', which is a profoundly short-sighted perspective. This is also the heart of the problem that Bonhoeffer saw in the German church excluding Jewish believers from congregations on racial grounds. This was not merely a secondary or 'ethical' issue, but a theological and salvation issue because it concerned the gospel of Jesus Christ.

For Bonhoeffer, salvation is impossible to talk about in abstraction from real life, that is, life in communion with others as with God. In the same way that sin entails a 'fall' from God and others in the world, salvation is about reconciliation with God and others in the world. The huge mistake in much of Western Protestantism is that we have separated God and others in our theology and discipleship, considering salvation to be something that relates to God directly and solely, while our life in the world is at best an outworking of that if we are up to it. For Bonhoeffer, faith in the salvation of God in Christ is intrinsically a faith that concretizes in earthly obedience. My ascent to a belief in the event of salvation through Christ is inauthentic if it remains an isolated belief, devoid of any obedience. This is certainly risky talk. But Bonhoeffer is anxious over and against the human inclination to be masters of our faith. Faith of the sort that does not result in discipleship is not a faith *in Christ* at all, but a faith in one's own ability to believe in and of ourselves, positing a 'God' of religious self-actualization at the expense of repentance unto Christ's call to 'follow me' (cf. Matt. 4.19; 8.22; 9.9; 10.38; 16.24; 19.21, 28; Mark 1.17; 2.14; 8.34; 10.21; Luke 5.27; 9.23, 59; 18.22; John 1.43; 8.12; 10.27; 12.26; 13.36; 21.19, 22; see DBWE 8, pp. 479–80). Thus in *Discipleship*, he argues: '*only the believers obey*, and *only the obedient believe*' (DBWE 4, p. 63).

All this is to say that Bonhoeffer's understanding of salvation cannot be focused solely or primarily on us as individuals, but on *Jesus Christ* in his being 'for us' or 'for me'; his salvific work is the human existence 'for others' (DBWE 8, p. 501). The emphasis for Bonhoeffer is on the salvific Lord, not those who are saved per se. Otherwise, notions of being 'saved' inevitably end up turning away from the saviour and back inwards, away from the one who calls us to discipleship, towards us and what we get out of Christ. Such a view of salvation is prevalent and problematic, individualistic and insidious.

This is an important backdrop for approaching Bonhoeffer's language of Jesus Christ as the revelation of the God who is *pro nobis* (for us) and *pro me* (for me). God is *for* us rather than *against* us (Rom. 8.31–33) – that is true. However, the emphasis is on God in Christ. Indeed, faith in Christ alone means being 'torn out of imprisonment in one's own ego, liberated by Jesus Christ' (Kirkpatrick, 2024, p. 278). Faith in Christ, and in the salvation he has achieved in his incarnation, crucifixion and resurrection, can be wielded as an abstract principle, a status we confer on ourselves, which, rather than thrusting us more deeply into communion with God and others in the world, secures us ever more deeply in ourselves, without any costly discipleship, without any genuine faith, without concrete obedience to Christ's commands, without a renunciation of our own lordship over ourselves, God and (not least) others.

This gets to the heart of what salvation *is* for Bonhoeffer. To be fair, his thought develops and his language changes over the course of his career (see Knight, 2019, pp. 210–24), but there is a plumb-line theme that is constant and could be summarized in the following way. Salvation is the action of God in Christ whereby human beings are incorporated into his fundamentally new humanity. In other words, Bonhoeffer's doctrine of salvation 'begins with the *person*, who assumes, recapitulates, and renews human existence in his life, death, and resurrection, and who opens this existence to us' (Knight, 2019, p. 212). In Jesus, God has revealed that God is not a God who is aloof, introspective or self-absorbed. Rather, the very essence of God is a freedom from all the trappings and inclinations within human beings that make us self-focused, anxious, coercive, imposing, ignorant, thoughtless, judgemental; I could go on! The point is that Bonhoeffer's God is not a God who is free just for God self, lost in abstraction and self-sufficiency. God has no obligation to creation, but has freely chosen not just to create a world that is called 'good' but to complete that work by establishing the fullness of God's freedom in that world. This is a freedom for and with the world as revealed in Christ.

To summarize briefly, the gospel stories witness to God's revealed word to humanity of who God is. This God is revealed to be the God who is for the world, and who loves it. In fact, God loved the world so much that he freely gave himself to that world through the free obedience of the Son, by the power and free agency of the Holy Spirit, offering God self to the world in the incarnation, crucifixion and resurrection of Jesus.

And whoever believed in him would not perish but have eternal life. Note the only definition of 'eternal life' in the whole Bible is offered by Jesus in John 17.3: 'And this is eternal life, that they may know you, the only true God, and Jesus Christ whom you have sent.' This does not overlook existence beyond death, but it is not the heart of it. Christ is God's word about what it means to be truly human, confronting humanity with its false notion of what it is (including its understanding of what eternal life is). Humanity does not exist for itself, but for God, for one another, and for the world within which it lives. That is what it means to bear the image of God. For Bonhoeffer, Christ is the only true human, the only human being who is ultimately free, because Christ is not a victim to the *cor curvum in se*, the heart turned in upon itself. Whether because of selfishness, egoism, insecurity, ignorance, or even the temptation to lose hope in God's goodness because of our suffering or enslavement, all of us become locked in ourselves and need saving. Some do not realize this as they consider themselves to have mastered their lives (or their relationships). But for Bonhoeffer, a fundamentally new humanity is required for a world that is locked in itself. Whether someone's self-isolation is through their own sin, or the assault of sin upon their own person which causes suffering, everyone needs liberation. Christ both is and enacts a new humanity that is not constrained by a preoccupation with himself, but he has freely bound himself to others, precisely because the person of Christ is God's self-revelation for and with others.

Faith and 'vicarious representative action'

The language Bonhoeffer uses to substantiate this is *Stellvertretung*, which is somewhat clinically translated as 'vicarious representative action', but it helpfully captures how he understands the saving work of Jesus Christ. He uses the term in different ways, but it essentially refers to the work that Jesus does because he is a person who is free. That is to say, he is free from the temptation of the heart turned in upon itself; he is free from any preoccupation with his individualism; he is free for and with the world that has become locked within itself, locked within its individualism and ideological tribalism. In contrast to a world that cannot help itself, Christ breaks the continuous battle of the *cor curvum in se*. Any human 'solidarity' that is experienced apart from Christ is based on basic commonality, shared experience and likemindedness, which excludes others who do not fit. Christ does not offer this sort of solidarity, but *vicarious representative action*, which is 'Christ's willing initiative to *stand in our place on our* behalf, to be our representative and thus to take everything we had coming to us and to give us all that he is as our own' (DeCort, 2018, p. 106). Christ upholds and ensures the genuine integrity and otherness of human beings who are distinctly not Christ himself, so that he can be and reveal himself to be 'one for the other' and the precise *other* 'who is for us from the creation of the world and now at the turning point of history' (DeCort, 2018, p. 106).

This is why salvation cannot be something reducible to individual souls being 'saved' from hell, annihilation or moral failure. Sin is far deeper than this, salvation is far bigger than this, and Christ is far more glorious than this! Matt Kirkpatrick explains it best: 'Bonhoeffer does not see Christ as an abstract being who provides for our salvation at the end of life, but the God-man who comes to redeem this life in all its rich, physical relationality' (Kirkpatrick, 2024, p. 269). Preoccupation with one's individual salvation is like eating fruit from a branch that has been broken off a tree; it might taste good when it has been acquired but will eventually rot and prove devoid of any substance and source whatsoever. Yes, Christ calls individuals to follow him and his call confronts them alone (*DBWE* 4, pp. 92–4). However, this call is an absolute demand on individuals to surrender their self-made individuality to him, to renounce our status and relationships on our own terms, and to give our allegiance to him as the one who mediates our individuality to us. We are no longer individuals in and of ourselves. We are individuals in relation to others through God's work in Christ, which is what true personhood is. It is no longer individualism whatsoever because it is inseparably bound to Christ and in his body, the church community. We might say that Christ saves human beings to live in the fullness of their true individuality, which is free for and with others in and through Christ.

In the death of Christ, God reveals God's judgement regarding the form of human existence that humanity has become locked in. At the cross, every individual is Adam/Eve. Each person stands alone before God (*DBWE* 1, p. 150). The cross is the actual means through which God in Christ allows human self-righteousness to appear right (after all, the Pharisees thought they were doing the 'right' thing), but through it, God justifies God self and God's intention for human existence. God usurps human judgements and horizons, thereby pronouncing or exposing humanity as a humanity both self-deceived and guilty (*DBWE* 12, p. 398; *DBWE* 14, pp. 608–9). 'In the resurrection of Jesus Christ his death is revealed as the death of death itself ... and the humanity-of-Adam has become the church of Christ' (*DBWE* 1, pp. 151–2).

Faith in Christ entails the recognition that God has acted decisively in history to enter and liberate humanity from its bondage to sin, slavery, suffering and ultimately death. Whether one is the cause or victim of sin, Christ has borne the burdens of both upon himself, binding both to himself and constituting a mediated relationship between one another via the cross. This does not diminish the reality of wounds inflicted and borne in the world (the next chapter considers this more fully), but takes them into God's costly work of reconciliation by bearing its implications in Christ's body.

This leads us into the significance of communion. Christ's work of salvation is a reconciliation of communion with God, with others and with the world. For Bonhoeffer, the Holy Spirit actualizes that which has been realized through Christ. Within human history, that is, the here and now of life, the reality of what God has done in Jesus breaks into the present by the Holy Spirit's presence (*DBWE* 11, p. 305). When people gather together as 'church' and share in Christ's word and sacrament anew, his new humanity is witnessed. The society called the 'church' is not necessarily the heart of the church. To witness the church in its true reality requires faith. But how does a person 'experience' the true reality of church and not just some earthly institution? Bonhoeffer answers that it

> certainly does not happen in communities that are based on romantic feelings of solidarity between kindred spirits. It rather takes place where there is no other link between the individuals than that of the community that exists with the church; where Jew and Greek, pietist and liberal, come into conflict, and nevertheless in unity confess their faith, come together to the Lord's Table, and intercede for one another in prayer. (*DBWE* 1, p. 281)

Indeed, Bonhoeffer also claims it is 'extremely dangerous to confuse community romanticism with the community of saints' (*DBWE* 1, p. 278). Sharing in the body and blood of Jesus is a witness to the reconciled humanity that people are a part of because of Christ. Feeling close to people when participating in bread and wine does not necessarily mean anything in and of itself, though it can be nice. Rather, acknowledging the disparate nature of human relations, the harm caused, the wounds yet to be healed, the presumptions not yet redressed; all of these things can be borne in Christ's brokenness as the raw material from which we are all made new. We remain sinners and sufferers together, but we witness our joining together as a reality of faith, and are reoriented to live in the light of this reality.

Liberation from otherworldliness and secularism

Later chapters will expand on the complexities of what this sort of new humanity involves, but for now it is hopefully clear as to why Bonhoeffer refuses to allow a severing between God and neighbour when we talk about salvation. Salvation is the reconciliation of communion with God, the world and (as a result) with our true selves. Ignoring conversations about racial reconciliation or reparations risks ignoring salvation in its fullest sense. There are complexities regarding how this outworks itself, and Bonhoeffer is alive to the risk of coercion, imposition and abuse that can happen in Christian communities in the name of Christ. It is worth considering two extremes for how we can sometimes weaponize or distort the reality of the gospel in our worldly existence.

In Philippians 2.12–13, the Apostle Paul encourages the fledgling Christian community to take seriously the reality of Christ's reconciling work:

> Therefore, my beloved, just as you have always obeyed me, not only in my presence, but much more now in my absence, work out your own salvation with fear and trembling; for it is God who is at work in you, enabling you both to will and to work for his good pleasure.

But how do we work out our salvation, let alone with fear and trembling? In an essay called 'Thy Kingdom Come', Bonhoeffer offers two extremes to help us avoid any misunderstanding: otherworldliness and secularism. *Otherworldliness* is no more than religious escapism. 'When life begins to be difficult and oppressive, one leaps boldly into the air and soars, relieved and worry free, in the so-called eternal realm' (*DBWE* 12, p. 286). *Secularism* grasps sole responsibility to build God's kingdom for God and establish salvation through human initiative, so 'faith is compelled to harden into religious convention and morality, and the church into an organization of action for religious-moral reconstruction' (*DBWE* 12, p. 287). These extremes are two sides of the same coin, a lack of faith in God's kingdom, and instead, belief in the kingdom of self. Against these perspectives, Bonhoeffer retorts: 'Whoever evades Earth in order to find God finds only himself. Whoever evades God in order to find the Earth does not find the Earth as God's Earth … in short, he finds himself' (*DBWE* 12, p. 288). For Bonhoeffer, Christians misunderstand the gospel if they think they can super-spiritually detach from the world into an otherworldly bliss and wash their hands of the world that has failed to be faithful (as though the church itself is). But nor can the institutional church consider itself to be the instigator of an imperial Christianity, lamenting or squashing those in the world that fail to comply with its own 'Christian' ideals. Salvation is eternal life, or, to put it differently, life that is pregnant with the eternal, which means living fully in the world in a way that is continually rediscovering one's orientation within the world that is reconciled by God in Christ.

The universality of the cross: Bonhoeffer's doctrine of election

Some people may have read this chapter and felt I am evading the 'ultimate' question. I hope the next chapter will ground this one in terms of how Bonhoeffer saw the relationship between 'ultimate' and 'penultimate' questions. But the question does remain as to where Bonhoeffer stood regarding themes such as God's final judgement and whether all or only some will be saved. To ask such a question first would be to commit the mistake he highlights in his rebuttal against individualistic notions of salvation. However, his eschatology and thoughts on the 'end' do require a brief note, and my sincere thanks to Corey Tuttle for the work he is doing in this area.

First, it is important to note the influence of Karl Barth on Bonhoeffer in this regard. Barth was famous for redressing the doctrine of election espoused by the Reformation tradition. This doctrine claimed 'that God divides humanity into two groups, those elected for eternal life, and those elected towards damnation' (Tuttle, 2022). This was a radical departure and a doing away with a perspective that is prevalent today among many, not least among evangelical Calvinists (Tietz, 2021, p. 370). For Barth, in Jesus Christ, God elects God self as the subject and object of election, electing God self for rejection and unification with God. In Christ, God says No and Yes to humanity, and in so doing, God is gracious in enfolding humanity into unity with God through including all in Christ, as Christ is the only rejected one (Barth, 1994a, p. 101). Tuttle shows that Bonhoeffer found Barth's redressing of the traditional Reformation to be gripping. However, Tuttle also draws our attention to Bonhoeffer's thinking before he came across Barth, where he gestures at a particular perspective on salvation and the eschatological end (*telos*) of creation that perhaps anticipates Barth's doctrine of election, whereby all are included in God's saving work.

Bonhoeffer does not use the term 'universalism' to describe this idea, but deploys the word *apokatastasis* (or *apocatastasis*), a Greek term that refers to the restoration of all things. He uses the term in his earliest and latest writing, and suggests a specifically Christian universalism rather than a pluralistic one. Tuttle actually notes 12 occasions on which this term is used. The fullest account of this is in *Sanctorum Communio*:

> We must not speak of a dual outcome here without at the same time emphasizing the inner necessity of the idea of apocatastasis. We are unable to resolve this paradox. On the one hand, the concept of the church, as Christ's presence in the world which calls for a decision, necessarily demands the dual outcome. The recognition that the gift of God's boundless love has been received without any merit would, on the other hand, make it seem just as impossible to exclude others from this gift and this love. The strongest reason for accepting the idea of apocatastasis would seem to me that all Christians must be aware of having brought sin into the world, and thus aware of being bound together with the whole of humanity in sin, aware of having the sins of humanity on their conscience. Justification and sanctification are inconceivable for anyone if that individual believer cannot be assured that God will embrace not only them but all those for whose sins they are responsible. But all statements in this regard only express a hope; they cannot be made part of a system. (*DBWE* 1, pp. 286–7)

What is clear is that Bonhoeffer considers that the cross has a universality to it, and that universality not only extends to all people, but enfolds all people. Yet, and crucially, he seems wary of making this into 'part of a system' which could make a doctrine of universal salvation abstract. Tuttle summarizes that '[Bonhoeffer] was content with letting the logic of reprobation and *apokatastasis* exist simultaneously while trusting that, somehow, in the end all would be saved' (Tuttle, 2022).

This raises lots of questions, and Tuttle's continuing work will hopefully offer more clarity on how Bonhoeffer's thoughts on universal salvation might relate to his more contemporary concerns about the situation in Germany, and how Christian theology and ethics (of salvation) impact the church's engagement with the world. But one thing is worth mentioning here, which is that whatever he thought, Bonhoeffer did not have a theology that overlooked sin and judgement. For him, the work of salvation was costly; it must be taken with the utmost seriousness. My own experience is that many who advocate for a theology of universalism appeal to the 'love' of God in a manner that diminishes (or juxtaposes it against) the judgement (or even the 'wrath') of God, and that is not the approach Bonhoeffer takes. Bonhoeffer lived in a time where racial divides and exclusion were legitimized by the church, and distinguishing itself along racial lines distorted its nature and work so that it became apostate. And yet, Bonhoeffer's view of salvation and discipleship meant that he identified vicariously with the apostate church, with the state zeitgeist, as well as with those victimized by the church and state. His understanding of salvation in Christ meant that he vicariously bore the guilt of the church and state genuinely upon himself as his participation in the life of Christ. In Gethsemane, Christ's disciples rejected him as they fell asleep, but Christ bound them to himself through his suffering and prayer. In the same way, Bonhoeffer considered his vocation (and that of all disciples) to be one where he was bound to a world and church in its godlessness and apostasy through his suffering and prayer for and with it. It is not that Bonhoeffer had an overly optimistic view of humanity that he looked towards apokatastasis, but rather, because he believed no one could escape the will of God in Christ, even in their rejection of him, for Christ has borne that into himself too.

Conclusion

There is a popular spiritual song that contains the words, 'We will wait till Jesus come to carry our loved ones home.' Some popular sources suggest that this song emerged not with an eschatological emphasis but with a historical and spatially salvific one. A very famous ship during the transatlantic slave trade was *Jesus of Lübeck*. Some sources suggest that the *Jesus* referred to in the song is not the incarnate, crucified and resurrected Jesus, but the maritime vessel that had been given to Sir John Hawkins (a cousin of Sir Francis Drake) in 1564 by Queen Elizabeth I. Some sources have suggested that 'The original meaning of that song to the slaves was literally going back home to Africa, as when they were sold by Hawkins, he promised them he would have returned to collect the slaves' (Scott, 2018).

Hawkins was the pioneer of the triangular trade, extracting Africans from Sierra Leone and transporting them to Spanish colonists in the so-called New World for extraordinary profit (Olusoga, 2021, pp. 50–2), which earned him high esteem with both queen and country. In the sixteenth century, much would have been passed down through oral tradition among the African slaves. One of my students once questioned the legitimacy of linking the song directly to *Jesus of Lübeck*, rightly suggesting that such a tradition of association would be more likely found in Virginia where Hawkins sold his slaves.

Linking this particular song to a particular ship may be tendentious, and it is quite common for people to find contemporary meanings that were not necessarily there in the first place. That said, I cannot help but feel a sobering discomfort at the thought that an English slave ship was transporting Black souls across the dreaded middle passage going by the name of *Jesus* (for a commentary that relates this to Christ's Passion, see Hall, 2021, pp. 17–34). The significance of this parallels the experience I shared at the beginning of the present chapter regarding my time in Rome. While I think there is much that Christianity in the West can celebrate (I am no iconoclast), there is much that also needs interrogating, and potentially redressing through openness to the perspectives of those who are not quintessentially White and Western. Some have been nervous about this call for attending to our history and current state of affairs, suggesting that Western colonialism was 'not all bad' (Biggar, 2023). Others have worked to remind us that it was not just the Christian West but the Muslim world that also operated in slavery, citing the Barbary Corsairs as a rebuttal against postcolonial work (Webb, 2021). Such a reflex may be rooted in a sincere desire to bring balance to various discussions, but it ultimately overlooks that we must account for the 'Christianized' posturing behind our particular history, a history that legitimized itself through appeals to the promulgation of a gospel of 'salvation' to others. Islamic nations can answer for themselves. My concern is that we (those who are White Western Christians) do not deflect the responsibility away from ourselves, but face it as those who worship a suffering saviour and not a dominative imperium. This 'facing up' includes considering our understanding of salvation, which can sometimes focus on the sorts of questions that are seemingly important for some of us, but incidental and evasive as far as other people are concerned, leaving language such as 'gospel' and 'salvation' as nothing but religious, hypocritical jargon.

In 1996, the 'Festival of the Sea' celebrated Bristol's history in the shipping industry, performing its narrative identity as a city of maritime heritage. However, the BBC, Harlech Western Television (HTV West) and *Evening Post* coverage cited nothing of Bristol's prosperity through the transatlantic slave trade (see picture by Forbes, 1999). In addition, certain people groups were 'evacuated' and excluded from key spaces in the festival (Atkinson and Laurier, 1998). I became aware of this in the wake of the Ferguson shooting on 9 August 2017, where Michael Brown was shot dead. Surrounded by White people who pointed the finger at America (not dissimilar to how our nation did after the war of independence), and who asserted 'I'm not racist', I reflected deeply on Michael Brown's death while studying for Baptist ministry at Bristol Baptist College. Its building is situated in Clifton, the most prosperous part of Bristol, within in a building that was undoubtedly constructed off the back of chattel slavery.

To this day, I think that many of us White Westerners have a pathology deeply wired inside of us that thinks we need to and know how to save Black, Brown and Jewish (i.e. non-White) people. Of course, we would all deny it, but I have seen and experienced the racialized tendencies on a personal and institutional level that posit White people as the salvific source, and, with unconscious reflexes, treat 'others' as the ones who need us for their salvation. But do we really believe we need others? Do we live as though our salvation is wrapped up in the lives of those who have been dehumanized and perpetually ignored. I believe my salvation is wrapped up in the lives and stories of those who have experienced the world 'from below', to use Bonhoeffer's term, because it is within suffering, sin and sorrow that God has chosen to reveal God self. The following song captures some of this, as I continue to wrestle with my own sin for the sake of salvation and genuine communion.

Mrs Ferguson

Mrs Ferguson, how do you do?
Here's a letter I had meant to send your way
Mrs Ferguson, it's taken time
For I've been struggling to find what words to say
And that's the problem, my words get heard whilst yours are gone
And the White man gets to speak when it was you who lost your son
In this world, the TV hides your cries away
And they tell the likes of me back here that everything's ok

In these White walls
Built with bright gold
Stained with red blood
Poured from black souls' veins
Brought on brown ships
Across the blue sea
Under grey skies clouding my eyes
To make me colourblind

Mrs Ferguson, how did you feel
When I told you I'm not prejudiced at all
Mrs Ferguson, now I see it's not enough

THE WHITE BONHOEFFER

To say we're both made in God's image when you fall
In my defence, I claim equality is won
And embrace distorted dreams with a chess board and a gun
While the strange fruit we are eating [from southern trees], familiar to taste
Was sold back here in Clifton or thrown out with the waste

From these White walls
Built with bright gold
Stained with red blood
Poured from black souls' veins
Brought on brown ships
'Cross the blue sea
Under grey skies clouding my eyes
To make me colourblind
And God's not colourblind

Mrs Ferguson, how can I say
I am sorry for ignoring all your tears
Mrs Ferguson, shall we look
And maybe open up the very thing I fear
To lament a shameful story that sowed wounds upon the earth
And made the bells of time and justice ring
Please guide me to the one who bears the scars of all your pain
So we can offer him the worship of our sorrow when we sing

To these White walls
Built with bright gold
Stained with red blood
Poured from black souls' veins
Brought on brown ships
'Cross the blue sea
Under grey skies clouding my eyes
To make me colourblind

(Penned November 2015)

5

Creed and Story

Between the years 1794 and 1799, William Wilberforce, the famous abolitionist, sometimes worshipped at Holy Trinity Church in Clapham, London, alongside his political enemy, George Hibbert. I discovered this while reading David Olusoga's *Black and British: A Forgotten History* (Olusoga, 2021, pp. 218–19). Olusoga's thesis is correct in that much of the history of Britain overlooks those who are, in hindsight, on the wrong side of the story. I had never heard of George Hibbert! In some ways, though, it is unsurprising. Popular history celebrates Wilberforce but forgets or ignores Hibbert. Furthermore, the stories that have been told about abolition have often deliberately omitted the agency of Black and female abolitionists. I imagine (or hope) that William Wilberforce would have rejected the historical narrative crafted by his two sons, who demoted key players and totally erased others from the story:

> The contributions of the black abolitionists, Olaudah Equiano, Mary Prince, Ottobah Cuguano, the Sons of Africa and others were also redacted, and a similar fate befell the female abolitionists, like Elizabeth Heyrick and Hannah More. The slave rebellions that had nudged the nation towards final abolition were likewise forgotten … The notion that the enslaved people had played a role in their own emancipation, that liberty had been demanded and fought for, rather than simply given, was for the most part forgotten. (Olusoga, 2021, p. 232)

The stories we are told form what we believe, and in turn, what we believe forms the stories we tell and the way we tell them. All the details, nuances, emphases, characters, actions, postures, silences, morals, conflicts, loves, losses; all these things are wrapped together in crafting our imaginations, that is, what we believe, who we are, and how we live. It may seem banal to some that Wilberforce's story was foregrounded at the expense of others, but it demonstrates the intention of those who sought to tell a story of triumphalism, individualism and exceptionalism, centred on the White male hero who allegedly embodied the sort of 'British values' that his authors and 'Christian' nation wanted to present as their own. Arguably, a more authentic story would recognize the invaluable role that Black men and women played in bringing the transatlantic slave trade to an end.

Bonhoeffer's life involved a constant struggle to notice and learn from the particularity of people's stories and experiences within his conviction that there was a universality of sorts to the Christian message, regardless of race, nation, gender, ability or whatever other distinction might be used to demarcate human existence. For him, the gospel was a word from God to all creation, but the word of God would take form in an embodied, incarnational way (i.e. Christ), not because God changes but because creation is so varied and contingent that God's word takes form within the different peculiarities of creaturely life in order that God's word is always in a sense grounded. Some people may consider the subject of race to be unrelated to the core of the 'gospel' or may be wrestling with how to relate our knowledge of God to how we live. For Bonhoeffer, though, 'Our ability to know God, and to know what we are meant to do, are exactly the same' (Kirkpatrick, 2024, p. 325). The question is not about whether the way we live in relation to others matters, because it does, and I hope most of us can agree. Rather, the key question here is about how we live in this world fully without making 'the world' and all its complexities totally determinative of *who* God is, in and of themselves. I sense that this may be an especially significant concern for those White Christians who are wary of subjects like race 'taking over the church' and issues of social justice gaining prevalence. I sympathize a lot, and hope what I offer here may enable us to frame some of the core convictions and beliefs we have in a way that does not evade or relativize the complexity of earthly existence alongside those who do not experience this earthly existence the way we do.

Ultimate belief in a penultimate story

In his essay, 'Ultimate and Penultimate things', Bonhoeffer articulates a grammar, or orientation, for living fully in the world as those whose identity is governed ultimately by God. He presents a vision of the Christ reality as something that is both ultimate and penultimate:

> In Jesus Christ we believe in the God who became human, was crucified, and is risen. In the becoming human we recognize God's love toward God's creation, in the crucifixion God's judgment on all flesh, and in the

resurrection God's purpose for a new world. Nothing could be more perverse than to tear these three apart, because the whole is contained in each of them. Just as it is improper to pit against one another a theology of the incarnation, a theology of the cross, or a theology of the resurrection, by falsely absolutizing one of them, such a procedure is false as well in any consideration of Christian life. A Christian ethic built only on the incarnation would lead easily to the compromise solution; an ethic built only on the crucifixion or only on the resurrection of Jesus Christ would fall into radicalism and enthusiasm. The conflict is resolved only in their unity. (*DBWE* 6, p. 157)

Bonhoeffer does not want us to categorize aspects of Christ's nature and person, which sometimes does happen. Some believers have only disdain for the world, but we witness in the incarnation of Christ that the world is affirmed as God's world. Conversely, some disciples may consider our present earthly state to be all that there is. However, the ultimate reality is that God has come to the world in Christ and judged it via the cross, offering new life through a total break with the old through the resurrection. That reframes this earthly existence in its current form as a penultimate one, affirmed for the sake of the ultimate, and now pregnant with opportunities to witness Christ's hope and rebirth while sin and suffering abide.

For Bonhoeffer then, 'Christian life neither destroys nor sanctions the penultimate' (*DBWE* 6, p. 159). An absolute focus on the here and now enslaves people to the possible never-endingness of the present, rendering them bereft of any hope in ultimate justice. This typifies more liberal or progressive streams of the church today, and Bonhoeffer calls it the 'compromise' approach (*DBWE* 5, p. 154). Those who strive to build God's kingdom themselves may find themselves disillusioned, exhausted or faithless in the face of overwhelming suffering and injustice, particularly if they lack the resource to effect what they seek (Billings, 2015, pp. 75–6). In contrast, a myopic preoccupation with ultimate things and a so-called 'after life', as some may call it, is simply to reject the gospel of Jesus Christ. This posture is often exemplified by conservative evangelicals and is what Bonhoeffer calls (negatively) religious 'radicalism' that sees the earth as fit for nothing other than to burn (*DBWE* 6, p. 153). Christians' penultimate existence is necessary as the spatial and temporal here and now that enables believers to 'prepare the way' for others to witness the ultimate reality of Christ. The means and ways by which we prepare the way for people to witness Christ must reflect him as the ultimate and penultimate reality. As such, living in the penultimate requires taking the 'this-worldliness' (see *DBWE* 8, p. 485) of the penultimate seriously. Otherwise, 'The ultimate word of God, which is a word of grace, becomes here the icy hardness of the law that crushes and despises all resistance' (*DBWE* 6, p. 153). It is one thing for a person to go to church and hear the word of God in a manner that does not harm them. However, hearing a gospel preached or embodied in a community that dehumanizes someone, forcing a yoke of slavery or racial conformity upon them; this is a masquerade of White religion and not a faithful witness to Christ. Therefore,

> What has been pushed into the depths of human misery, what is lowly and humiliated, will be raised. There is a depth of human bondage, of human poverty, and of human ignorance that hinders the gracious coming of Christ ... If Christ is to come, all that is proud and high must bow. There is a degree of power, of wealth, and of knowledge that is a hindrance to Christ and the grace of Christ. (*DBWE* 6, p. 161)

Ross Halbach relates to our failure as White Christians to live in the reality of the penultimate, and not just the ultimate, suggesting that we often cultivate a 'form of cheap grace' that tries to 'domesticate the ultimate into something at one's disposal' which will 'serve as an evasion of actually being with someone in the temporal moments of his or her pain' (Halbach, 2020, p. 42). Bonhoeffer notes how this relates to slavery:

> Concretely stated, slaves who have been so deprived of control over their time that they can no longer hear the proclamation of God's word cannot be led by that word of God to a justifying faith ... it is necessary to care for the penultimate in order that the ultimate not be hindered by the penultimate's destruction. Those who proclaim the word yet do not do everything possible so that this word may be heard are not true to the word's claim for free passage, for a smooth road. (*DBWE* 6, p. 162)

It is no wonder that Bonhoeffer observed a reaction against Christianity from many Black youths when he visited Harlem (*DBWE* 10, p. 315). An almost gnostic obsession with 'heaven' left many Blacks experiencing not heaven but hell on earth 'in the name of Jesus' as creaturely life was relativized or disdained in line with a distorted gospel of White supremacy. I would suggest that this religiously radical posture is exhibited by those who refuse to recognize the penultimate importance of reparations for Britain's (and the church's) involvement in chattel slavery, with its contemporary implications.

This being said, we cannot straddle the ultimate and penultimate, as though it is some sort of balancing act or existential tension. Bonhoeffer articulates it provocatively to his fiancée, Maria: 'Christians who venture to stand on earth on only one leg will stand in heaven on only one leg too' (*LL92*, p. 64). Christian disciples live fully in this penultimate existence – with all the particular complexities it entails – as those illuminated within it by the ultimate word that Christ is Lord of all things. Without upholding the penultimate in space and time, Christians may hinder people who suffer from receiving and coming to faith, or from even continuing in it. After all, 'It is hard for those thrust into extreme disgrace, desolation, poverty, and helplessness to believe in God's justice and goodness' (*DBWE* 6, p. 162). Sadly, because of its emphasis on universality and catholicity, which are good things, though not ultimate realities, the church in the West has often lacked the theological dexterity and imagination to navigate the particularities and peculiar differences that mark human life for vast numbers of people.

Something that was significant about Bonhoeffer was that his beliefs and interpretation of his creed would be crafted over the course of his life through relationships that refracted and reframed the universals that his story had assumed. In particular, it was through experiences of those who suffered in different ways within the penultimate that his sociotheological imagination developed.

Narratives of suffering

Mark Thiessen Nation discusses the strong theme of German nationalism in Bonhoeffer's early theology (Nation, 2022, pp. 51–8). During a year in Barcelona, the young Lutheran presented a series of three lectures, one of which made an apology for war and violence as something that was sanctified by God for the sake of the people (*Volk*). In the complex argument, he stated, 'I will have to do to those enemies [of the state] what my love and gratitude toward my own people commands me to do, the people into whom God bore me' (*DBWE* 10, p. 372). Much of this content was imbibed from his teachers, most of whom were German nationalists (Bethge, 2000, p. 127).

Bonhoeffer had long exhibited an openness and genuine willingness to learn from others. To use the language discussed in this chapter, he took the penultimate seriously, with all its particularity, complexity and immanent limitations. From childhood he felt the impact of life's contingencies, as during the First World War, Walter, Dietrich's second-oldest brother, died from shrapnel wounds on 28 April 1918. The impact on his family resulted in his mother Paula, who was normally 'full of courage and optimism' (Leibholz-Bonhoeffer, 1971, p. 5), moving in with a neighbour for some time with depression. Father Karl stopped recording the family memoirs for ten years (Bethge, 2000, pp. 27–8). Dietrich navigated this loss in tandem with having to sleep in a different room from his twin sister Sabine. Having previously enjoyed reflecting together at night on the concepts of death and eternity, Dietrich experienced a deep loneliness over this separation, and it was around this time that he 'composed a cantata on the Psalmist's lament: "My soul is downcast within me"' (Gardiner, 2018, p. 24).

Bonhoeffer's appreciation for the penultimate appears to have also been formed a lot from his experiences in other countries and cultures. Christiane Tietz notes that, 'For a young man of his generation, Bonhoeffer gained an extraordinary amount of experience abroad' (Tietz, 2016, p. 13). In 1924, during a visit to Tripoli, Bonhoeffer enjoyed a reception with a Bedouin chief. However, something apparently went awry, and Bonhoeffer noted that 'We had often tried in vain and had clumsily sought to react correctly to a particular situation in Africa' (DBWE 9, p. 98). This may well be one of the first experiences he had of not 'fitting in' to a place. In addition, he witnessed the 'brutality and vulgarity' with which Arabs were treated like slaves by Italian soldiers: 'one can understand their [the Arabs'] bitterness and callous fear' (DBWE 9, p. 116).

Clifford Green opines that these early experiences 'anticipate Bonhoeffer's association with other marginal groups in the future, such as African Americans in New York' (DBWE 10, p. 5). As mentioned already, during his year in New York (1930–31), Bonhoeffer witnessed the problem of racism, and was deeply affected by the African American community's suffering. Reggie Williams writes:

> By recognizing the situated, localized nature of learning, we gain a better understanding of the various life-factors that shape it and we equip people who are not members of the same formative communities to recognize the social value of empathy and to interact in healthier ways. (Williams, 2021, p. 82)

While in America, Bonhoeffer's engagement in the life of the African American church, as well as its community and wider literature, was unusually deep and immersive (DBWE 10, pp. 271, 295). He was even told by a White colleague that he was spending too much time with Blacks (Cone, 2013, p. 42). James Cone foregrounds Bonhoeffer as a standout example of Christian courage and solidarity, highlighting Bonhoeffer's immersion in all aspects of Black life to the point of becoming affected by it on more than an intellectual level, while others, such as Reinhold Niebuhr, maintained a 'critical distance' in their association and advocacy (Cone, 2013, pp. 41–2), possibly due to an innate anxiety to control the parameters of their own imaginative formation.

Back in Germany, Bonhoeffer taught confirmation classes in a particularly deprived area in North Berlin. Against the advice of others, he decided to live among the people he was serving. In February 1932, he wrote to his American friend Paul Lehmann about witnessing the 'most dreadful living conditions. With my very limited means, I am almost unable to help at all. And now to preach the gospel under these circumstances!' (*DBWE* 11, p. 94). He was having to reconfigure what the good news of Jesus Christ was for the particular people living in this run-down part of the city.

In August 1933, he wrote to his grandmother Julie Bonhoeffer following his experience with the Bethel community, which had been 'established to look after those with disabilities' (Kirkpatrick, 2024, p. 216). Bonhoeffer wrote that 'The time in Bethel has made a deep impression on me' (*DBWE* 12, p. 157). His reflections are telling and are worth quoting at length:

> Here we have a part of the church that still knows what the church can be about and what it cannot be about. I have just come back from the worship service. It is an extraordinary sight, the whole church filled with crowds of epileptics and other ill persons, interspersed with the deaconesses and deacons who are there to help in case one of them falls; then there are elderly tramps who come in off the country roads, the theological students, the children from the lab school, doctors and pastors with their families. But the sick people dominate the picture, and they are keen listeners and participants. Their experience of life must be most extraordinary, not having control over their bodies, having to be resigned to the possibility of an attack at any moment. (*DBWE* 12, pp. 157–8)

For someone who was well built and sporty, musically talented, intellectually astute, politically aware, socially adept; all these factors became a particular horizon that Bonhoeffer was confronted with as he worshipped alongside those who would be considered 'unsuccessful' and weak in worldly (and certainly in Nazi) terms. This was one of the many moments where he realized, as he came to write later in life, that 'God became a poor, wretched, unknown, unsuccessful human being' (*DBWE*

15, p. 111). This optic continues to emerge in Bonhoeffer's imagination as his letter to Julie continues:

> Today in church was the first time this really struck me, as I became aware of these moments. Their situation of being truly defenseless perhaps gives these people a much clearer insight into certain realities of human existence, the fact that we are indeed basically defenseless, than can be possible for healthy persons. And it is just this abrupt alternation, between standing there healthy and falling down sick, which must be more conducive to this insight than being healthy all the time ... What utter madness when some people today think that the sick can or ought to be legally eliminated ... Anyhow, our concept of sickness and health is pretty ambiguous. What we see as 'sick' is actually healthier, in essential aspects of life and of insight, than health is. (*DBWE* 12, pp. 158–9)

Eleanor McLaughlin notes the helpfulness of this reflection, but she also highlights how Bonhoeffer 'comes perilously close to falling into the trap of depicting disabled people as, in [Nancy] Eiesland's term, "spiritual superheroes"' (McLaughlin, 2024). Anticipating the sweeping generalizations that can be made especially in liberal wings of the church today, Bonhoeffer projects his well-intentioned hermeneutic on those who experience limitations that are not the common experience of many people. His reflection is helpful, and reflections such as these are helpful, provided that they do not lead us to draw conclusions that are divorced from the agency and particular story of those who may narrate their experience differently. Following this experience, Bonhoeffer nevertheless concluded that aligning the church to the state was impossible in light of the direction that both church and state were going. In this letter to his grandmother, he revealed the dramatic change in his views about this: 'The issue is really Germanism or Christianity, and the sooner the conflict comes out in the open, the better. The greatest danger of all would be in trying to conceal this' (*DBWE* 12, p. 159).

The view from below

When he was in prison, Bonhoeffer wrote a short essay for his fellow conspirators, seeking to make sense of the 'unsuccessful' results of trying to remove Hitler from power, and to offer hope regarding what had been achieved, and how they might understand their situation now. The essay,

'After Ten Years', ends with a final paragraph entitled 'The View from Below':

> It remains an experience of incomparable value that we have for once learned to see the great events of world history from below, from the perspective of the outcasts, the suspects, the maltreated, the powerless, the oppressed and reviled, in short from the perspective of the suffering. If only during this time bitterness and envy have not corroded the heart; that we come to see matters great and small, happiness and misfortune, strength and weakness with new eyes; that our sense for greatness, humanness, justice, and mercy has grown clearer, freer, more incorruptible; that we learn, indeed, that personal suffering is a more useful key, a more fruitful principle than personal happiness for exploring the meaning of the world in contemplation and action. But this perspective from below must not lead us to become advocates for those who are perpetually dissatisfied. Rather, out of a higher satisfaction, which in its essence is grounded beyond what is below and above, we do justice to life in all its dimensions and in this way affirm it. (*DBWE* 8, p. 52)

What might be overlooked by some of us as we read this, is that Christians are not solely (or primarily) called to help those who are less fortunate. Of course, we must seek justice and advocate for those who are downtrodden and overlooked. However, Bonhoeffer is touching on something far deeper and arguably more disquieting. He is suggesting that God's very glory and revelation is offered through those who are looked down on, marginalized and considered to be of less value. The travesty of British history is that we narrated a justification of triumphalism in the name of the White Christ, shackling and oppressing Jesus because he did not (and still does not) cohere with what Matthew Kirkpatrick calls our 'worldly heritage' (Kirkpatrick, 2024, p. 219). I would argue even further, that we White Westerners continue to look for the successful Jesus, the powerful, useful, productive, triumphant, exceptional, nationalistic, brand-worthy, feel-good Jesus (see Rah, 2015, p. 58). As a result, we find conversations about race and Whiteness to be inconvenient at best, and anti-Christ at worst (because Christ is White). But God is the God of the oppressed. To an extent, White Christians like myself must always hear Jesus' call to discipleship as an invitation to penitence and to re-imagining what it means to be human at the behest of and at the feet of those who experience their humanity as belittled, relativized or crushed.

Penultimate polyphony

So what does it look like to live fully in the penultimate in light of the ultimate? How do Christian communities all witness and witness to the ultimate Word of God spoken in Jesus Christ, as distinct communities that are so different and made up of people with such different experiences and stories? How do we confess Jesus Christ as Lord in an ultimate sense, offering a creedal belief concerning the ultimate reality of God's judgement and grace, while not diminishing the uniqueness of particular people and groups who would bring nuance, contingency or critique to these very universal claims of Christian faith? Is there even anything universal that could be said about the gospel of Jesus Christ? There is much that could be discussed, but I wonder if the Black church holds a key insight for wrestling through this struggle with integrity and humility, in a way that avoids the polarization of universal and particular, ultimate and penultimate, and which achieves the unity in conflict that Bonhoeffer talks about. To return to a previous quote from his time in Harlem, Bonhoeffer writes this:

> Anyone who has heard and understood the Negro spirituals knows about the *strange mixture of reserved melancholy and eruptive joy* in the soul of the Negro. The Negro churches are proletarian churches, perhaps the only ones in all America. (*DBWE* 10, p. 315, my emphasis)

This was not just a cerebral observation for Bonhoeffer; it was deeply affective on a visceral level (Tarassenko, 2024, p. 19). Ruth Zerner writes that 'black worship, particularly in song, was so overwhelming and personal for him that he found it difficult to analyse in writing' (cited in Tarassenko, 2024, p. 19). In later life, Bonhoeffer reflected on his love for the 'Negro spirituals' which 'sing with moving expression about the distress and liberation of the people of Israel ... the misery and distress of the human heart ... and love for the Redeemer and yearning for the kingdom of heaven' (*DBWE* 15, pp. 457–8). Bonhoeffer was also bewildered as to why many White Americans really enjoyed hearing them while simultaneously participating in the racism of society. Black life in America entailed immeasurable suffering. Community culture and worship entailed eruptions of protest and sorrow that cried out because of their hope in the love and solidarity of God in Christ. They embodied lament and joy together, proclaiming the justice and love of God amid their particular plight and pain, witnessing to an ultimate hope by way of their penultimate struggle. The womanist theologian Cheryl A. Kirk-Duggan describes the spirituals as a means of 'exorcizing evil' through casting out their grief before God as a community (Kirk-Duggan, 1997, p. 109). The pathos of oppression and dehumanization would be interwoven with cries of defiance and certainty of justice because God is the God of the oppressed. Life is horrendous, and Jesus will make all things new.

These two aspects of human life, sorrow and joy, protest and thanksgiving, lament and praise, have been difficult to ground in some White churches, due perhaps to the individualism that governs much of our way of life. It is in the ability to live fully in the midst of seemingly competing experiences that we experience what Bonhoeffer describes as the 'polyphonic' life. As he was a musician, it is unsurprising that terms like this aided his thinking. I have written elsewhere:

> Polyphonic music involves the simultaneous play of several lines of melody that digress and stand independently, yet find their continuity and essential basis in the whole. Melodies that play in counterpoint to others might create a sense of dissonance, certainly for those unfamiliar with its texture, but they are often playing within the bounds of the *cantus firmus* [firm song]. The beauty of polyphonic music is that its contrapuntal voices are held together amidst their distinct and sometimes dissonant unity ... To use the apostle Paul's words, disciples are 'sorrowful, yet always rejoicing' (2 Cor. 6.10). The polyphony of life in Christ is a liturgical freedom to celebrate all things that bring joy and thanksgiving alongside grief and lament. (Judson, 2023, p. 79)

I have also suggested that the Black church embodied the metaphor of polyphony in a way that is not remotely problematic when we consider their context. The lack of lament in much of the Western church today is partly down to our inability to reckon with sorrow, suffering and sin alongside joy, goodness and beauty.

Blackness and Whiteness in the penultimate

Without an openness to the reality of Christ taking form in both the ultimate *and* penultimate sense within of our own and others' lives, the teaching of Jesus could all too easily become co-opted or manoeuvred into a programme of self-deprecating subservience, falsely leading disciples to serve the devil rather than Christ himself. For example, when Jesus encourages people to 'love your neighbour as yourself' (Mark 12.31), this can sometimes mean *we* love *our neighbour* (whoever that is) according to *our* imaginative horizons of what it means to love and be loved. But I think part of being human in the creaturely sense is that we recognize our limitations regarding what and who love is. I do not love my children the same way I love my wife or my friends. Likewise, I think discernment, humility and openness is needed when I seek to love those whose racialized experience has been very different from mine. The point of recognizing the penultimate is that we should do all we can in order not to hinder people being able to witness God's word in Christ. That goes for me too. I need to recognize the ways in which I hinder my own witnessing of Christ in my encounter with others, and whether I act in racialized ways within the penultimate at the expense of Christ's ultimate word. For many who live in predominantly White areas, claiming that there is not a problem of race only reinforces the racialized norms that perpetuate the White flight that occurs in urban areas in particular, and which overlooks the anxiety of White folks to have control over the question regarding who is their 'neighbour'.

The Western church has a dark shadowside within its (penultimate) history, one of deploying certain Bible verses to exacerbate a socio-cultural status quo that condones violence upon others for the sake of 'order' in society. Tragically, it is (at least sometimes) from a sincere desire to be faithful to Christ that these evils have been committed, either actively or passively. It is understandable (for this author at least) that movements have arisen whereby Black slaves have responded towards slave masters through revolution, violence and even murder. Such action is not as much of a departure from orthodox Western Christianity as might be assumed. For example, Thomas Aquinas, the famous medieval theologian of virtue and vice, remarks that 'it is much more lawful to defend one's life than one's house. Therefore neither is a man guilty of murder if he kill another in defense of his own life' (Aquinas, 1948, p. 1465). Yet here, Aquinas (a pre-modern Western theologian) qualifies the appropriateness of such violence, which, for him, is based on the perceived 'order' of society. As such, slaves are never permitted to strike their masters, though the opposite is apparently permitted (Aquinas, 1948, p. 1468). This is a classic example of where those in positions of authority and power are presumed to have the best grasp of justice and truth, and of God's providence and care. Therefore, his claim that 'the governor of a city has perfect coercive power' reveals a dangerous idealism that overlooks the potential for corruption in the depths of the human heart that asserts power over others (cf. Jer. 17.9). The poor are always accountable, but the rich and powerful are less so. Aquinas seems to try and make space for violence within the 'natural order' of things, which negates any redressing of that order through the agency of those who are constrained in the underside of society. Considering the stories or perspectives of those who are enslaved or oppressed would probably be non-sensical for Aquinas, as it was for progressive, White abolitionists in the modern era, who were passionately opposed to slavery, but not so interested in opening themselves to the Black slaves regarding the ways and means of their liberation.

This is one of the ways in which the penultimate and the ultimate become hazy and dangerous. There is no middle ground. There is a unity in conflict. When is something ultimate and a total 'given' without room for particularity and difference? Bonhoeffer himself struggles at points with this way of framing things. In *Discipleship*, he addresses slavery in a way that is problematic for some readers. He initially makes a case to assert that Christ has bound believers together on a level that is deeper than any shared history or race. In other words, Christ judges the divide between Jew and German, binding them together in the visible church community (*DBWE* 4, pp. 233–5). Being a disciple of Jesus has an impact beyond one's own personal salvation, 'but also their relationships throughout all of life' (*DBWE* 4, p. 235). He then raises the story of Onesimus in the book of Philemon, highlighting Paul's reference that Onesimus is a brother not just in the Lord but also 'in the flesh' (Philemon 16). For Bonhoeffer, this is significant in that Paul is challenging 'privileged' believers who might behave one way towards fellow believers in church, only to treat them differently in the world. This is a 'dangerous misunderstanding' of the Christian life (*DBWE* 4, p. 235). While Onesimus may return and resume his place as Philemon's slave, the point for Paul, according to Bonhoeffer, is that he is now a brother in Christ, and therefore, a brother in the world, that is, in the penultimate. Therefore, Philemon should treat him as an equal, not as a slave, given that the dividing wall of hostility separating Jew and Gentile, slave and free, male and female, has been destroyed, making them one in Christ Jesus at baptism (Gal. 3.27–28).

Bonhoeffer's interpretation is interesting in that he upholds the absolute Lordship of Christ in identifying who people are in an ultimate sense. Yet there are other points where Paul appears to at least acknowledge a penultimate givenness of slavery. Many of us like to quote Paul: 'There is no longer Jew or Greek, there is no longer slave or free, there is no longer male and female; for all of you are one in Christ Jesus' (Gal. 3.28). But at times for Paul, a slave remains a slave in the penultimate, and a woman remains a woman, a Jew remains Jewish. Could this be that Paul does not allow the ultimate to reframe how he lives in the penultimate, taking slavery as a divinely given mandate when it should actually be dismantled? Does Paul (and Bonhoeffer) confer more agency on the privileged and powerful, those with social resource and narrative capital? Valentina Alexander notices the problems with the book of Philemon, and imagines a letter from the slave, Onesimus, and what his perspective may have been, as though he were writing to his former slave master. She proposes Onesimus' thoughts:

> I [Onesimus] wish so much to be reunited with the brothers and sisters and return to continue the Lord's work at home. This is what Paul advises and I would like to follow his advice, but as I have explained, I cannot return without making it clear to you [Philemon] that I should return your brother, free in the body and in the spirit to serve the Lord with you. If this is unacceptable to you in your flesh, then I pray that the Lord will make it acceptable to you by His Spirit. If you deny His Spirit, the chains will be yours and not mine, and in sorrow I shall have to find another place to live out my freedom in the Lord. (Alexander, 2014, p. 188)

One way of interpreting Galatians 3.28 is that people are now a slave and/or a woman in a manner that has recognized and affirmed their ultimate identity in Christ, bestowing value on them both in and against their penultimate particularity. For example, a slave does not necessarily need to become free to be a disciple of Jesus, though I would argue that it is incumbent on their 'master' to offer them freedom if their master is indeed a disciple too. A woman does not need to squash or defer her womanhood to achieve full discipleship status.

Following this thinking, I would infer that, in Christ, there is no longer Black nor White, for we are ultimately all one in Christ Jesus. Yet – and this point penultimately links to the first – all people should be afforded equal status and honour in both the church and world within the particularity of their person and situation in a way that reckons seriously with their peculiar experience. Jew and Gentile are in fellowship within a communal crucible that navigates their distinct and conflicting particularities. Similarly, Black and White are in fellowship within a communal crucible that navigates *their* distinct and conflicting particularities, and this includes redressing the troubled history of their penultimate life together which has benefited Whites. To ignore this story is to ignore the penultimate. Bonhoeffer suggests that Paul's statements for slaves to remain slaves 'are certainly not a justification or a Christian apology for a shadowy social order ... Rather, it is valid because of the fact that Jesus Christ already has brought about an upheaval of the whole world by liberating both slave and free' (*DBWE* 4, p. 238). One can sense him pushing the reality of the gospel in its ultimate sense here and gesturing at the sentiments hypothesized through Onesimus by Alexander. Bonhoeffer is trying very hard to speak something ultimate without disregarding the damage caused by overlooking or absolutizing the penultimate. For Bonhoeffer, the reality that Christ took the form of a slave/servant is a witness to the overturning of the world's social order, and that the church expects nothing from the world, making space for its own polity from within the church community (*DBWE* 4, 240–1). The church's life together is one that witnesses to the world a total (ultimate) overcoming of all social and political structures. Yet profoundly (and challenging any ungrounded idealism) this witness occurs within the particularity of all people who live in a wonderful yet wounded penultimate world where the story of sin and suffering abides.

> They [Christians disciples] are to remain in the world in order to engage in the world in a frontal assault ... The world must be contradicted within the world. That is why Christ became a human being and died in the midst of his enemies. It is for this reason – and this reason alone! – that slaves are to remain slaves, and Christians are to remain subject to authorities. (*DBWE* 4, p. 244)

This is one place in *Discipleship* where Bonhoeffer wrestles with the penultimate, articulating a way by which people live in 'uncompromising discipleship' in their 'following Christ according to the Sermon on the Mount' while the world is what it is (*DBWE* 13, p. 285). I am not sure that he quite satisfies those who experience life 'from below'. Perhaps it would be helpful at this juncture to turn to those who do, and Bonhoeffer's thought would benefit from the perspective offered by the great African American mystic Howard Thurman.

Thurman recalls the awful heritage within the White Western church of using New Testament passages about slavery to enforce the servitude of Black people. Thurman reminisces about his grandmother, who was born a slave and grew up on a plantation near Madison in Florida. In later life, the young Howard spent time with her and she asked him to read portions of the Scriptures for her. He was struck that she never asked for passages from the Pauline epistles. One day, after asking her why, she responded:

> 'During the days of slavery,' she said, 'the master's minister would occasionally hold services for the slaves. Old man McGhee was so mean that he would not let a Negro minister preach to his slaves. Always the

white minister used as his text something from Paul. At least three of four times a year he used as a text: "Slaves, be obedient to them that are your masters ..., as unto Christ." Then he would go on to show how it was God's will that we were slaves and how, if we were good and happy slaves, God would bless us. I promised my Maker that if I ever learned to read and if freedom ever came, I would not read that part of the Bible.' (Thurman, 1996, p. 20)

Thurman's life and work has been oriented towards navigating the abusive manner by which the White Christians' faith has often profited the powerful at the expense of the poor and oppressed. We cannot ignore this penultimate reality. His famous work, *Jesus and the Disinherited*, continues to have a tremendous impact on Black populations seeking a faithful way in the face of lynching, segregation and, in these days, racism in its different guises. Thurman offers a concrete way of being human amid dehumanization and systemic evil, rooted in the Spirit of Christ who bestows fresh courage and hope upon the oppressed. '[Jesus] recognized with authentic realism that anyone who permits another to determine the quality of his inner life gives into the hands of the other the keys to his destiny' (Thurman, 1996, p. 18). Folks like myself may never understand fully the agonizing grit that enabled Thurman to offer a word of hope amid the temptations around him towards either passivity or violence. Uprising and revolt is understandable from my perspective, though tragic and horrible. Yet, without dismissing the impetus behind such movements, I am stunned by Thurman's firm resolve that Black disciples' enemies (White slave masters, racists, ignorant bystanders) must not determine the actions and self-determination of Black people created in the image of God, who call on the name of Jesus. How disarming for those who seek to conform people according to their own image! Thurman is a nonconformist in the best sense, or even better, he is one seeking conformation to Christ alone in the most profoundly penultimate sense as a witness to the ultimate reality of God in Christ.

Bonhoeffer observes the unbearable arduousness of discipleship when the world loses all integrity and becomes demonic (*DBWE* 4, p. 247). And yet, like Thurman, he continues to believe that faithfulness to Christ must come before any reactionary evil on the part of those who suffer. It would be interesting to compare and contrast the work of Thurman and Bonhoeffer further, somewhere beyond the scope of this book.

Conclusion

On 24 February 2022 (though it feels like yesterday) Russia invaded Ukraine. The Russo-Ukranian conflict had been going on since 2014, but this invasion was the largest attack on a country in Europe since the Second World War. The news of this gripped many people in the West. Many people in the UK offered their homes to refugees. My parents themselves hosted a family for a year. The husband of this particular family had been granted permission to leave his country with his wife and children as both his brothers had already been killed in the conflict. This was a time for humanity to recognize their common worth and for our nation to show compassion and welcome to strangers, in many ways embodying those words of Jesus from Matthew 25.35, 'I was a stranger and you invited me in.'

I do not mean to diminish the generosity of people like my parents who gave of themselves (far more than the government offered financially) gladly and willingly to help people who were just like them. And yet, that is perhaps the thing: Ukranians do look just like us, they are predominantly White. Moustafa Bayoumi documents the many clumsy (and revealing) comments made in Western coverage of the war, which noted the shock of seeing 'civilized' Western people fleeing their homes, which was clearly more disturbing and shocking than seeing the pictures of presumably 'primitive' Black or Brown people doing the same (Bayoumi, 2022). The amount of coverage afforded to this war is also telling of the significance placed upon it in contrast to other conflicts. Eva Połońska-Kimunguyi (2022) offers the view that 'whether the war is covered or not, whether civilian fighters are seen as heroes or suspects, whether refugees are deemed worthy or not, largely depends on the racial background of its subjects. Racism remains a dominant organizing force of the global politics of war.'

Furthermore, reports show that those 'non-White' people fleeing Ukraine itself were treated according to nationalistic/racialized grounds. Jessica Orakpo, a Nigerian medical student, was refused a place on a bus heading to Poland, and despite claiming to be pregnant, she was told, 'If you are Black you should walk' (Akinyemi, 2022). A report by Virginia Pietromarchi shows that this sort of treatment was not unique, which is suggestive that times of crisis do not necessarily exclude racism and draw people together, but perhaps illuminate its pervasive influence.

The wide-open arms that were extended by the UK towards (White) Ukranians represents a tremendous contrast against our country's attitude towards those people who sought to come to Britain from non-European, non-White countries, who were also fleeing their homes because of war. Many might not admit it, but one cannot help but sense the inherent reflex within our White Western sensibilities, as well as the deployment of our legislation, that posits people from Syria, Nigeria, Palestine or Iran as inferior. There is a common sense that 'those people' are used to suffering and not so affected by it, as though that makes it less of a concern. White people are undoubtedly more eligible to come here, partly because they are perceived to be cleverer and able to contribute to society, but they are racially defined as more like us and therefore imagined as more capable of 'fitting in' to Britain without threatening 'British' identity, whatever that really is.

I am obviously caricaturing and over-simplifying attitudes that may not be verbalized in quite this way (though I have heard some extraordinarily ignorant and short-sighted things within Oxford University). Nevertheless, I would encourage the reader to ponder whether this is a perspective that partly directs their own horizons, as it indeed seeks to narrate mine at times. Admitting this takes courage and requires both humility and self-awareness, but admitting it must surely be the first step to dealing with it. Just because somebody comes to our country who bears a darker skin complexion does not mean they are less human, less worthy or less in need of being embraced, and that includes those who reach our shores illegitimately. For example, if I suddenly had to flee my home and lost everything, I for one would certainly not anticipate and prioritize the particular and peculiar governmental procedures that would interrogate the legitimacy of my hope to plead asylum there. There are undoubtedly systems that must be upheld for the sake of ensuring an appropriate level and capacity of service economically and spatially. My point is that the partiality shown towards White people exposes something of the creed by which our 'Christian' nation lives. Bonhoeffer claims there should be no such partiality, for all are human. Being a Christian means that 'we are to take part in Christ's greatness of heart, in the responsible action that in freedom lays hold of the hour and faces the danger, and in the true sympathy that springs forth not from fear but from Christ's freeing and redeeming love for *all* who suffer' (*DBWE* 8, p. 49, my emphasis).

It is to this end that I share a song inspired by those brave people who fled their homes and sought refuge in the 'free' Western world. Many tried to reach Europe from Syria by crossing the Mediterranean Sea in boats. Some of them made it, while many drowned. Those with skilled professions, as well as children, vulnerable adults and articulate English speakers were considered less important than their White Ukranian neighbours. Their story needs to be told, and I think it needs to disturb us and inject life into our humanity.

What are you going to do?

We used to stand proud and strong
No one could ever bring us down
A time when smiles grew easily
And happiness was all we knew
The only tears we ever cried
Were from the laughter we couldn't hide
There was no place back then for pain
But now we see our hopes and dreams
Are washed beneath the crashing sea
And God, you told us You'd be there

Why do you ignore my cry?
How long till I drown?
I won't last much longer
What are you going to do?

I thought this world was made for me
To rule as though I was a king
And others told me I could be, O I could be
Anyone and do anything
I led my life from the highest height
Where wind and waves don't beat nor bite
And peace is promised for everyone who cares to try
But these dark depths exhaust my course
No where to shield me from the force
Of this life decrying, love denying, light defying void

Why do you ignore my cry?
How long till I drown?
I won't last much longer
What are you going to do?

It seems to me that just a few
Will reach the end free from despair
But all the rest of us will find

THE WHITE BONHOEFFER

We're far too precious not to care
And God who lives in heav'n above
Assures us He's a God of love
then simply says that His grace is enough
Whilst thousands die lost out at sea
And all they leave is a memory
For those who watch but will not intervene

Why do you ignore my cry?
How long till I drown?
I won't last much longer
What are you going to do?

(Penned October 2015)

PART 2

Works and Witness

6

Dissertations and Lectures on Christology

In this second half of the book, we will work our way through Bonhoeffer's main publications, represented by volumes 1–8 (minus vol. 7) of the *Dietrich Bonhoeffer Works*. I was encouraged to read the later volumes for my PhD thesis (vols. 9–16), which are far bigger and hugely informative, though these earlier works continue to have an abiding influence on how people understand Bonhoeffer. They also exhibit much of the thinking he was developing in his letters, essays, sermons and other genres of writing that are found in the later volumes. I am not going to give an all-encompassing summary of each publication, but engage in some of the key themes that carry some import for considering the subject of race in Bonhoeffer's project.

Approaching Bonhoeffer's work for the first time, it makes sense to begin with his earliest publications. However, his first two monographs are dense and highly technical pieces of work. They can be trickier to navigate than books such as *Discipleship*, *Life Together* and *Letters and Papers from Prison*, which we come to later on. If you are new to Bonhoeffer, you may prefer to return to this chapter later. Nevertheless, these early works *are* worth the effort.

Sanctorum Communio (DBWE 1)

Sanctorum Communio translates (from Latin) to mean 'The Communion of Saints', and this, Bonhoeffer's doctoral thesis, explores *A Theological Study of the Sociology of the Church*. Joel Lawrence notes: 'Although Sanctorum Communio is a work that seeks to explore the sociological and theological nature of the church, one cannot but recognize the central role that Christ plays in this work' (Lawrence, 2010, p. 13). Christology provides, for Bonhoeffer, the ontological basis both for and through which to understand the sociology of the church.

The basic task of *Sanctorum Communio* is to use theological/doctrinal language and sociological concepts to assess what the church essentially *is*. He articulates an understanding of Christian community that takes seriously the complex social relations that operate within its polity. Rather than merely using idealistic language or abstract (religious) notions of 'church', he grapples with the wealth of modern philosophy and sociology to envision the church as a reality that lives and breathes and bleeds in the crucible of worldly existence, where sin, suffering and social ambiguities are always present. He initially begins by articulating a definition of what it means to be a person, and what personhood entails.

For Bonhoeffer, a person is not simply an individual who autonomously identifies themselves and others through a supposedly pure lens of separated objectivity. The idea that a person can perceive and observe anything in a full, infallible and unfractured sense is illusory (*DBWE* 1, pp. 47, 78). There is no individuality that is fully independent of others, nor of one's understanding of themselves. Conversely, however, a person is not solely reducible to a mere part or cog in a communal 'body' that exists at the expense of particular people being joined together. A person is not a person simply by joining the herd, or the collective spirit. Rather, a person is to be understood in social terms as an *individual* who is *in relation to others* (*DBWE* 1, pp. 66, 80). On the one hand, there is no isolated individuality, but nor is there a dissolution of individuality through becoming absorbed within a crowd. True personhood recognizes genuine individuality that is inseparably bound in a basic social relation with others.

One of the key ways Bonhoeffer tries to describe the integrity of the 'structure' of human personhood is through referring to what he calls the 'I–You' relationship. Rachel Muers notes: 'When Bonhoeffer critiques "abstract" theological and anthropological thought, his constructive response to the persistent danger of abstraction is to keep returning theology to the I–You encounter, an encounter that is always concrete, always happening in the middle of things' (Muers, 2019, p. 200). Understanding the church in this sense requires a Christologically redemptive account of human sociality. While his thought 'develops and deepens' later, this book is mature and full of rigour (Mawson, 2018, p. 146). A key argument Bonhoeffer makes is that one cannot separate being 'in Christ' from being in the church community (*DBWE* 1, p. 140). 'Community with God exists only through Christ, but Christ is present only in his church-community, and therefore *community with God exists only in the church*' (*DBWE* 1, p. 158). Christian faith entails an inherent sociality because it is the very self-isolation of fallen humanity that Christ overcomes on the cross (*DBWE* 1, pp. 121, 227–8). Through vicariously bearing the sinful solitude of humanity 'in Adam', Christ binds humanity's individualism to himself and condemns it, thereby reconstituting human individuality as something that is free in relation to and for others. Christ is the *new humanity*, within whom individuals are bound together as his body, the church. If Christ is the foundation of Christian personhood, which is bestowed from outside one's isolated individualism, then a Christian essentially finds the basis of their existence not from within the self-reductive consciousness of a private faith but within the enfleshed community of Christ.

A further, related point is that Christ alone mediates the essence of the church community to itself. Bonhoeffer criticizes the view that a sense of strong faith might derive from 'romantic feelings of solidarity between kindred spirits' (*DBWE* 1, p. 246). Instead, the differences that inevitably cause struggle and conflict between people, who may even experience 'strangeness and seeming coldness' alongside one another, are the essential means by which Christ mediates his presence. Experiences that may seem negative or uncongenial serve as an acute opportunity for faith in Christ alone, who himself has borne and crucified human isolation (*DBWE* 1, pp. 192, 281). If this is so, then it is not necessarily in the psychologically or emotionally enjoyable where Christ is most real, but within distress, disturbance, and perhaps even within the failure to 'fix' problems that leave groups feeling disparate and tribally opposed to one another.

One of the issues that can sometimes arise in conversations about race and racial reconciliation is that there is a common anxiety among White folks to relativize the gulf between people, maybe by seeking to articulate one's pseudo-understanding of the other, not least as White people try to grasp what it means to be Black. Yet this betrays an innate need in us to have someone worked out in our own minds. Bonhoeffer is suggesting that it is precisely in our inability to understand others fully that Christ can be present among us, confronting us through the alien 'other' who eludes our grasp, and who therefore evades our epistemological mastery over them. All we can do is accept them in the name of Christ, recognize their perspective and seek to live in faith that Christ alone can mediate our relationship.

Bonhoeffer would also challenge an approach to faith and community that may subtly streamline others to serve our own 'experiences' of communal like-mindedness within the community. This would be an unfortunate domestication of Christ-in-others that potentially neuters the genuine You that is another person, thereby soothing the ego of those who struggle to exist alongside others. Unity, a term that takes on a different sense here than elsewhere, cannot be crafted by *our* ability to relate to *them* any more. Otherwise, *they* will always be confined to *our* understanding of *them*, which is only a phantom understanding of the genuine *them* whom we encounter in Christ, and through whom we encounter Christ as well.

Much of the difficulty that can occur in conversations about race is that White people like myself are keen to truly understand the experience that Black and Brown people go through. What is in many ways a very worthy intention – demonstrating a desire for solidarity alongside others – is problematic in that it may inadvertently seek to enfold the reality of another into the constraints of a White person's purview. To use a limited analogy, it would be difficult to explain to a two-dimensional cartoon character what it is like to be in three dimensions. Furthermore, this cartoon character would never be able to become three-dimensional, no matter how much it tries to understand. I can never indwell the story of a Black person fully, and nor should I deceive myself into thinking I can fully indwell their story. This is a limited (and I hope not overly offensive) parable for appreciating the limitations of a White person understanding the extent of Black existence. It can be helpful for us to learn what it means to be White by allowing ourselves to be disrupted in our assumptions, norms and criteria for assessing the world around us. This is not to say that we can only learn anything about ourselves from Black people, but I think we would struggle to truly face the conflicting reality in ourselves as White people unless we rub shoulders with someone who is Black or Brown, who genuinely confronts us in our Whiteness. Otherwise, race and racism will remain a theory in our heads, and never move beyond our isolated selves.

Act and Being (DBWE 2)

In Bonhoeffer's *Habilitationsschrift* (his second doctoral thesis), published as *Act and Being*, he builds upon his earlier work by foregrounding theological epistemology. This project reveals the influence that philosophy had at the time on theology regarding how one understands revelation conceptually. Bonhoeffer's Berlin education enabled him not only to perceive the trends in the academy, but this yielded tools to synthesize the two main schools of theological thought to illuminate a way forward which utilized philosophy for theological thinking, albeit critically (Bethge, 2000, p. 113). For him, revelation as a concept must be afforded its own self-constitutive essence, otherwise it falls prey to the abstraction and egotistical introspection of the 'heart turned in on itself' (*cor curvum in se*). Revelation in its dynamic genuineness cannot be reducible to that which is empirically verifiable alone, as that is no longer something truly revealed; nor can it be suspended as something perpetually elusive and, by implication, never actually *revealed* beyond its abstract, non-substantial transcendence. Revelation cannot be construed as either of these alone. Bonhoeffer's claim orients his discussion: 'The concept of revelation must ... yield an epistemology of its own' (*DBWE* 2, p. 31).

This working philosophical concept of revelation is then related to the biblical revelation of Christ. Bonhoeffer's logic suggests that the church is not something that adds Christ to itself as its own possession, as something revealed once but not necessarily anew. Rather, the church is 'the community of faith created by and founded upon Christ ... as the new human, or rather, as the new humanity itself' (*DBWE* 2, p. 112). To know Christ as the genuine 'real' and revealed (on his own terms) Christ is only possible through dynamic, spatiotemporal participation in word and sacrament within the church community of faith (Tietz, 2016, p. 19). Rather than making this move purely out of religious principle, Bonhoeffer substantiates what he means on a visceral, incarnational level: 'Through such proclamation of the gospel' in word and sacrament, 'every member of the church may and should "become Christ" to the others' (*DBWE* 2, p. 113).

If revelation cannot be reduced to epistemological introspection, but occurs through dynamic engagement within the concrete church community, it follows that any epistemological preconditions for how we understand ourselves and one another are wrought from faith in Christ, not abstractly, but as he is encountered anew in the church. This means in many ways that any 'preconditions' we have about God and the world are judged and maybe reconstituted as people indwell the gospel story in word and sacrament while rubbing shoulders with one another in the embodied community. Bonhoeffer's undergirding argument is that Christian individuals can only know themselves as those who ultimately do not know themselves (*DBWE* 2, p. 124). The God who has given God self to humanity in Christ is the one who truly and fully knows us, and who reveals who we are as God freely reveals God self ever anew. 'God freely chose to be bound to historical human beings and to be placed at the disposal of human beings. God is free not from human beings but for them' (*DBWE* 2, p. 91). It is in God's freedom for humanity in Christ that God has chosen to be 'haveable' (*DBWE* 2, p. 91) in an encounter with others from beyond the confines of human epistemological constraints and self-isolation. Encounters with others are therefore encounters with God, or at least opportunities for an encounter with

Christ, in a way that is genuinely open to his revelation because one is confronted by the milieu of others who are Christ's concrete presence on earth (*DBWE* 2, pp. 112–13). Genuine faith in Christ is therefore not derived from within the self. Instead, faith is derived from and directed towards Christ who reveals himself anew within the physical bodies and absences, the spoken words and silences, the praises and laments of the church through word and sacrament, so that he is recognized in creation *extra nos* through the other (*DBWE* 2, pp. 158–9). Selfhood, faith, and I would even argue doctrine, find their impetus in Christ in a way that is continually mediated by and directed towards him through and alongside others.

This means believers in the church essentially *are* Christ to one another by the Spirit's mediation. Christ reveals himself ever anew in a dynamic, contingent sense, through the concrete other (*DBWE* 2, pp. 126–8). Bethge summarizes the obvious link with *Sanctorum Communio*: 'In all respects, it is dialogical sociality – a sociality that is permanently and already fulfilled, yet permanently fulfilling itself anew, both vertically and horizontally' (Bethge, 2000, p. 135).

Bonhoeffer's dialectic of faith (the transcendent aspect) within the church community (the concrete, ontological aspect) serves a theological and ethical epistemology that is possibly attempting to break out of the constraints of Western thinking, by using Western philosophy to do so. What is interesting is that he develops this grammar for understanding an encounter with Jesus Christ in theory. Yet his experience in Harlem among the Black community is the outworking of his theory in practice, and it was only in practice that he could outwork what he was advocating in his early doctoral work. He arguably anticipated what would be a profoundly transformative encounter by rubbing shoulders with African American sisters and brothers in worship, but he probably had no idea how much it would disrupt his 'phraseological' thinking (*DBWE* 8, p. 358), drawing him away from 'pure' intellectual work towards concrete engagement with the reality of God and the world in Christ, the Christ who would call him to faithfulness beyond the confines of esoteric academia, and beyond his previous theological imagination.

Lectures on Christology (DBWE 12, pp. 299–360)

Bonhoeffer's *Lectures on Christology* take his two dissertations further in terms of making the Christological grounding for sociality and epistemology more explicit. In these lectures, he is continuing to use language to push for a view of reality that is borne both from and ultimately within the revelation of God in Christ.

Bonhoeffer claims that humanity is unable to place itself into the truth of reality because of the 'heart turned in on itself' (the *cor curvum in se*). Any truth about God, the world and self is confined within the isolation of human subjectivity. The truth or *logos* of reality (from the Greek meaning 'word') is something we cannot help but derive from within ourselves as individual units. However, Christ the 'counter Logos' confronts the 'human logos' from beyond itself as a person. Christ is not a concept of truth, but truth embodied in fleshly reality, what might be called personal transcendence. The person who is truth reveals to humanity that 'Nothing can be known about [either] God or human being, until God has become a human being in Jesus Christ' (*DBWE* 12, p. 352). Bonhoeffer claims, 'the counter Logos [i.e. Jesus] appears, somewhere and at some time in history, as a human being, and as a human being sets itself up as judge over the human logos and says, "I am the truth, I am the death of the human logos"' (*DBWE* 12, p. 302).

In the human inclination to achieve epistemological mastery over others, Christ undercuts the questions we ask about others that are often an attempt to categorize and dominate them. Analytical questions such as *how* or *what* are illuminated by Christ as nothing other than an attempt to get the measure of a person and understand them on my terms, attempting to enfold them into my self, and not accepting them on their own terms as a distinctly different being. Michael Jinkins summarizes to say that 'when we are confronted by Jesus Christ we are confronted by that reality that calls reality into question' (Jinkins, 1999, p. 93). The only question we can really ask of Jesus when our categories and frameworks are usurped is, '*Who* are you?' This question can only be genuine for those whose own frame of reference has already been superseded by Christ, in whose death and resurrection the human logos is convicted and disempowered (*DBWE* 12, pp. 305–7).

This does not negate any sense of human truth whatsoever, but as Joel Lawrence clarifies, 'it is only through the coming of Christ that the logos is countered with a Truth that it cannot grasp on its own' (Lawrence, 2010, p 19). Christ is 'for me' (or *pro me*) by presenting himself as a stumbling block for human truth, in order to achieve humanity's freedom from its own introspection (*DBWE* 12, pp. 314–15). 'The stumbling block, which we accept, is that our faith is continually tested. But this teaches us to pay attention to the word. Faith comes through temptation' (*DBWE* 12, p. 358). Temptation perpetually draws humanity to revert to the human logos, yet this context is where genuine faith occurs, because those who look to Christ experience the real truth about themselves not from within themselves, but from Christ who counters their own pseudo-truth about reality.

Let me try and contextualize this. When confronted by a person who expresses an experience of suffering and marginalization because of the colour of their skin, I may respond with a laudable desire to understand them better. This is helpful to an extent, yet it is fraught with danger and risk. If I ask about the nature (*what*), reason (*why*) or meaning (*how*) within someone's suffering, I may well be asking questions that are derived from and ultimately directed to myself, because I want to console myself regarding this other person's perception of reality. However sincere and humble I try to be, there is an extent to which I will never understand another person fully. More specifically, I will never understand or embody their enfleshed reality.

My posture towards others who are not like me may inadvertently be within a semiotic world that I have created and continue to dominate. Any enquiry, listening or openness may merely synthesize that person's alien experience within my own logos (*DBWE* 12, p. 301) in my pious attempt to 'grasp' them. As such, any experience or challenge, any suggestions or cries for justice will risk being manoeuvred about and utilized from within my view of reality, which may be open to different perspectives, but only inasmuch as I can remain master of the world within which I live and move and have my being (cf. Acts 17.28). To lament racism with such a paradigm does so without any willingness to have my very paradigm judged by Christ, who confronts me through others, and wants to lead me into a new truth that I cannot be in control over.

That is not to say that questions about racism and racial suffering cannot be asked. The point is that Christ reconstitutes our questions and inquisitiveness into the question he compels us to ask: '*Who* are you?' This question must require my renouncing any inclination towards epistemological mastery by witnessing the revealed reality of Christ here and now within contingent suffering. A Black person is not an *idea* of a Black person; they are real, more real than I will ever be able to mentally grasp or articulate. They are true in a dynamic, enfleshed sense, and their existence, including their suffering, is always contingent, never reducible to an *idea* of suffering. That does not even touch on understanding it fully. Knowledge and understanding of racism in the sense Bonhoeffer is describing is penitently conscious of my (White) human limits as they are revealed by Christ, the one who is a concrete *who* and not a *what*. Rainer Mayer reminds us that Christ is the key, the one who gives meaning as we encounter those with whom we encounter difference. 'Bonhoeffer has bound transcendence to the *sociological reality of the community and the other*, but ... Community and fellow man must be understood in the light of Christ' (Mayer, 1981, p. 188). This means that the goal of any attempts towards justice or racial equality must be open to hearing from Christ in a genuinely transcendent way, as White people like myself humbly recognize our concrete limitations in the crucible of Christ's enfleshed community.

This all means that Christ continually mediates in real time and space what it means to be human within the concrete contingencies of life together. Christ confronts individuals anew through one other, effectively calling them to participate in his life as we rub shoulders with one another under word and sacrament, which arrests the individual self from basing human self-understanding on theological (ideological) abstraction. Bonhoeffer states: 'Even the church, as the presence of Jesus Christ – God who became human, was humiliated, resurrected, and exalted – must receive the will of God every day anew from Christ. For the church, too, Christ becomes, every day anew, an offence to its own desires and hopes' (*DBWE* 12, p. 360). Being human entails our daily resisting the temptation to explain or resolve human existence, with its joys and sorrows, within the magisterially isolated self. We must confess the perpetual allure of epistemological introspection. Bonhoeffer is calling believers to recognize their genuine need for one another, so that we might be liberated by, and drawn into life's confusions, struggles and experiences, as a dynamic way of finding freedom from the *cor curvum in se* in Christ, rather than seeking to resolve epistemological limitations within the self that judges others.

Conclusion

On 29 August 1932, Bonhoeffer delivered an address at the International Youth Conference in Gland. In this remarkable piece, his concern was that the church was allowing the world's logic to define how it understood itself and its message, rather than the reality of God in Christ breaking through to reconfigure the imaginations of God's people. 'Only with clear eyes on reality, without any illusion about our morality or our culture, can one believe' (*DBWE* 11, p. 376). In the tense and wounded tumult of a post-First World War Europe, Bonhoeffer offered a claim that challenged the entrenched nationalism of different nations by pointing to a gospel that transcended all national particularity: 'We encounter Christ in the brother, the German in the Englishman, the Frenchman in the German' (*DBWE* 11, p. 377). These words strike a prophetic tone in a divided and bruised continent. Bonhoeffer recognized that his encounter with the living Jesus was wrapped up in his encounter with those who had recently been enemies. Their true selves were realized as they were subjected to the uniqueness and dynamic differences of one another, across national boundary lines, language, culture, yet recognizing the givenness of one another in their particularity.

If we encounter Christ in our sister and brother, this means that the White British person encounters Christ in the African, as well as the British citizen of African Caribbean descent. As I embrace the distinct *You* that is a person from a different context, I am both affirmed and challenged regarding who I think *I* am. Rather than looking at a mirror made in my image, I am looking at a mirror made in God's image, a real person who offers a reality I have to reckon with, making me potentially a bit uncomfortable at points because certain assumptions and 'givens' are disrupted, while potentially offering torrents of grace provided I am willing to learn and be transformed alongside my sister or brother.

We have a phrase in my church that we use regularly. For us, a gospel church entails 'rubbing shoulders' alongside those with whom we have nothing in common. On one level, that is the heart of the kingdom of God. However, I must be careful as a pastor of a predominantly White church that I do not end there. If we rub shoulders with one another and are not formed by one another in a manner that enables us to become more like Christ, we have a problem. Potentially, rubbing shoulders with one another (i.e., interacting in close quarters as an embodied community of believers) without growing and bearing fruit could cause harm to those who bring distinct gifts that could, but sometimes do not, shape the community. That is why I am tentative about saying that my Black sisters and brothers will encounter Christ through Whites like me. On one level, I think I do represent Christ to the Black and Brown folks in my church, and I am humbled that they express gratitude for my ministry and the fellowship of the church. However, I think there is a lot more to be said for being attentive to the ways in which most of us White folks can and should learn from our kin from a Global Majority Heritage, particularly given that, in my context at least, they are a minority. I regularly feel so anaemic in my understanding of hospitality. I am learning that not wanting to bother others with asking for prayer displays false humility, self-sufficiency and pride. I am realizing that the Lord's Supper is as much about *who* we are sharing it with, as *what* we are actually sharing. There is much work to be done to disentangle people like myself from assumptions about what we perceive to be truly human, when it is often White human. Practices and traditions are maybe comfortable for many of us, but can be truly painful for those for whom an understanding of the gospel is culturally different. For many, Christian faith is not overwhelmingly focused on individuals, as I heard a hugely reputable Christian economist say in a class where I teach. To reduce it to this is more a matter of culture than Scripture. I cannot prescribe all the moral specifics for this. However, the role of a theologian, and I suppose the role of a preacher, as I also am, is to point to what (or *who*) is real. Such proclamation inevitably informs our morals and behaviour, but we must begin with the real, and Bonhoeffer's early work is an intellectual attempt to extricate himself from the constant allure of the heart (and mind) turned in on itself. As his work seeks to communicate, we can only encounter freedom from ourselves when we are confronted and encountered and liberated from ourselves by others. I would suggest that Whiteness is a phenomenon that is both extensive and elusive. I cannot spell out the depths of the issues, as I am suffering from the same malady. I do not know fully what it means to be White, but need guidance and grace on the part of my Black sisters and brothers to highlight where I am making assumptions that are not normative for everyone. Anthony G. Reddie encourages us: 'White people may be prone to collusion with Whiteness and be impacted and affected by its sinful strains, but they are not predetermined to be constrained by it' (Reddie, 2009, pp. 50–1). The field of Black theology may sometimes exhibit a frustration and even a sense of rage over White people's continual reversion to see the whole world through our own frameworks and sensibilities. I think sometimes I need to be told that I am being inadvertently racist, and I take hope in the reality that I can repent and grow to be a humbler and less imposing presence in the world. But saying that, I must do this in relationship with those who are genuinely placed to guide me in this from without. The addressing of my own Whiteness is shaped by those with whom I rub shoulders, and therefore the presence of Black folks in my church, in Oxford University, and in my friendship circles, offers prophetic leadership in my life and thought.

To end this chapter, I want to share the last poem Bonhoeffer wrote. It expresses a childlike desire to embrace the reality of life, the joy and the sorrow, in a way that can be faithful to Christ, knowing that some things will be confusing and difficult, but undergirding it all is a desire to be in fellowship with others, through whom God shares the gift of God self with us.

'By Powers of Good'

1. By faithful, quiet powers of good surrounded
   so wondrously consoled and sheltered here –
   I wish to live these days with you in spirit
   and with you enter into a new year.
2. The old year still would try our hearts to torment,
   of evil times we still do bear the weight;
   O Lord, do grant our souls, now terror-stricken,
   salvation for which you did us create.
3. And should you offer us the cup of suffering,
   though heavy, brimming full and bitter brand,
   we'll thankfully accept it, never flinching,
   from your good heart and your beloved hand.
4. But should you wish now once again to give us
   the joys of this world and its glorious sun,
   then we'll recall anew what past times brought us
   and then our life belongs to you alone.
5. The candles you have brought into our darkness,
   let them today be burning warm and bright,
   and if it's possible, do reunite us!
   We know your light is shining through the night.
6. When now the quiet deepens all around us,
   O, let our ears that fullest sound amaze
   of this, your world, invisibly expanding
   as all your children sing high hymns of praise.
7. By powers of good so wondrously protected,
   we wait with confidence, befall what may.
   God is with us at night and in the morning
   and oh, most certainly on each new day.

(DBWE 8, pp. 548–50)

7

Creation and Fall

Within some Western thinking, there is a pervasive illusion that human beings can create for themselves, as well as from within themselves, a genuinely new beginning. Of course, one may start a new job, buy a new coffee cup or receive a new member into the family. However, while these things are new on a certain level, they do not happen from nothing. There is a history of connections, conversations, actions within a meshwork of stories, as well as material collisions that occur to constitute the 'new' that happens. Therefore, there is a certain extent to which nothing in this world is 'out-of-the-ether' new. The modern 'discovery' of the supposed 'New World' is a case in point.

At the dawn of the Enlightenment, European explorers marked a new epoch, but this was not a truly new beginning. The settlement and expansion of Western civilization into what became the Americas and Africa marked a colonial moment (Jennings, 2010, pp. 24, 83), where all that had existed before from the beginning became refracted (or distorted and dislocated) through an imaginary lens of 'new beginnings' for the (White) human race. People who sailed the seas to these different lands encountered (or, were confronted by) groups that already inhabited these spaces. Indigenous people, tribes, families and societies had dwelt in these lands for generations. They loved, worked, played, fought, reconciled and learnt together within the contours of the landscape and the ebbs and flows of the rivers and tidal currents. The meshwork of flora and fauna gave life to the people and in many ways constituted who they were (Jennings, 2010, p. 49). The land had always been there, giving shape and meaning to those who received it as a life-giving gift to be treasured. White Christians did not appreciate this fully, that these lands were not really 'new' at all, but were already inhabited by people who bore God's image there.

The image of God and a doctrine of creation

I share all of this to set the scene for exploring *Creation and Fall*. This book is a publication of some lectures Bonhoeffer delivered at the University of Berlin in 1932–33, offering a theological exposition of Genesis 1—3. At the time, this method of interpretation prompted biblical scholars and systematic theologians to respond with indignation or indifference respectively, being either too theological or too biblical for the different schools of thought. Eberhard Bethge highlights that this method of theological interpretation of Scripture is no longer regarded as problematic, but at the time it prompted biblical scholars to accuse Bonhoeffer of being too theological, while systematic theologians claimed he was too biblical. Yet Bonhoeffer was pursuing a way of reading Scripture for its primary purpose (Bethge, 2000, p. 217). Bonhoeffer viewed Genesis not primarily as an archaeological text, nor as a philosophical document, but as part of the Christian Bible, and his lectures interpret this ancient creation account Christologically, for Christ reveals the beginning and end (or goal) of all things (*DBWE* 3, p. 22). The church reads Genesis 1—3 through God's revelatory word in Christ (cf. John 1.1–5). It is a true text that tells the story of humanity's beginning, not as a beginning that we can reach towards or behind and verify as truth in an empirical sense, nor is it something that we can springboard off existentially to replicate another beginning like it, because this beginning is an identity marker that continually grasps humanity from beyond itself.

> No one can speak of the beginning but the one who was in the beginning … God alone tells us that God is in the beginning … No question can go back behind the creating God, because one cannot go back behind the beginning. (*DBWE* 3, pp. 29, 30, 31–2)

Humanity finds itself located in the middle of things, living between the beginning and the end, yet able to witness their beginning.

Bonhoeffer claims God created heaven and earth in unconditioned freedom. In an act that is unrepeatable and unbound by human conceptions of divine sovereignty, God freely creates out of nothing. 'Nothing' in this original sense is not a primordial possibility that exists in conjunction with God to link creation somehow to the divine; it is truly nothing. God's very act of creating is a divine negation of 'nothing' as God's word wills something called 'light' into existence (*DBWE* 3, p. 34). Bonhoeffer's doctrine of *creatio ex nihilo* (creation out of nothing) relates the creation narrative to the resurrection of Christ, where light shines in the darkness of death and nothingness (*DBWE* 3, p. 35).

Bonhoeffer argues that creation is not an extension of God's being. It rests entirely in God's gracious hand and will continually depend on the divine upholding to exist, and yet God also bestows creation with its own unique form. Creation exists before God as that which is distinctly not God, which means it can, with essential integrity, truly belong to God because it is not God (*DBWE* 3, p. 39). What binds God to creation is not God's being, but God's word in the world (*DBWE* 3, p. 41). A critical point here is that Bonhoeffer refuses to accept that creation reveals who the Christian God is. This is in keeping with his rejection of natural theology (see *DBWE* 12, p. 383; *DBWE* 14, p. 133; *DBWE* 15, p. 301; *DBWE* 16, pp. 240, 592). Natural theology holds that human beings can decipher and discern who God is and what God is like within perception and reason. Bonhoeffer rejected this view. He would argue that we can of course know God as the creator and worship God as such, but it is only in Christ that we know that the creator is this God, rather than a general creator deity. Without Christ, our understanding of the creator is incomplete and open to distortion. This may sound a little restrictive and exclusive, but that is because, for Bonhoeffer, creation is not what it should fully be. Because of sin, humanity has a distorted perception of God, creation and itself. While some people may look at world history and seek to interpret the nature of God through current events (as the Reich church did), Bonhoeffer would claim emphatically that Christ is Lord of creation, and anything happening in the world must ultimately be measured against his person and work.

There are a few contextual things to note. First, Bonhoeffer is drawing on an Old Testament story attached to ancient Israel and modern-day Jews. With the rise of National Socialism, Bonhoeffer foregrounds this ancient story which does not draw upon German notions of blood and soil, but of Jewish blood and toil. It should not be lost on us that many Black Christians have found meaning and significance in the Scriptures of ancient Israel. While many of our White churches today oftentimes ignore or gloss over the seemingly alien and difficult passages of the Old Testament, Black Christian experience has drawn deeply from the wells of the Old Testament.

Second, Bonhoeffer makes a big deal of the nature of 'new beginnings' in these lectures. This motif was throughout the rhetoric of Adolf Hitler in his rise to power (Bergen, 1996, p. 10; Bethge, 2000, p. 648; DeCort, 2018, pp. xx, 76–7). There was a 'semi-religious mystique' developing around Hitler as the emerging *Führer*, who offered dreams of a golden age and new beginning for Germany after the devastation of the First World War (Bosanquet, 1968, p. 95). Bonhoeffer's reference to the beginning was a sharp attack against all narratives that incited Germany to attempt its own self-actualization, and enact its own new beginning. There is no true 'new beginning' for those locked in the complexity and confusion of worldly life. There are always other people, other groups within other spaces, and human lives are interconnected with the earth to the extent that any change in the world is never from within a vacuum.

The concept of the 'image of God' is not referenced directly in the Scriptures very much, but has historically carried significant import in many streams and traditions of the church. One of the key places where it is used is in the creation story. Genesis 1.26–27 reads:

> Then God said, 'Let us make humankind [*Ādām*] in our image, according to our likeness, and let them have dominion over the fish of the sea, and over the birds of the air, and over the cattle, and over all the wild animals of the earth, and over every creeping thing that creeps upon the earth.'
> So God created humankind [*Ādām*] in his image,
>   in the image of God he created them [him];
>   male and female he created them.

While this is the only occurrence in Genesis 1—3, Bonhoeffer offers an understanding of the *imago Dei* (image of God) that carries far-reaching implications for the relationship between doctrine and ethics. To put it simply, he describes the *imago Dei* as 'freedom'.

'Freedom' is a loaded word, especially in the context of a book about race and racism. I am reminded of the African American spiritual etched upon my memory these days, which remembers the souls and bodies of Black slaves:

> Oh freedom, oh freedom,
> oh freedom over me.
> And before I'd be a slave,
> I'll be buried in my grave.
> and go home to my Lord/God and be free.

Bonhoeffer's use of the word *Freiheit* in German is being deployed in a different way here and it can be helpful to frame his conception of freedom with three additional words: 'relationship', 'creatureliness' and 'obedience'.

The freedom of the *imago Dei* is a dynamic *relation* (DBWE 3, p. 63). It is not something that humankind 'has' in itself. Freedom is not something that can be drawn upon from within or identified on oneself like skin colour or anatomical make-up. For Bonhoeffer, there is nothing in humanity's being, in and of itself, that makes it free. It is in its relationship with God and others that humanity is genuinely free. This is a comportment to the world that embodies God's freedom, who freely 'wills not to be free for God self but for humankind' in an act that is not obligated, but gratuitous. God freely begets and bestows upon humanity a dynamic freedom for God, but also, both simultaneously and inseparably, for one another as well. Therefore, freedom cannot be reduced to an individual. Genesis 2.18 highlights that it is not the human as an individual but the aloneness of that individual which is not good. Contrast this to Genesis 1.31 in the first creation narrative, where all that God had made, including humankind as 'male and female', is very good. The *imago Dei* is not a static *category*, but a dynamic *practice* of freely giving and receiving love in communion, and, through this, 'God's self enters into God's creation' (*DBWE* 3, p. 63).

Humanity's freedom is therefore dependent on both a vertical and horizontal dimension (Bethge, 2000, p. 135). 'Community with God by definition establishes social community as well. It is not that community with God subsequently leads to social community; rather, neither exists without the other' (*DBWE* 3, p. 63). An obvious implication for our purposes would be that I cannot claim to be free and loving in my relation to God if I am simultaneously inhibiting or disfiguring my relationship with another. To be specific, I cannot delude myself that I can achieve intrapersonal or individual flourishing in isolation from those whose lives are impacted by my attempts to flourish. My freedom finds its basis in a relationship of love for and with others. I may think that I am 'free' to get a promotion, or to live in a particular part of the country, or to buy certain foods and clothing. However, if that 'freedom' depends on others being stifled or encumbered, then I am not free at all. It is when I live for the sake of others' flourishing, that I live in freedom in this sense, even and especially when it may impact my own individual sensibilities and preferences.

Freedom as a *relation* naturally links to the second aspect of the *imago Dei*, which concerns humanity's free *creatureliness*. People are God-like in an unfathomable, creaturely sense whereby God recognizes the divine self in human creatures (*DBWE* 4, pp. 281–2). They are created, not the creator, finite, not infinite, limited, not limitless. There is no unbridled, abstract autonomy for human creatures because human *being* is not ultimately self-constituted (*DBWE* 3, p. 62). The image of God celebrates defined, temporal, spatial, creaturely boundaries. These boundaries are not to be understood in an oppressive sense, but as a beautiful, if fragile, gift of grace, without which humanity would have no substance to its being and sink into the void and abyss of nothingness (*DBWE* 3, pp. 58–9). Freedom embraces creaturely limits as an embodied gift inaugurated from humanity's origin in God as the means of being free for one another before God in the created order. As Bonhoeffer poetically puts it elsewhere, 'Only through discipline does one learn the secret of freedom' (*DBWE* 8, p. 512). Humans are confronted by the other as their frontier, their limit, and therefore as a gift that engenders their freedom. As those who are set to rule over creation, human beings are distinct from creation, but in a way that is bound inseparably to it. '[I]n my whole being, in my creatureliness, I belong wholly to this world; it bears me, nurtures me, holds me … Humankind is derived from a piece of earth. Its bond with the earth belongs to its essential being' (*DBWE* 3, pp. 66, 76). People relate within a created, bodily existence, sharing limits with other bodies. Human being is de facto creaturely, which means true humanity is fundamentally grounded in the reality of time and space. Even and especially when it comes to their knowledge of God, human creatures are bound to God not despite but through their place in the earth within which God has created them.

Third, the *imago Dei* encompasses free *obedience* to God's word (*DBWE* 3, pp. 84–5). The only way to be truly free in a theological sense is to obey God's commands, trusting God in childlike innocence. Free humanity does not derive its own sense of right and wrong from within itself because it is free to obey God in in unbroken and simple clarity (Reed, 2018, p. 109). In simple terms: Adam does not think for himself about what is good for him, because he believes God knows, so Adam freely obeys God's word without question (*DBWE* 3, pp. 86–7, 98).

Free *relation*, *creatureliness* and *obedience* are terms that articulate the *imago Dei* for Bonhoeffer. He considers both the tree of life and the tree of the knowledge of good and evil to be iconic representations of how God fixes the necessary conditions for the *imago Dei* (Lawrence, 2013, p. 117). As the earlier chapter on Creation and Space shows, the commandment to refrain from eating the fruit of the tree of the knowledge of good and evil is, for Bonhoeffer, a spatiotemporal referent from which humanity encounters the centre and limit of its freedom ever anew. God has thought of all that humanity needs to flourish alongside the rest of creation with God. The problem comes when freedom is transgressed, assaulted, dismissed or claimed, in what Bonhoeffer identifies as sin.

Falling away from freedom

In Genesis 3, Adam and Eve eat from the tree of the knowledge of good and evil. Bonhoeffer refers to the 'Fall' (as it is sometimes called) as being something that occurs in an ambiguous 'twilight' (*Zwielicht*). The *how* or *why* this happens is utterly unanswerable (*DBWE* 3, p. 104). No direct answer is attainable for such questioning, other than a strange, indirect one.

> The *twilight* in which what has been created and what is evil appear here cannot in any way be made an unmixed light without destroying something that is decisive. The ambiguity of the serpent, of Eve, and of the tree of knowledge as creatures of God's grace and yet as the place where the voice of evil is heard must be preserved as such; it must on no account be crudely simplified and its two aspects be torn apart to make it unambiguous. (*DBWE* 3, p. 104)

The serpent raises a seemingly innocent question concerning the authenticity of God's word (*DBWE* 3, p. 106). It is precisely this insidious and pious nature of temptation that makes it so dangerous. It is not stark, but subtle in positing the notion of being responsible, and even good, so that it might gain power over humankind (*DBWE* 10, p. 401). The serpent appears to be on God's side by dangling a postulate that cloaks itself in God's word as a disguise (*DBWE* 3, p. 106).

A key thing to highlight is that the voice of evil is 'veiled in the garb of piety' (*DBWE* 3, p. 107). The serpent's very question uses God's word to usher its hearer away from God towards itself. Even the most orthodox answer (Gen. 3.2–3) is sometimes not enough to resist the serpent's temptation (Barth, 1994b, CD IV/1, p. 434), and can be the very thing through which the human heart is deceived and turned in upon itself. Speaking for God as though God is constrainable within our ideals, rather than turning towards the actual living God, transplants God's dynamic word into a dead, fallen, human word. Truth becomes a concept or proposition, not a person who is free (John 14.6).

Humanity entertains the alluring possibility that God might not know what is best, that God might not be the God of freedom who offers freedom for humanity. This results in human *disobedience*. God's word is assimilated into human words and ideals, directing humanity towards nothingness (*DBWE* 16, p. 487). Humanity goes behind the word of God in the attempt to somehow validate God's word on humanity's own terms (*DBWE* 3, pp. 106, 109). God is no longer the Lord whose word receives simple obedience, and humanity is promptly flooded with the natural impulse to hide, only to later try and justify its disobedience (Gen. 3.12–13).

Humanity also transgresses its *creatureliness*. Adam and Eve grasp beyond their God-given, life-constituting limits, within which they encounter their true potential. They want to be *sicut Deus*, like God, like the creator, which could only be a non-creaturely, non-human, non-being (*DBWE* 3, pp. 115–16). To try and become like God would mean self-determined solitude and isolation for human creatures (*DBWE* 10, p. 396). By acquiescing in the serpent's objective advice, humanity rejects its creaturely limits and particularity, leaving it simultaneously divided and alone (*DBWE* 3, pp. 119–20, 122).

Adam and Eve also elect for themselves the unfreedom of introspection through their 'ontic inversion into the self, the *cor curvum in se*' (*DBWE* 2, p. 46). They now find their *relation* to God and one another to be unwelcome and abhorrent. Their rejection of the *imago Dei* in the Fall is a vertical rejection of God and a corresponding, horizontal rejection of one another (Greggs, 2016, p. 86). Rather than being a gracious gift of relational freedom *for* one another in their differences, they withdraw *from* each other, threatened and seeking freedom *from* one another *for* themselves. This is merely an evasive and oppressive pseudo-freedom that trips them up to fall into naked self-shame (*DBWE* 12, p. 201).

The notion that human sinfulness is biologically hereditary and therefore inevitable is not only theologically distorted and fatalistic, but oppressive and repulsive. It paints humanity as a tragic race that is not really enslaved to sin, but perpetually determined to sin as a robotically cosmic inevitability. Barth echoes Bonhoeffer, explaining, 'there can be no doubt that the idea of a hereditary sin which has come to man by propagation is an extremely unfortunate and mistaken one … "Hereditary sin" has a hopelessly naturalistic, deterministic and even fatalistic ring' (Barth, 1994b, *CD* IV/1, p. 434). The whole point of Genesis 1—3 is that humanity's dynamic 'Fall' should not happen, should not exist, and should never be explained because it would then be in some ways justified. God does not will humanity's rejection of human freedom. No theorizing about sin can comprehend the horror of its implications in the world, and we cannot evade the seriousness of God's word about the rejection of our humanity.

Through sin, creation is marred by its image-bearers. The world is intrinsically turned in on itself because those who were set to rule and steward it have failed to be free *for* the world. God still upholds the world that has fallen from its origin, even while it is assailed by sin to the extent of suffering decay, destruction and death (*DBWE* 1, p. 108; *DBWE* 11, p. 267). Many of the tragic and wicked occurrences in the world are therefore not commensurate with God's will, but in opposition to it (*DBWE* 3, p. 126; *DBWE* 10, p. 518). Humanity is enshrouded within its own fallen twilight, and cannot pinpoint from an effective vantage point what is God's good, finite creation and what is the assault of sin on creation. 'That the world has fallen and that sin now rules and that the creation and sin are so intertwined that no human eye can see them as separate, that every human order is the order of the fallen world and not of creation, all that is not seen in its seriousness' (*DBWE* 11, p. 363). Humanity often tries to understand itself in relation to itself, rather than in relation to God and others. It discerns its limits by transgressing them and disregarding those who inhabit others spaces. It navigates its actions within an accountability structure that derives not from the heart of creation but from its own epistemological dominion over all things. Nevertheless, Bonhoeffer suggests:

> Humankind is not permitted to remain alone in its sin; God speaks to Adam and halts him in his flight. Come out of your hiding place, out of your self-reproach, out of your cover-up, out of your secrecy, out of your self-torment, out of your vain remorse. Confess who you are, do not lose yourself in religious despair, be yourself. Adam, where are you? Stand before your Creator ... Adam tries to excuse himself with something that accuses him ... As though one could use sin itself as an excuse – the inconceivable folly of humankind! Just because you are a sinner, stand before me and do not flee. (*DBWE* 3, pp. 128–9)

Rather than standing penitently before God, Adam speaks defensively and correctively to God while hidden in the bushes, clothed in his shame and guilt, 'appealing from God the Creator to a better god, a different god' (*DBWE* 3, p. 129). It is in this state that the grace of God continually comes to humanity in freedom, not merely setting up the conditions for humanity to live but revealing God self freely, ultimately coming as the only truly free human being, Jesus Christ.

Conclusion

Bonhoeffer offers an approach to sin that considers it to be personal in both an intra-personal and inter-personal sense. Sin has implications for how we understand and treat both ourselves and others. Any account of sin must therefore account for its intrinsic sociological and cosmological dimensions without which we perpetuate the very sin we are seeking to address regarding human individuality and communality.

To give a historical example, we can consider the writings of Gomes Eanes de Azurara (Zurara), a chronicler who documented the arrival of Black slaves in Portugal at the behest of Prince Henry 'the Navigator' in 1444. During the early stages of the modern slave trade, White European Christians encountered their own 'serpent's question' through the buying and selling of Black slaves. Rather than living in freedom, protesting the awful treatment of fellow human beings, challenging the assault upon others' God-given finitude and heeding Christ's call to love their neighbour as themselves, many misconstrued God's image in others and, consequently, in themselves. Zurara warped his Christological hermeneutics and concocted distorted notions of 'providence' to understand and thereby legitimize this irreversible evil (Jennings, 2010, pp. 16–18, 90), while penitently enjoying the benefits. Willie James Jennings illuminates the dangers and self-deception of the serpentine piety that hypnotized Europeans such as Zurara, who sought to discern a 'reason' or means by which God was in this horrific activity. What is most sobering for some readers is that he was deeply moved to tears by the agony and misery exhibited from Blacks, yet failed to recognize Christ suffering within the flesh and blood of these fellow humans (Jennings, 2010, pp. 20–1). In fact, his tearful and sorrowful response dexterously shifted his gaze away from his neighbour's freedom, focusing instead on his own pseudo-freedom as a pious and religious means of assuaging any personal responsibility. In *Creation and Fall*, Bonhoeffer exposes the evil of crafting a theological justification for evil. In the same vein, Nathan Kerr challenges believers who, in his view, are guilty of reinforcing an oppressive status quo upon marginal communities by blurring the lines between what God has or has not willed (Kerr, 2009, pp. 50–1). God wills freedom, but that does not mean individuals or groups are autonomously permitted to dehumanize, coerce or impose themselves upon others at will. This is not freedom at all, but unfreedom, which results when those bestowed with the image of God reject God's image.

When a person is dying from terminal illness, suffering racial injustice, facing redundancy or traumatized from an abusive relationship, inciting God's sovereign will to help that person (and ourselves) to make sense of the situation could inadvertently concoct a theological justification for that situation, and in turn evade the call of Christ himself. In such instances, the principalities and powers of a sinful world absorb Christianity into its machinations under the auspices of 'God's will', and providence is yoked upon individuals who become enslaved to the snake-like order of the day. Evoking providence and 'God's will' to sovereignly explain suffering, evil and sorrow is not so different from asserting the 'orders of creation' doctrine that Bonhoeffer opposed, due to the way German Christians conflated 'God's will' with worldly history. We cannot conflate a fallen world with God's good creation. Bonhoeffer asserts that not everything is simply 'God's will', though 'in the end nothing happens "apart from God's will" (Matt. 10.39), that is, in every event, even the most ungodly, there is a way through to God' (*DBWE* 8, pp. 226–7).

We cannot regard 'the way things are' synonymously with the way God intends. In Christ, we witness that truth is a person and not an idea, so faith is rooted in the person and work of Christ, rather than our lofty concepts about him. Christ does not offer an epistemological explanation for suffering and evil, certainly not one that human beings can go behind God's word to grasp. Bonhoeffer warns us against any attempt to explain *how* or *why* evil occurs. 'The question why there is evil is not a theological question, for it presupposes that it is possible to go back behind the existence that is laid upon us as sinners. If we could answer the question why, then *we* would not be sinners' (*DBWE* 3, p. 120). It is unsurprising therefore that many Black theologians are uninterested in the subject of theodicy (the philosophical problem of God in relation to suffering). John Swinton demonstrates how this modern posture developed, and why it is problematic to a life of Christian faithfulness (Swinton, 2018, pp. 30–45). Trying to understand and verify God's 'plan' within worldly suffering further exposes the serpentine hubris of human sinfulness and tempts people over the precipice of rejecting the biblical God, who calls us to faith and righteous action. For Bonhoeffer, any explanation of sin and suffering is ultimately suspended in Christ's lament on the cross, 'My God, my God, why have you forsaken me?' The key thing is to respond to God's call in freedom, that is, to be freely relational, creaturely and obedient in and through Christ, and not to turn our hearts inwards. The juxtaposition of these things is captured poetically in one of Bonhoeffer's prison poems.

Fortune and Calamity

Fortune and calamity
that rush to strike us and overwhelm,
are at first
barely distinguishable

like heat and frost to the fingertips' sudden touch.
Like meteors
hurled from far above the earth,
brilliant and threatening,
they steer their course over our heads.
Victims stand dumbstruck
before the rubble
of their lusterless, everyday existence.

Grand and sublime,
destroying, conquering,
fortune and calamity,
invited and uninvited,
make ceremonious entry
into shattered people's lives,
adorning and robing
those they visit
with solemnity and blessing.

Fortune is full of horror,
calamity full of sweetness.
Inseparably both, the one and the other,
seem to issue from the eternal.
Great and terrible are both.
People from far and near
come running to see
and gape
half envious, half shuddering
at enormity,
where powers above the earth,
blessing and destroying,
appear
in a confusing, forever entangled
earthly drama.
What is fortune? What calamity?

Only time divides them.
When the unfathomable thrill
of sudden event
turns to tiresome, tortuous duration,
when the day's endlessly dragging hour

finally unveils to us calamity's true form,
then most people turn away,
disillusioned and bored,
weary of the monotony
of calamity's familiar tune.

This is the hour of faithfulness,
the hour of mother and lover,
the hour of friend and brother.
Faithfulness transfigures all calamity
and quietly envelops it
in gentle, celestial resplendence.

(*DBWE* 8, pp. 441–2)

8

Discipleship

When I mention Dietrich Bonhoeffer in conversation, many Christians who are familiar with his name usually remark on his popular book, *The Cost of Discipleship*, or *Discipleship as* it is called in the *DBWE*. The German title is *Nachfolge*, which translates as 'following after' and encapsulates the whole of the book succinctly, which is a theological treatise centred on the Sermon on the Mount in Matthew 5—7. Like many other Christians, when I first read this book, I found it to be a heart-warming and inspiring devotional text that I could draw on during my quiet time, and then quote in pithy form to demonstrate that I was taking my discipleship seriously. I may be the only one, but I sense that there are others who, like me years ago, do not fully perceive the theological depth and astounding radicality of this book. As I came to it during my PhD studies, I considered that I would be on familiar ground, but was disturbed and, if I am honest, harrowed by the intensity of it. From my own experience, but also from numerous conversations with other Christians, reading *Discipleship* with both an awareness of Bonhoeffer's own socio-political context, as well his undergirding Christology, makes this book much more than a 'nice' Christian classic.

Contextualizing *Discipleship*

Bearing in mind what I have said above, and also recalling what I said in Chapter 5, we need to recognize that the 'radical' nature of *Discipleship* is vulnerable to being co-opted to serve numerous ideological leanings within our current culture wars. This tendency is evident in some ways the Scriptures have been used in the past to oppress others. Bonhoeffer's thinking in general can sometimes make him vulnerable to being interpreted differently, given that he is not quite so verbose and watertight as others. However, it is possibly in *Discipleship* more than anywhere else that readers may sense an affinity with Bonhoeffer's rhetoric regarding the uncompromising call of allegiance to Christ alone, but read this from within the context of different social and political horizons, therefore translating what 'allegiance' means in divergent ways. Such an optic inevitably engenders contrasting perspectives on what it means to be truly 'radical' today. Therefore, it is important that *Discipleship* is read with two things in mind. First, one must bear in mind the context within which the book was written. Contrary to much thinking in the White Western world, theology is always, at least to a necessary extent, worked out from within a context. Bonhoeffer is no exception, and we do him a disservice if we fail to be attentive to the historical situation and specific audience he was directly addressing in each of his works. Second, we would do very well to read *Discipleship* in the overarching narrative of his whole life and thought. In suggesting this, I do not want to diminish the somewhat polemical nature of *Discipleship*. Far from it! Rather, I would encourage us to consider his writing here as an emphatic clarion call that stands as a contrast against other writings that are less absolute and pointed in their content. Joel Lawrence also recognizes the candid nature of *Discipleship*, suggesting that it therefore requires some careful parsing and expansion so that Bonhoeffer is not diminished to what he says here (Lawrence, 2010, pp. 47–9).

For all of us, when our personal situations become fraught with danger and risk, we naturally form a sharp focus on what is ultimately most important. For example, if my house suddenly went up in flames, I would be solely concerned about getting my family out of the house, and would have little or no concern for any personal documents or sentimental valuables, though of course those things are important when the crisis has abated. People will naturally prioritize different aspects of the Christian life depending on their context and positioning in the world, while others would foreground other (contrary or complementary) aspects of life and Scripture. I would encourage readers to approach *Discipleship* in a manner that is attentive to this.

Such a lens through which to approach *Discipleship* is one that Bonhoeffer himself proposes from his reflections in prison. In a letter to Eberhard Bethge (21 July 1944), written on the day after a failed attempt to assassinate Hitler, he remarks:

> I thought I myself could learn to have faith by trying to live something like a saintly life. I suppose I wrote *Discipleship* at the end of this path. Today I clearly see the dangers of that book, though I still stand by it. (*DBWE* 4, p. 486)

He notes some dangers to the book, though he still maintains its value and importance. These dangers are what need highlighting and expanding if we are to read *Discipleship* appropriately today, especially in relation to the subject matter of this book. Earlier in prison, Bonhoeffer writes:

> One can and must not speak the ultimate word prior to the penultimate. We are living in the penultimate and we believe the ultimate ... In *Discipleship*, I only touched on these ideas ... and never developed them properly. *That will need to be done later.* (*DBWE* 8, p. 213, emphasis mine)

His understanding of the 'ultimate and penultimate' has already been explored in Chapter 5. The penultimate represents the provisional, earthly existence that has been judged and reconciled in Christ, who is the ultimate word regarding all that is penultimate. Bonhoeffer's *Discipleship* foregrounds the ultimate, which lends itself to a particular interpretation of the Sermon on the Mount that stands on its own, but could benefit from some development, as Bonhoeffer intimates. Christian Gremmels rightly explains that the radical nature of *Discipleship* can 'only become dangerous if the penultimate is being confused with the ultimate' (*DBWE* 4, p. 308).

I have unpacked Bonhoeffer's understanding of the penultimate (discipleship in our earthly, spatiotemporal, provisional lives) in Chapter 5, and this aspect provides the necessary development of *Discipleship* for a full account of race and racism. Indeed, without recognizing the time and place within which we witness Christ, who is the ultimate Word of God, there is no context to receive and respond to Christ's ultimate call. Without the penultimate, the gospel becomes a gnostic ideal, rather than a concrete call to follow Jesus here and now. Bonhoeffer's omission (or lack of foregrounding) of the penultimate is understandable, though he later suggests its content would be more whole if the crisis at hand had not necessitated a tunnel-vision approach to its content.

Like the Sermon on the Mount which he discusses, Bonhoeffer could be misappropriated here to belittle and suppress conversations around race and racism. I would go even so far as to say that the piety exhibited through certain interpretations of the Sermon on the Mount may inadvertently manipulate racialized suffering and sorrow for oppressive purposes, legitimizing evil. Bonhoeffer maybe risks this at points in purporting his understanding of absolute allegiance to Christ. It will be helpful to expand Bonhoeffer's reading of Jesus' radical teaching here, lest the theological interpretation offered becomes at best incomplete or, at worst, anaemic to those who are not White, as Bonhoeffer and I are. It seems that Bonhoeffer's close friend and supporter Ruth von Kleist-Retzow (his fiancée's grandmother) perceived this need, writing to him that she anticipated further development of the links and content he had omitted (Pejsa, 1991, p. 260). This chapter will start to attempt just that.

Radical obedience to Christ

Discipleship exhorts readers to a life of radical obedience to Christ by faith, through a strict obedience to the Sermon on the Mount. Christ's call breaks any immediacy between the individual and the world. 'Christ has untied the person's immediate connections with the world and bound the person immediately to himself' (*DBWE* 4, p. 93). Any self-knowledge or individual knowledge of God is now mediated to disciples by Christ alone, a notion the world hates (*DBWE* 4, pp. 62, 94). My knowledge, understanding and action is based on what Christ calls, not through my own autonomous impulses.

The call of Christ means, 'The disciple is thrown out of the relative security of life into complete insecurity (which in truth is absolute security and protection in community with Jesus)' (*DBWE* 4, p. 58). Faith in Christ requires obedience, 'otherwise Jesus' call dissipates into nothing' (*DBWE* 4, p. 63). Those who sorrow over a lack of faith and struggle to obey Christ's call are merely disobedient, which is symptomatic of 'cheap grace' and prompts self-forgiveness, rather than the forgiveness bestowed by costly grace through concrete repentance (*DBWE* 4, p. 67; also, *DBWE* 13, p. 408). Bonhoeffer's concept of 'cheap grace' arguably developed during his time in Abyssinian Baptist Church in Harlem, where he witnessed the segregation and oppression of Black people by White Christians (Rah, 2015, p. 202; Reynolds, 2016, p. 134). Faith in *Christ* (rather than in ourselves) must involve penitent action in response to him, with the hope of receiving a grace that is costly (cf. 1 Cor. 6.8–13). Those who are blessed to share in Christ's life have therefore renounced any entitlement or presumption to individualistic happiness in and of itself. 'They mourn over the world, its guilt, its fate, and its happiness' (*DBWE* 4, p. 103). But disciples do not remotely despise God's world. 'No one understands people better than Jesus' community. No one loves people more than Jesus' disciples – that is why they stand apart, why they mourn' (*DBWE* 4, p. 104). The sorrow disciples bear arises from witnessing the misery of the world in a way that is only possible through Christ, who mediates their relation to the world (and themselves), for his own sake.

There are similarities here to Bonhoeffer's earlier work. One's moral agency is not determined by one's own self-enclosed matrix, like a computer using various algorithms to work out a solution to different problems. A disciple's life and action is constituted by Christ's call, which comes to them from beyond themselves, beyond their ideas and latent assumptions, confronting them with a call to lay down the very sensibilities that have otherwise been afforded lordship over their life. This is the locus from which Bonhoeffer lays a hermeneutic to read the Sermon on the Mount. The teachings of Christ are not the moral and ethical framework in and of themselves as a goal. The goal is Christ, and the Sermon on the Mount is descriptive of a life that is commensurate with the call of Christ as Lord. Mourning is not blessed in and of itself. Christ is the point of discipleship, not mourning, or peacemaking, or forgiveness, or any other aspect of his teaching in and of itself. All of these things are ultimately for Christ's sake, and they take shape through the means and ways that Jesus calls his disciples to live in fellowship with and through allegiance to him.

Allegiance to Christ means living under the cross, which involves suffering, rejection and death (*DBWE* 4, p. 85). Bonhoeffer famously writes, 'Whenever Christ calls us, his call leads us to death' (*DBWE* 4, p. 87). This language is intense for some readers, but perhaps not unfamiliar for Bonhoeffer's seminarians at the time. *Discipleship* was a culmination of his teaching from Finkenwalde, where he was training pastors for the Confessing Church to stand fast in their faithfulness to Christ amid numerous pressures from the Nazi regime. The likelihood of war loomed and Bonhoeffer could see no Christian legitimization in this. Those who refused conscription were often sent to concentration camps, while those who joined the military would later write what can only be described as confessions to Bonhoeffer regarding the atrocious acts they were obliged to commit. An uncompromising stand for Christ against Hitler would entail the very real possibility of death. However, Joel Lawrence rightly explains that there is more going on in this 'call to death' that Bonhoeffer highlights:

> When Bonhoeffer focuses his attention on the cross in *Discipleship* he does not do so out of a morbid fascination with guilt and death, but with the theological conviction that it is in the place of Christ's great agony and suffering that we see the doorway to life. The cross is not an end in itself but is a means to an end: life for others. (Lawrence, 2010, pp. 27–8)

Disciples are called to participate in Christ's life, which means potentially suffering and dying with him. As disciples struggle in a world where they are hurt or despised, they take on the sin, suffering and need of Christ because they are in him. This binds them Christologically to the whole world that causes him harm (*DBWE* 4, pp. 139–40, 144–5, 152–5). Discipleship involves a daily sorrow over sin and guilt in the world, a dynamic petition for faith to be obedient while praying in hope that deliverance will one day come (*DBWE* 4, p. 157). Disciples do not fatalistically acquiesce in the violence of the world, nor do they necessarily orchestrate a forceful revolution for God. Rather, they remain faithful to Christ by loving enemies through prayer and acts of justice and mercy. This cruciform obedience through faith is disciples' participation in Christ's existence (*DBWE* 4, pp. 94–6).

Suffering evil

There are inevitably some challenges that arise in reading Bonhoeffer's *Discipleship* when we consider the complexity of this penultimate world as it awaits and anticipates Christ's final return. An obvious problem for some readers of the Sermon on the Mount arises regarding Jesus' teaching in relation to evil. In Matthew 5.38–39, Jesus says, 'You have heard that it was said, "An eye for an eye and a tooth for a tooth." But I say to you, Do not resist an evildoer.' Bonhoeffer draws on the Old Testament law of retribution which was established to uphold justice. He claims this law is both affirmed and ultimately completed in Christ, and therefore concludes: 'According to Jesus' words, such just retribution takes place only in not resisting it' (*DBWE* 4, p. 132). The command to 'not resist an evildoer' means that Jesus 'releases his community from the political and legal order' which would otherwise bind them to something or someone other than Christ (*DBWE* 4, pp. 132–3).

Obedience to Christ means overcoming the evil of evildoers 'by allowing their evil to run its course … Suffering passes when it is borne. The evil comes to an end when we permit it to pass over us, without defense' (*DBWE* 4, p. 133). Evil is resisted and defeated by not retaliating against it as though the evildoer themselves were an adversary. The original Greek verb for 'resist' is *anthistēmi* and is a term for 'setting oneself against' another, or doing battle against them, so it has an aggressive reactionary sense rather than a merely resolute sense (Danker, 2000, p. 80). In other words, non-resistance means non-retaliation, but this does not mean it is unresponsive. Evil is usurped of its power by disciples who 'give witness to it just as Jesus did, because otherwise the evil person will not be engaged and overcome ... Suffering willingly endured is stronger than evil; it is the death of evil' (*DBWE* 4, p. 134). Not resisting evil is not strictly passive, though it is certainly not violent; it is actively non-violent in its response towards evil (Wink, 2003, p. 10–13).

How does this claim fare for people who have experienced oppression, dehumanization and terrorism due to the colour of their skin? Might Bonhoeffer (and Jesus) only be referring to the Christian community here? Bonhoeffer answers that 'Jesus says: because you live in the world and because the world is evil, that is why the statement is valid: do not resist evil' (*DBWE* 4, p. 135). Bonhoeffer seemed wary of non-violence as a categorical principle because it might not necessarily be grounded in the reality of Christ. He later reflects in *Ethics* that people born into such structures and principled systems such as an absolutist scheme of non-violence are 'ethically emasculated ... others who venture to act in free responsibility amid the pressures of daily life are crushed by the machinery of all-pervasive rules and regulations' (*DBWE* 6, p. 286). Of course, Martin Luther King Jr is a famous figurehead for non-violent resistance. Both King and Bonhoeffer draw on the Sermon on the Mount in their thinking, as well as the influence of Gandhi (Roberts, 2005, pp. 67–70). Unlike Bonhoeffer, King is criticized by some as developing an abstract principle of non-violence, whereas many scholars claim Bonhoeffer held to this orientation with a keen attentiveness to the very rare contingencies arising in a complex and conflicted world that is real and penultimate (Williams, 2021, p. 191). He does not unpack this fully in *Discipleship*, but it seems reasonable, given his involvement in the conspiracy, to argue that Bonhoeffer considered allegiance as something that may entail going beyond the idealism of a rigid non-violence precisely because of allegiance to the Christ. This view is contested by scholars such as Mark Thiessen Nation, who offers an important corrective against the relativization of Bonhoeffer's strong emphasis on peace and love for enemies (Nation, 2022, esp. pp. 58–82). Notwithstanding Nation's claim, I would suggest that a categorical appeal to peace and non-violence from those who occupy places of security and consolation can sometimes place a yoke upon others that hinders their ability to know the love of Christ in their lives, particularly if a Christian is placing that yoke upon them from the privilege of a racially secure vantage point.

Christine Schliesser clarifies that 'What seems to be the climax of the disciple's renunciation and passive suffering paradoxically turns into the starting point of the disciple's acceptance of responsible action' (Schliesser, 2008, p. 84). There is clearly an active aspect to bearing suffering, which may manifest itself through protest and lament, or might entail the refusal to act a certain way. One's response to evil cannot be prescribed. Jesus is not that specific because he is enfleshed in the reality of the penultimate. That said, the Sermon on the Mount does describe a prevalent posture that entails non-violent resistance against evil.

Loving enemies

In Matthew 5.43–44, Jesus teaches, 'You have heard that it was said, "You shall love your neighbour and hate your enemy." But I say to you, Love your enemies and pray for those who persecute you.' Such a passage might be misappropriated to silence the cries of those who suffer from evil, marginalization and injustice. However, on the contrary, Jesus is commanding disciples to *love* their enemies and *pray* for them as the faithful means of overcoming evil. Jesus' disciples experienced enemies daily, for people hated and cursed them because of their allegiance to Christ and the threat this entailed to the dominant socio-economic and religio-political order. Their conformation to Christ represented an embodied non-conformity in the world as it was (*DBWE* 4, pp. 137–8). Bonhoeffer interprets this passage as follows:

> In prayer we go to our enemies, to stand at their side. We are with them, near them, for them before God. Jesus does not promise us that the enemy we love, we bless, to whom we do good, will not abuse and persecute us. They will do so. But even in doing so, they cannot harm and conquer us if we take this last step to them in intercessory prayer. Now we are taking up their neediness and poverty, their being guilty and lost, and interceding for them before God. We are doing for them in vicarious representative action what they cannot do for themselves. Every insult from our enemy will only bind us closer to God and to our enemy. Every persecution can only serve to bring the enemy closer to reconciliation with God, to make love more unconquerable. (*DBWE* 4, p. 140)

Jesus is surely commanding disciples to evoke blessings on their enemies as an aspect of this. However, that cannot be the only form of prayer here. As the next chapter demonstrates, Bonhoeffer understood Jesus to have prayed the entire psalter, which included lament and, most significantly, the imprecatory psalms. Praying for enemies through lament and protest is also obedient to Christ, without ignoring or diminishing the reality of suffering and evil for those oppressed by racism. To love enemies as those also created in the image of God necessarily includes questioning and challenging the ways those people are acting. As Brian Brock articulates, 'Christians dare to raise questions about the ethos of their age out of hope in a Jesus whose power to heal challenged the ruling powers and ethos of the first century' (Brock, 2019, p. 37). Loving and praying for enemies is another example where passivity or evasion is not an option, but where agency is given to disciples in their suffering. While recognizing the 'safe spaces' that are necessary for those who are oppressed to express themselves fully, it is incumbent on White church communities to subject themselves to the stories and suffering of those whom they may be inadvertently harming. As James Poling explains:

> Those who are in positions of power need to hear the voices of those who suffer from abuse or deprivations just as surely as those who suffer cry out to be heard. Only through this kind of conversation can humanity be restored to both oppressed and oppressor. (Poling, 1991, pp. 14–15)

Part of this loving and praying for enemies entails the possibility of giving witness to one's anger. Bonhoeffer claims that anger causes the alienation of disciples from both God and one another (*DBWE* 4, p. 123). However, evil rightly prompts a very legitimate and understandable anger for those whose allegiance is to God's kingdom. One way of working through this is to regard it concretely. One cannot simply not be angry, but can allow their anger to find its basis in Christ, who ultimately overcomes his enemies by bearing suffering alongside his protest against it in lament. There is more that could be said about anger, but it seems that anger is acknowledged as a natural aspect of human life, and is also something that carries great risk of leading people into sinful and harmful thoughts or actions if it is not borne in prayer (in its broadest sense). Discipleship is always concrete, always happening in the middle of life, but it is always for the sake of Christ, who is the ultimate reality over this penultimate existence in all its complexities and contingencies.

Conclusion

As a British Baptist minister, I have been particularly inspired and challenged by the story of Sam Sharpe. Sharpe is known by many as a prophetic Christian figure who led a slave revolt in Jamaica in 1831–2.

The histories of most Black slaves in the Caribbean were less well documented than the pedigree details of horses from that time (Reid, 1988, p. 56); Sam Sharpe is known and remembered. It is believed that he was born in 1800 but was executed by the British government on 23 May 1832 (Bleby, 1853, p. 129). He was named by his master, Samuel Sharpe, a lawyer and proprietor of Coopers Hill Estate in Montego Bay, St James (Reid, 1988, pp. 54–5). Sharpe became 'known within the Black and enslaved community of his time as "Daddy Sharpe," "Ruler Sharpe" and "preacher to the rebels" because he was one of, if not their primary leader' (Reid-Salmon, 2021, p. 2).

Sharpe possessed significant intellectual, oratorical and administrative abilities, which contributed to his influence and effectiveness among Black slaves for instigating an attempt to pursue justice for himself and others (Bleby, 1853, p. 112). Sharpe intended to facilitate a revolt in the form of industrial action, as his primary concern was for just treatment of slaves in accordance with their God-given freedom. Bleby writes:

> The plan proposed to be acted by Sharpe was that of passive resistance, and to fight only in case the 'buckras' [White men] used force to compel them to work as slaves. He thought that if they all 'sat down' and refused to go to work again in the capacity as slaves after Christmas, carefully abstaining from offering violence to any person, it would be a very difficult thing for the masters to force such an immense body of people to work against their will. (Bleby, 1853, p. 113)

The irony is that Black slaves were treated as though they were worthless and not human, yet they were critical in upholding the British economy (Braithwaite, 1977, p. 25). By disrupting the system, Sharpe hoped to redress the injustice of his people's treatment, but in a manner that flew in the face of the 'gun and whip, treadmill and shackle' that were used against them (Braithwaite, 1977, p. 25). That said, Sharpe was not a naive idealist. The preparation for the work strike involved months of detailed planning, which drew on secret trails, networks of communication and the existing market systems (Higman, 1998, pp. 262–3). Furthermore, while Sharpe perhaps hoped for a non-violent protest, he would have likely anticipated the possibility of violence from Whites (Reid-Salmon, 2012, pp. 9–10).

Despite the poise and calm resolve of Sharpe and his adherents, the response of the Whites was aggressive and violent. Consequently, despite his alleged intention not to bring harm to others, Sharpe's call from Christ to pursue the liberation of his oppressed Black sisters and brothers meant that he sought this end through the exercising of a freedom not bestowed by his slave masters but afforded to him by the gospel of Jesus Christ, even if that regrettably involved violence. It is this perspective and dilemma that intimates one of the points of departure for many theologies of liberation.

Bonhoeffer was not himself a liberation theologian. In many ways, he remained operative within the White Western framework within which Protestant theology emerged. He was not 'radical' in that sense. He was, however, radical in a way that continually questioned the legitimization of any action, pointing instead to Christ, who alone is the one who justifies our actions, or, rather, his actions through us. Bonhoeffer sought an authentic perception of reality, which entails a genuine basis for human freedom and questions things as they are, never assuming to fully know how things should be.

After the quelling of the Jamaican Christmas rebellion, many slaves faced the inevitability of their execution at the hands of the 'Christian' British government. A Presbyterian missionary, Hope Waddell, was an eyewitness to these events. He remarked how, with rope around their necks and white caps on their heads, loaded in oxen-drawn carts, 'they simultaneously commenced a hymn, in which all joined with great composure and fervency ... On each of the melancholy occasions, the unfortunate men met their death, with a fortitude and cool deliberation that astonished all who beheld them' (Waddell, 1863, p. 65). Sam Sharpe startled those who witnessed his execution, assured that he was held by the grace of God over and against anything that human beings might do to him. His resolve is captured in his famous claim: 'I would rather die upon yonder gallows than live in slavery' (Zoellner, 2020, p. 187). This remark demonstrates the freedom of a man whose life is allegiant to Christ alone, not to the systems that would otherwise place the extent of his freedom upon him.

When Bonhoeffer was summoned for court martial in Flossenburg concentration camp, he turned to Payne Best, a British prisoner of war who had become a recent companion, requesting that Best relay a message to his friend George Bell. Bonhoeffer asked Best to 'tell him that this is for me the end, but also the beginning' (*DBWE* 16, p. 468). Such was the life of another who died on the gallows, born with the privilege and autonomy of many White folks, and yet found freedom in the call of Jesus Christ to discipleship. The following poem intimates something of the ways in which this freedom is encountered by Black and White alike.

DISCIPLESHIP

Stations on the Way to Freedom

Discipline
If you set out to seek freedom, then you must learn above all things
discipline of your soul and your senses, lest your desires
and then your limbs perchance should lead you now hither, now yon.
Chaste be your spirit and body, subject to yourself completely,
in obedience seeking the goal that is set for your spirit.
Only through discipline does one learn the secret of freedom.

Action
Not always doing and daring what's random, but seeking the
    right thing,
Hover not over the possible, but boldly reach for the real.
Not in escaping to thought, in action alone is found freedom.
Dare to quit anxious faltering and enter the storm of events,
carried alone by your faith and by God's good commandments,
then true freedom will come and embrace your spirit, rejoicing.

Suffering
Wondrous transformation. Your hands, strong and active, are fettered.
Powerless, alone, you see that an end is put to your action.
Yet now you breathe a sigh of relief and lay what is righteous
calmly and fearlessly into a mightier hand, contented.
Just for one blissful moment you could feel the sweet touch of freedom,
Then you gave it to God, that God might perfect it in glory.

Death
Come now, highest of feasts on the way to freedom eternal,
Death, lay down your ponderous chains and earthen enclosures
walls that deceive our souls and fetter our mortal bodies,
that we might at last behold what here we are hindered from seeing.
Freedom, long have we sought you through discipline, action,
    and suffering.
Dying, now we discern in the countenance of God your own face.

(*DBWE* 8, pp. 512–14)

9

Life Together and Prayerbook of the Bible

In the Spring of 1935, after 18 months of pastoring two German congregations in London, Bonhoeffer returned to his home country to take up the role as director of one of the Confessing Church's seminaries at Finkenwalde (*DBWE* 14, p. 16). He would now be responsible for the formation of gospel ministers during this turbulent time of Germany's history. Finkenwalde was something of an experiment in new monasticism, explored through his conviction that the church needed serving through this rigorous mode of discipleship together.

Life Together

Life Together was written as a summation of the pattern and purpose of the Finkenwalde community. Some of the key themes presented in *Life Together* provide a rich grounding for the Christian community and how that relates to the subject of race.

Bonhoeffer offers an unavoidably practical perspective on Christian community, which is strictly Christological in its orientation. 'We belong to one another only through and in Jesus Christ' (*DBWE* 5, p. 31). This means '*first*, that a Christian needs others for the sake of Jesus Christ. It means, *second*, that a Christian comes to others only through Jesus Christ. It means, *third*, that from eternity we have been chosen in Jesus Christ, accepted in time, and united for eternity' (*DBWE* 5, p. 31). Christ is the foundation, mediator and goal of Christian community. This is obvious and orthodox in theory, but carries sobering implications as it is anything but utopian, forcing communities to navigate many complexities and challenges. This form of community cannot seek to generate and maintain unmediated relationships of spiritual like-mindedness or ideals. It cannot fixate on worldly notions of success (*DBWE* 5, p. 35). Christ reveals himself to individuals concretely through others in this community, confronting, comforting and calling one another as bearers, proclaimers and bringers of salvation (*DBWE* 5, p. 32).

Bonhoeffer is anxious to distinguish between Christ's community and those that easily mistake him for other societal ties. Christian community is never *ideal*, but a *divine* reality. Some people may be driven to realize a great or pious community within wholly fallible intentions. 'Those who love their dream of a Christian community more than the Christian community itself become destroyers of that Christian community even though their personal intentions may be ever so honest, earnest, and sacrificial' (*DBWE* 5, p. 36). Visionary efforts to secure a 'pure' or 'zealous' community may appear faithful, even selfless, but abstract idealism ignores Christ's establishment and mediation of his community. Relationships derived from an *ideal* of community reject the grace of God that confronts individuals concretely through *real* believers (*DBWE* 5, p. 47). 'By sheer grace God will not permit us to live in a dream world even for a few weeks and to abandon ourselves to those blissful experiences and exalted moods that sweep over us like a wave of rapture' (*DBWE* 5, p. 35).

Bonhoeffer highlights a distorted vision of Christian community. If people do not fit a dominant ideal or aesthetic (verbally, visually, economically, culturally etc.), their place in the community (and the gifts they bring as a member) is diminished, precluded or contorted due to pious attempts to 'help them fit in' the body. As an example, it is not inherently sinful for the leadership of a church to be all White, but it does engender an embodied aesthetic for the Christian life which is particular and not universal. Without attentiveness and action to own (and potentially redress) this, the particular becomes myopic and closed-minded, excluding others. Many churches have languages and postures that are not necessarily anything to do with Christ, but are wrapped up in the particularity of their ethnic or socio-cultural context.

Underlying a lot of racism and unconscious Whiteness in the church is an ideological aspiration oriented towards the self-possessed White man (Higton, 2023, pp. 14–19). This aesthetic carries a thick allure that belittles or marginalizes the vulnerable, the suffering and anyone who does not exhibit the self-sufficiency, consolation and magisterial dominance of the 'normal' believer (Reddie, 2023, p. 53). However, Bonhoeffer argues, 'The exclusion of the weak and insignificant, the seemingly useless people, from everyday Christian life in community may actually mean the exclusion of Christ; for in the poor sister or brother, Christ is knocking at the door' (*DBWE* 5, pp. 45–6). White readers should not be quick to label Global Majority Heritage sisters and brothers as weak. That would play into the issue being addressed. Rather, embracing those who challenge false ceilings, boundaries and stereotypes placed upon those who are not necessarily living according to the script of the White world we inhabit makes them critical and indispensable parts of the Christian body.

Reggie Williams summarizes that for Bonhoeffer, 'idealized humanity was an obstacle to encounters with the incarnate Christ, and thus to real Christian community' (Williams, 2019, p. 383). In Christ, believers are called to embrace a 'new' form of community that binds them together as reconciled sinners. On this basis, the community 'begins to grasp in faith the promise that is given to it' and can learn to live alongside one another in and through Christ alone (*DBWE* 5, p. 35). By embracing and making space for the expressions, perspectives, bodies and spiritualties of those who do not fit a White aesthetic, the community opens itself to receive the real Christ, and lays down the inclination to seek that which is made in its own image. They resist the temptation of what Martin Luther calls misdirected love, which is nothing other than idolatry.

Bonhoeffer also claims Christian community is a *spiritual* reality, as opposed to a 'psychic' or 'emotional' reality. 'Within the spiritual community there is never, in any way whatsoever, an "immediate" relationship of one to another' (*DBWE* 5, p. 41). Christian community is mediated by Christ, which means there are boundaries between individuals that must be acknowledged and respected, rather than belittled or assaulted. Believers cannot construe relationships through 'the natural urges, strengths, and abilities of the human soul' (*DBWE* 5, p. 38). The psychic community seeks unconstrained (and therefore unaccountable) intimacy with others and regards the boundaries (and particularity) of the other to be abhorrent, preferring the romantic notion of total 'fusion' between (the self-absorbed) *I* and (the dominatable) *You*. Such a view is self-deception, an insidious pseudo-love. The God-given boundaries between persons are totally dissolved in the psychic community because Christ no longer structures relationships in freedom, other than being flagged as a justification for assailing another's boundary in the name of love. The desire for immediacy in community is seductively egotistical because it fails to respect a person genuinely as *You*. In such a context,

> self-centred, strong persons enjoy life to the full, securing for themselves the admiration, the love, or the fear of the weak. Here human bonds, suggestive influences, and dependencies are everything. Moreover, everything that is originally and solely characteristic of the community mediated through Christ reappears in the nonmediated community of souls in a distorted form. (*DBWE* 5, p. 41)

In communities governed by 'nonmediated' relationships, love appears selfless and makes the most striking of sacrifices, but is a covert mode of selfish self-love (cf. 1 Cor 13.2–3).

> Self-centred love loves the other for the sake of itself; spiritual love loves the other for the sake of Christ. That is why self-centred love seeks direct contact with other persons ... It wants to do everything it can to win and conquer; it puts pressure on the other person. It desires to be irresistible, to dominate. (*DBWE* 5, p. 42)

Selfish, self-serving 'love' consumes the dignity and freedom of others. When relationships between Whites and 'non-Whites' are structured within the psychic (unmediated) community, everything merely serves the self-assertion of the dominant party. Any genuine sincerity to love the other fails to accept that Christ alone can mediate the communal love that is sought so earnestly. There is an anxiety in many of us White folks that longs to feel affirmed by our Black and Brown sisters and brothers. We do our best to relate to their experiences, but to do so is to risk imposing ourselves on their space and enfolding their perspectives into our White bodies. I will never be Black, and it is as a White man that I navigate my relationship with others by recognizing Christ who stands between us, thereby safeguarding the particularity of another. I cannot synthesize people's lives and experiences into my own horizons, committing epistemological colonization as a means of defining Blackness on my terms at my table. Instead, I let Christ remind me that my relationship with those who are different from me is established at Christ's behest, not my own, and I must renounce the presumption that I can fully 'get where they are coming from' as a White guy. Relationships between Christians that do not recognize this mediated reality are potentially coercive, abusive, imposing, narcissistic and dangerous. Such communities will only ever serve the egos of dominant parties, and the best thing for them is their dissolution and death (*DBWE* 5, p. 43).

Prayerbook of the Bible

Bonhoeffer's last formally published work provides a vital part of this book. *Prayerbook of the Bible* gives some clear content for how Bonhoeffer approached prayer, and a few clues regarding his own cultural sensibilities. However, it also offers a creative way of navigating the subject of race and racism through what is essentially a Christological appropriation of the psalter.

As his life developed, Bonhoeffer depended upon the psalms every day, knowing many of them by heart, to the point that much of his thought and speech was permeated with them, particularly during times of helplessness and struggle (Krötke, 2019, p. 177). He first developed his appreciation for the psalter from his experience of English monastic life (Brock, 2007, p. 74).

Brad Pribbenow argues that Bonhoeffer offers a distinctly unique contribution to psalm interpretation by offering a 'two-pillar' hermeneutic (Pribbenow, 2018, p. 93). For Bonhoeffer, the psalms are, first, *prayers*, but, second, they are *prayed by Jesus Christ*, during his incarnate life and now in eternity, for and with the church. Prayer is not primarily about offering one's own experience to God, but about 'finding the way to and speaking with God ... For that one needs Jesus Christ' (*DBWE* 5, p. 155). Such an approach bridles prayer with the intention to rescue disciples from the narrow-minded optic of individualism that is prevalent in much of the White Western church. Disciples participate in the prayers of Christ, who has borne the entirety of human nature on himself before God through his own prayer (*DBWE* 5, pp. 158–9). Bonhoeffer would even claim that disciples must pray 'against our own heart in order to pray rightly' (*DBWE* 5, p. 157).

Context is key here. The ideology and self-referential deification of Hitler's Arian vision was dominant, having stolen the hearts and minds of a nation. Bonhoeffer was seeking a means of prayer that would direct Christ's followers against the warped desires and dreamy hopes of an introspective, National Socialism (*DBWE* 5, p. 145). What may sound constrictive is a safeguard against the prayer of an unbridled, isolated self. One does not pray through the horizons of White Germany, but in step with the Jewish Jesus.

Christ's appropriation of the psalter means that he, who has suffered the fullness of torment, pain, guilt and death for all humanity, has borne the entirety of human nature on himself before God in prayer. The psalter 'can become our prayer only because it was his prayer' (*DBWE* 5, p. 160). In this way Bonhoeffer also harmonizes the psalter and Lord's Prayer, suggesting they validate and echo one another (*DBWE* 5, pp. 58, 157–8, 162). Bonhoeffer also cites the antiphony and repetition of the psalms as reminders that we do not pray alone. Whether gathered or scattered, individuals pray as part of Christ's community. Individuals need the prayers of the community, and give themselves over to the community in individual prayer as well (*DBWE* 15, p. 506).

Bonhoeffer classifies the psalter into ten different categories: (1) creation; (2) the law; (3) history of salvation; (4) the messiah; (5) the church; (6) life; (7) suffering; (8) guilt; (9) enemies; and (10) the end.

Psalms of *creation* witness to the wonder of the world created by God. The world exists for Christ's sake, and so Bonhoeffer encourages believers to pray in thankfulness for the materiality that has enabled human existence (*DBWE* 5, pp. 163–4). John Colwell clarifies, 'What is passing away [in redemption] is this material world's order (or disorder) rather than its materiality' (Colwell, 2007, p. 37). Black slaves were right to reject a White Christ who did not care about their earthly freedom in creation.

Psalms about the *law* acknowledge God's word and command in Jesus Christ, longing never to be separated from it. For Bonhoeffer, the deepest anxiety of new life in Christ is the possibility of not recognizing God's will, so Christians pray desperately for God not to hide it from them (*DBWE* 5, p. 164; cf. Ps. 119.19). Brian Brock notes: 'Only one nemesis fills the psalmists with dread: that they will take up God's statutes but God will no longer reveal what is required for living today' (Brock, 2007, p. 88).

Psalms on the *history of salvation* (such as Ps. 78, 105, 106) recount God's covenant loving kindness and action in history, witnessed ultimately in Jesus Christ. We pray these psalms for Christ's sake, thanking him and confessing our guilt as we petition him to remain faithful to his promise, both now and in its fulfilment (*DBWE* 5, p. 165). Abstract concepts of salvation have been deployed to sanction slavery, Jim Crowe law and contemporary racism. Some argue that modern colonialism was not all that bad and that many good things came out of it for the sake of the gospel. However, such a perspective overlooks the distortion of the 'gospel' that was expanded in the first place, diminishing the mutual gift-giving or 'joining' (Jennings, 2010, p. 113) that could have resulted if the Western church adopted the ways and means of Jesus in its mission. Salvation is a critical biblical word for many Black Christians, encompassing physicality and concrete freedom.

Messianic psalms announce and culminate in Christ's coming. Jesus referenced himself as the messianic fulfilment prophesied in the psalter (*DBWE* 5, p. 166; cf. Luke 22.44). While many psalms are attributed to David, Christ appropriated them to himself and gave them their full, or ultimate, meaning.

Psalms about the *church* relate the temple of Jerusalem to the Body of Christ in the world. The church celebrates God's presence on earth in his body amid all joy, yearning and anxiety. The church is the continuation (not replacement) of the story of God's people, fulfilled and reconstituted in Christ (*DBWE* 5, pp. 167–8).

Bonhoeffer poses a category of psalms about *life*. Certain people suppress visible earthly blessings. However, 'in doing so they want to be even more spiritual than God' (*DBWE* 5, p. 168). The psalms about life pray for 'life, health, peace, and earthly good' (*DBWE* 5, p. 168). In them, 'we recognize all these as evidences of God's gracious community with us and thereby hold fast to the knowledge that God's goodness is better than life' (*DBWE* 5, pp. 168–9). When creaturely life is upheld for the sake of the ultimate, believers pray the psalms about life faithfully.

Psalms about the *end* offer hope in God's ultimate victory over sin and death, founded upon the resurrection of Christ. These psalms are not as explicit. 'To be sure, the Psalms pray for community with God in this earthly life, but they know that this community does not end with this earthly life, but continues beyond it, even stands in contrast to it' (*DBWE* 5, p. 176). Along with all creation, the psalms of the end long hopefully for the day of Christ's return (cf. Rom. 8.19–23).

I have reserved analysing Bonhoeffer's discussion regarding psalms of suffering, guilt and enemies until last, as these are representative of what is overlooked and evaded in many White churches.

Suffering

Bonhoeffer remarks that 'The Psalter has rich instruction for us about how to come before God in a proper way in the various sufferings that the world brings upon us' (*DBWE* 5, p. 169). The psalter faces the bitterness of suffering 'as a severe ordeal of faith, indeed at times they no longer see beyond the suffering' (*DBWE* 5, p. 169). These psalms direct believers 'away from ourselves and towards God in Christ ... allowing [these prayers] to challenge and unravel our assumptions and ideas' (Mawson, 2019, pp. 132–3). This does not diminish personal struggles that people go through, but disrupts the spiritual smugness of White triumphalism present in the bourgeoisie or National Socialists. Bonhoeffer is not perturbed by seemingly blasphemous language of the lament psalms as even in the bleakest of situations they still address God (*DBWE* 5, p. 170).

Bonhoeffer claims, 'No single human being can pray the psalms of lamentation out of his or her own experience. Spread out before us here is the anguish of the entire Christian community throughout all time, as Jesus Christ alone has wholly experienced it' (*DBWE* 5, p. 169). He asks, 'how should we pray those prayers of unspeakable misery and suffering, since we have hardly begun to sense even remotely something of what is meant here?' (*DBWE* 5, p. 56). Here, he reveals his own privileged horizons, which are different from those for whom suffering is very familiar (Bethge, 2000, p. 19). Nevertheless, he is making a radical statement contextually. First, he is drawing on the Old Testament to inform the church's prayers. Second, he is encouraging people like himself to embrace the language and life of other members of Christ's body through the mediation of Christ's prayer. He and others like him enter the space occupied by those who live 'from below, from the perspective of the outcasts, the suspects, the maltreated, the powerless, the oppressed and reviled, in short from the perspective of the suffering' (*DBWE* 8, p. 52). Anyone who is not familiar with suffering participates in the prayers of others through Christ. Christ prays the psalms of suffering vicariously *for* and *with* the world, so the church prays Christ's prayers of suffering in his body.

Because Christ is *with* us in prayer, there is 'no longer any suffering on earth in which Christ, our helper, is not with us, suffering and praying with us' (*DBWE* 5, p. 170). Christ's prayer ensures that our prayer always has a certainty of a hearing, bringing comfort amid suffering (*DBWE* 5, p. 171).

Bonhoeffer's aim is to redress a regular claim by some who apparently 'can't relate to these psalms'. One's lack of suffering is not primarily important because Christ calls them to lament and suffer alongside him in prayer. Additionally, for those who are enshrouded in despair and a sense of desolation, words are given as a gift to hold a person when they have no prayer to muster for themselves (*DBWE* 5, pp. 55–7).

Guilt

There are fewer psalms about the forgiveness of sins than some may expect. 'Christian prayer is diminished and endangered when it revolves exclusively around the forgiveness of sins. There is such a thing as confidently leaving sin behind for the sake of Jesus Christ' (*DBWE* 5, p. 171). Bonhoeffer is wary of a pious and self-absorbed spirituality that exhibits itself through a zealous 'wallowing' in guilt at the expense of concrete repentance and action in the world (see *DBWE* 4, p. 67).

Psalms of guilt may prompt disciples to confess personal sins. 'The Christian will find scarcely any difficulty in praying these psalms' (*DBWE* 5, p. 172). However, disciples are called to pray these psalms regardless of whether they identify their sins or not. In Christ, we confess our sins and repent through faith, not based on our self-judgement of sin (*DBWE* 2, p. 124). To only confess the sins I *perceive* in *myself* would be to ignore Christ's revelation of sin (*DBWE* 4, p. 157).

Bonhoeffer juxtaposes David against Christ to navigate the problem of Christ praying these psalms. 'David spoke here of his own guilt. But Christ is speaking of the guilt of all people ... which he has taken upon himself and borne' (*DBWE* 5, p. 166). Jesus prays for the forgiveness of sins which he has made fully his own (*DBWE* 5, p. 172). Understood like this, prayer is expanded far beyond tangible, individual sins. Christ calls the church to participate in the world's guilt which, in him, it bears *for* and *with* the world vicariously.

Bonhoeffer also suggests that 'one can speak of one's own innocence in a self-righteous manner, but do we not realize that one can also pray the most humble confession of sin very self-righteously?' (*DBWE* 5, p. 172). It is none other than Christ's innocence that the psalter appeals to. No one can lament their guilt without also responding through discipleship to Christ. At the same time, their innocence is found in Christ, who demonstrated his own innocence by bearing the world's guilt on himself (cf. Rom. 8.21). He further argues, 'It is a thoroughly unbiblical and destructive idea that we can never suffer innocently as long as some kind of fault still remains in us' (*DBWE* 5, p. 173). Those who suffer for a godly cause suffer innocently and ultimately suffer with God (cf. *DBWE* 4, p. 87; *DBWE* 6, p. 346). People align themselves with God's cause through a life of penitent obedience as Christ himself demonstrated. Psalms of innocence are prayed by the community that confesses its guilt before God. 'That we really are with God and, therefore, really innocent is demonstrated precisely in this, that we pray for the forgiveness of our sins' (*DBWE* 5, p. 173). This means believers can pray the psalms of innocence faithfully because they repent of any self-righteousness, for the sake of Christ and the world reconciled in him.

Enemies

The vengeance (or imprecatory) psalms are the most problematic part of the psalter for many Christians, with their candour causing some believers to set them aside (*DBWE* 5, p. 174). Bonhoeffer distinguishes between the motives behind these psalms and their content as part of God's word. Geffrey Kelly suggests that Bonhoeffer's integration of these psalms was a rebuttal against contemporaries such as Emmanuel Hirsch, whose interpretation of the Old Testament contained anti-Jewish ideology (*DBWE*

5, p. 174). Vengeance psalms contribute to the church's search for God's justice in an evil world, where the human desire for revenge arises, and must be voiced, borne and given to God for Christ's sake. Justice over evil is ultimately God's domain (*DBWE* 14, p. 967). Christ mediates the content of these prayers. Christ vicariously bore the world's evil as God's word of judgement against evil. Believers cannot pray this way in themselves as Christians are just as guilty for the evil and hostility that cause havoc in creation (*DBWE* 14, p. 964). Christ is the only truly innocent one who prays this psalm, placing everyone alongside one another as a humanity accused of evil and godlessness. These psalms are a wake-up call for those who might relativize the radical presence of evil.

> That was the end of all false thoughts about the love of a God who does not take sin very seriously. God hates and judges the enemies of God in the only righteous one, the one who prays for forgiveness for God's enemies. Only in the cross of Jesus Christ is the love of God to be found. (*DBWE* 5, p. 175)

For Bonhoeffer, the psalms of vengeance travel along the path of judgement, to mercy and forgiveness. In community, 'things have to come into the open; but they must also be tamed in and through prayer' (Zimmermann, 1973, p. 108). Without this, Christians muster self-forgiveness or forgiveness of others from within the deceptive resources of the introspective self. Christ places people alongside enemies who have become brothers and sisters before God at the cross (*DBWE* 14, pp. 391–2). Christ prays for vengeance by also offering himself vicariously for the sake of the wicked, reconstituting how these psalms are prayed (*DBWE* 14, p. 970). For Bonhoeffer, Christ genuinely *does* pray for the destruction of God's enemies and the eradication of evil under God's righteous judgement, but ultimately embodies the divine definition of God's judgement over the whole world (Pribbenow, 2018, p. 162). In Christ, God refuses the presence of evil and darkness in the world, and Christ both prays for and participates in the destruction of God's enemies freely *for* and *with* the world (*DBWE* 14, p. 969; cf. 2 Thess. 1.7–8).

Personally, I cannot relate easily to the words of the martyrs in Revelation 6.10: 'Sovereign Lord, holy and true, how long will it be before you judge and avenge our blood on the inhabitants of the earth?' However, this language, which is akin to the psalms of vengeance, offers comfort and agency to those who are oppressed as they seek God in the midst of evil, and challenges my own sensibilities as I participate in it. The language is part of the heritage of Black life, a biblical mode for putting oppressors 'on notice' regarding God's judgement and justice (Jinkins, 1998, p. 38). W. E. B. Du Bois highlights that the genre of lament 'breathes a hope – a faith in the ultimate justice of things. The minor cadences of despair change often to triumph and calm confidence' (Du Bois, 1989, p. 208). White Christian communities who pray these psalms, with careful caution and humility, may become more attentive to the harm we have caused others as we are confronted by the intense language (*DBWE* 5, p. 27). Thus, 'Christ leads me back daily to the gravity and the grace of his cross for me and all the enemies of God ... In this way the crucified Jesus teaches us to pray truly the psalms of wrath' (*DBWE* 5, pp. 175–6).

Conclusion

My friend George is a pastor in nearby Exeter. Since George Floyd's murder, he has been reading and reflecting on race, and has become proactive in cultivating a community that is attentive to its White Western particularity, seeking to be inclusive of others from contexts of a Global Majority Heritage. He has been delighted and encouraged to see the change in the church polity. One example he shared with me was of a woman from India who has felt increasingly comfortable praying in her extensive style, both in English and in her mother tongue. George has pushed back against criticism from a few White people in the church who find this difficult. He recently explained to me that he wants his church to be enriched and changed by the faith expressions non-White people bring, and for the fellowship (himself included) to be open to challenge regarding the dominant White Western culture. 'I don't want to tell [my Indian sister] to prayer shorter or in English. I want to tell everyone to pray more like her because the way they pray in India is incredible; she clearly believes in the power of prayer.' George is also part of the Baptist Union's Younger Leaders Forum and has built relationships with some Black people who guide and encourage him along the way in redressing some of the invisible assumptions people like him and I can sometimes make. Like me, he still probably acts out of ignorance at times, but he is keen to learn and grow and is not a 'racist' but believes that racism is contrary to the gospel. The church where he is a pastor is becoming increasingly multi-cultural, and the congregation are seeking to change so that their worship and life together embodies this diversity.

The reality and prayers of the Christian community described in *Life Together* and *Prayerbook of the Bible* reminds me of the sorrow and joy that Bonhoeffer experienced in Abyssinian Baptist Church, where the polyphony of life was witnessed before God. In his meditation on Psalm 119, Bonhoeffer remarks: 'It is a surprising observation that it is precisely in the psalms lamenting the oppression and the suffering of the righteous that praise for the kindness of God, who bestows wellbeing on his own, emerges most strongly' (*DBWE* 15, p. 501). It was not in the White churches where he observed this kaleidoscopic existence, but in the Black churches, which witnessed to the Black Christ. The following poem is possibly Bonhoeffer's most famous one, which marks the internal confusion and struggle of discerning who we are amid life's tensions and conflicts, ultimately finding it, and ourselves, rooted in Jesus.

Who Am I?

Who am I? They often tell me
I step out from my cell
calm and cheerful and poised,
like a squire from his manor.

Who am I? They often tell me
I speak with my guards
freely, friendly and clear,
as though I were the one in charge.

Who am I? They also tell me
I bear days of calamity
serenely, smiling and proud,
like one accustomed to victory.

Am I really what others say of me?
Or am I only what I know of myself?
Restless, yearning, sick, like a caged bird,
struggling for life breath, as if I were being strangled,
starving for colors, for flowers, for birdsong,
thirsting for kind words, human closeness,
shaking with rage at power lust and pettiest insult,
tossed about, waiting for great things to happen,
helplessly fearing for friends so far away,
too tired and empty to pray, to think, to work,
weary and ready to take my leave of it all?

Who am I? This one or the other?
Am I this one today and tomorrow another?
Am I both at once? Before others a hypocrite
and in my own eyes a pitiful, whimpering weakling?
Or is what remains in me like a defeated army,
fleeing in disarray from victory already won?

Who am I? They mock me, these lonely questions of mine.
Whoever I am, thou knowest me; O God, I am thine!

(*DBWE* 8, pp. 459–60)

10

Ethics

Before his arrest, Bonhoeffer was working on what he hoped would be his last major work (*DBWE* 8, p. 222). After his execution, scholars sought to work out a coherent order to his unfinished manuscripts to reproduce the posthumously published material referred to as *Ethics*. This chapter unpacks these essays in terms of race.

Unlike other chapters, where I have sought to pick out key themes, this one offers a summary of each essay, highlighting the main ideas that pertain to this subject. I recognize that this may make the following seem a little segmented, but will hopefully give a sense of the huge range of ideas and concerns that Bonhoeffer covers in this work for those who may not be familiar with it.

'Christ, Reality, and Good. Christ, Church, and World'

Bonhoeffer argues Christian ethics falls at the first hurdle by interrogating concepts of the 'good' because, with such a perspective, 'the decision has already been made that the self and the world are the ultimate realities' (*DBWE* 6, pp. 47–8). Encasing ideas of reality (such as 'good') within the self is the heart of the problem, because all concepts and ideals derived apart from Christ are not real (*DBWE* 6, p. 54). In Christ, 'I never experience the reality of God without the reality of the world, nor the reality of the world without the reality of God' (*DBWE* 6, p. 55). Paired concepts such as 'worldly-Christian, natural-supernatural, profane-sacred, rational-revelational' are nonsensical. 'This thinking fails to recognize the original unity of these opposites in the Christ-reality' (*DBWE* 6, pp. 58–9).

The church is not disconnected from the world, but lives within and witnesses to it (*DBWE* 6, p. 73). 'The space of the church is not there in order to fight with the world for a piece of its territory, but precisely to testify to the world that it is still the world, namely, the world that is loved and reconciled by God' (*DBWE* 6, p. 63). There is no dualism between God and the devil. Even in its godlessness, the world belongs to God in Christ (*DBWE* 6, p. 65). Nevertheless, the world often adopts isolation, withdrawing from its origin, and 'falls prey to unnaturalness, irrationality, triumphalism, and arbitrariness' (*DBWE* 6, p. 61).

To think racism does not ultimately matter to Jesus abstracts an understanding of God away from the world and incarnate Christ. We must also be wary of conceptualizing race too rigidly. Bonhoeffer warns against the risks of generating any conceptual truths or ideals above the living person of Jesus. White folks like myself may benefit from being carefully attentive to how we have inadvertently imbibed ideals and notions of what is good (sociologically, morally, politically etc.). Such abstractions have led to racialization and the prefigured judgements of ourselves and others along racial lines.

'Ethics as Formation'

Bonhoeffer analyses his nation's ethical disintegration by discussing prevalent frameworks which he considers perilously bankrupt (he says similar in *DBWE* 8, pp. 37–52). He laments that 'evil should appear in the form of light, good deeds, historical necessity, social justice' (*DBWE* 8, p. 38). Noble, moral and good 'principles' become co-opted to condone and serve evil. For Bonhoeffer, the Holocaust exposed the deep rottenness of Western moral sensibilities (Rasmussen, 1999, pp. 207–9, 214). Claudia Koonz (2005) bolsters Bonhoeffer's claim by showing that Nazism grew through narratives towards the 'good' and 'virtue' of German morality. The Western desire for an ethical 'framework' engenders a vision of God and creation that is fraught with danger.

Bonhoeffer suggests ethics is *not* about the 'good', which is often reducible to the epistemological dominion of an individual or tribal society. He challenges appeals to reason, ethical fanaticism, conscience, duty, self-justifying freedom, or private virtuousness, all attempts towards what Reggie Williams describes as 'mastery over others' (Williams, 2023). However, ethics becomes judged and reconstituted anew through Christ. Any 'ethics' is simply about 'being formed by Christ', who removes human subjectivity by conforming people to himself as the only truly 'real' human (*DBWE* 6, p. 93). Humanity cannot try to become like God, nor change into something alien. 'Human beings become human because God became human' (*DBWE* 6, p. 96).

'Heritage and Decay'

Bonhoeffer presents the context of the church in relation to the world, suggesting pointedly that Christianity and Western history is wrapped up in the people of Israel. Therefore, 'Driving out the Jew(s) from the West must result in driving out Christ with them, for Jesus Christ was a Jew' (*DBWE* 6, p. 105). Bonhoeffer traces how the Reformation 'radically desacralized' the relationship between state and church (*DBWE* 6, pp. 111, 114). One implication was that 'Christians' legitimized the machinations of slavery via the state while proclaiming Christ in church. The church would stick to prayer and theology, severed from the world's machinations, ignoring the reality of life revealed in Christ, who unites all things under his lordship. For sure, the church should not control nor should it seek to be the state, but it makes space for itself through proclaiming the gospel to the state (*DBWE* 6, p. 127). The church calls the state, and indeed the whole world, away from the decay and distortions that would otherwise engulf it. The 'restraining power' of the church is its means of being an ally for the world: 'Justice, truth, science, art, culture, humanity, freedom, and patriotism, after long wanderings, find their way back to their origin' (*DBWE* 6, p. 132). This 'origin' is not the church per se, but Christ who takes dynamic form in the church body.

'Guilt, Justification, Renewal'

This essay confesses the church's failure to Christ and the world, articulating its need to bear guilt over the historical moment. Renouncing its anxious desire for self-preservation, the church must renounce its own 'righteousness' or 'goodness' and bear those who suffer at the hands of a godless world. In addition, the church vicariously bears and confesses the world's guilt as its own. 'With this confession the whole guilt of the world falls on the church, on Christians, and because here it is confessed and not denied, the possibility of forgiveness is opened' (*DBWE* 6, p. 136). The church is not heroic or altruistic; believers are 'simply overwhelmed by their very own guilt toward Christ' (*DBWE* 6, p. 136). Bonhoeffer then gets specific:

> The church confesses that it has looked on silently as the poor were exploited and robbed, while the strong were enriched and corrupted.
> The church confesses its guilt toward the countless people whose lives have been destroyed by slander, denunciation, and defamation. It

has not condemned the slanderers for their wrongs and has thereby left the slandered to their fate.

The church confesses that it has coveted security, tranquillity, peace, property, and honor to which it had no claim, and therefore has not bridled human covetousness, but promoted it.

The church confesses itself guilty of violating all the Ten Commandments. It confesses thereby its apostasy from Christ ... It has not so proclaimed the righteousness of God that all human justice must see there its own source and essence ... By falling silent the church became guilty for the loss of responsible action in society, courageous intervention, and the readiness to suffer for what is acknowledged as right. It is guilty of the government's falling away from Christ. (*DBWE* 6, pp. 140–1)

These are not mere moralisms but 'vicarious representative action' at work. The church confesses the world's guilt, which it bears as its own because (in Christ) it is responsible and complicit in the world's evil. Only when it confesses its sin vicariously for and with the world can it be 'awakened to new righteousness and new life' (*DBWE* 6, p. 142).

'Ultimate and Penultimate things'

Bonhoeffer articulates a grammar for the form of Christ in the world, presenting a Christological vision of reality as both ultimate and penultimate. Christians cannot despise the penultimate world because it is affirmed by God in Christ. However, Christians cannot absolutize the world as it penultimately is. It has been judged and is being renewed through Christ alone. Ultimately, God has come in Christ, judged it via the cross, offering new life by totally breaking with the old through resurrection. Therefore, 'Christian life neither destroys nor sanctions the penultimate' (*DBWE* 6, p. 159). This is significant for a subject like slavery:

> Concretely stated, slaves who have been so deprived of control over their time that they can no longer hear the proclamation of God's word cannot be led by that word of God to a justifying faith ... it is necessary to care for the penultimate in order that the ultimate not be hindered by the penultimate's destruction. Those who proclaim the word yet do not do everything possible so that this word may be heard are not true to the word's claim for free passage, for a smooth road. (*DBWE* 6, p. 162)

'Natural Life'

The 'natural' is a lost concept in the West, having 'fallen into disrepute in Protestant ethics' (*DBWE* 6, p. 171). Bonhoeffer affirms the value and beauty of a creaturely life in its finite provisionality and transitory fragility, which is rooted in Christ but where sin abides. For him, 'natural' refers to the created and cosmological phenomena that are affirmed through Christ's incarnation in the midst of the world's fallen finitude (*DBWE* 6, pp. 173–4, 179). 'Natural' refers to a created world that suffers decay and confusion, which nevertheless belongs to Christ (*DBWE* 6, p. 186). All that is natural is loved by God. To be specific, God loves Black bodies, Jewish bodies, neuro-diverse bodies, damaged or disabled bodies. 'Among free, independent persons, conscious encroachment on the body of another means destruction of the first natural right of human beings and therefore a fundamental deprivation of rights and the destruction of natural life' (*DBWE* 6, pp. 188–9).

Disregard for the natural reduces the body to a means for something else, a thing or object to be used and exploited. Our bodies serve multiple purposes but diminishing the body exclusively to its utilitarian value disregards its worth. The body is an essential part of being human, and rejecting the natural complexity and beauty of natural life means bodies are missed or crushed. Appreciating the natural recognizes the wonder and woundedness of the world. This is significant for eco-theology, but for the sake of this book it serves against the commodification of bodies that occurred in the modern Western epoch. Black people are not a thing (*DBWE* 6, pp. 215, 217), and the enslavement of any people should be opposed (*DBWE* 6, pp. 214–15).

Here, Bonhoeffer is challenging Nazi euthanasia, specifically addressing the systematic execution of certain people to 'protect' the productivity of the German *Volk* (people). Many people groups were 'euthanized' through the 'ethical' desire to safeguard some by sacrificing others. Cries were silenced and ignored, and too many people lost due to the myopic visions of success, normality and human flourishing fed by the Nazi regime (*DBWE* 6, p. 183). Homosexuals, ethnic minorities and the disabled 'hindered' the aesthetic of a strong, 'pure' German race, and it was deemed ethically necessary for them to die.

I have a nephew and niece who, for different physiological reasons, would have died in the Third Reich. Human endeavour is sometimes too quick and ignorant to presume the criteria for a person's potential or purpose. In our limited (and fallen) horizons, we sometimes fail to recognize the true end to which all life may be directed (*DBWE* 6, p. 198). Our end and purpose is far beyond our own demarcations and preferences. 'Part of the very essence of joy is that it is spoiled by thoughts about purpose' (*DBWE* 6, p. 186). Retaining the 'natural' embraces life itself is an end worth celebrating through Christ.

'History and Good [1 and 2]'

In *Ethics*, two essays are both entitled 'History and Good', the second of which is more comprehensive in exploring the nature of responsibility within the reality of Christ. Bonhoeffer structures an understanding of responsibility as a *bond* with God and others, without which there is no one to be responsible to, for or with. Additionally, responsibility encompasses one's unique *freedom*, recognizing agency and accountability (*DBWE* 6, p. 257). Within this structure, responsibility finds its Christological essence in a life of 'vicarious representative action'. Bonhoeffer rejects concepts of the 'good' as a descriptor of life. Responsible people are simply 'to live' (*DBWE* 6, p. 253). Bonhoeffer uses the analogy of a parent, states-person or instructor, each of whom act on behalf of another in their respective capacity (*DBWE* 6, p. 258). In an all-encompassing sense, Christ vicariously represents all humanity:

> Jesus was not the individual who sought to achieve some personal perfection, but only lived as the one who in himself has taken on and bears the selves of all human beings. His entire living, acting, and suffering was vicarious representative action. All that human beings were supposed to live, do, and suffer was fulfilled in him. In this real vicarious representative action, in which his human existence consists, he is the responsible human par excellence. Since he is life, all of life through him is destined to be vicarious representative action. (*DBWE* 6, pp. 258–9)

Christian responsibility entails vicarious action. This cannot be abstracted into an 'ethical' framework, which, as the next chapter highlights, can become problematic. Nevertheless, Bonhoeffer defines 'vicarious representative action' (*Stellvertretung*) as 'completely devoting one's own life to another person' (*DBWE* 6, p. 259). Such action arises within a genuine, concrete encounter with others in history (*DBWE* 6, p. 261). Christ is the origin, mediator and goal of one's action, incorporating, though sometimes transgressing, certain 'values' and conditions in the contingent moment (*DBWE* 6, p. 259–60). Experience serves discernment, but it could also distort the optic guiding a person's action, hence the action is never constrained by a conceptual framework.

Bonhoeffer contextualizes his argument by mentioning the 'Scotsboro' case, where nine Black men were executed for the unproven accusation of rape against a White girl. He also highlights the refusal of German ministers to speak out on behalf of people beyond their immediate congregations. His point is that responsibility requires an imaginative dexterity regarding the scope of one's vocation (*DBWE* 6, pp. 295–6). Bonhoeffer proposes four criteria for self-examination:

- One's field of responsibility is based on Christ's call alone, never on abstract ethical 'principles' which inevitably displace Christ's lordship.
- Those who veer towards fanaticism, reform and transgressing 'limits' for the sake of 'freedom' must guard against arbitrary and unbridled enthusiasm (revolutionism).
- Those who veer towards caution, constraint and rule-keeping must not haemorrhage themselves from free responsibility (legalism).
- Action derived from within the self is an irresponsible disregard for true (responsible) freedom. Christ's call constitutes one's actions. (*DBWE* 6, p. 294)

Certain 'radicals' may be inclined to 'stick it to the man' and protest everything as a matter of principle without much concern for the structures that uphold human life and, provisional as they are, hold the world back from total chaos. Conversely, those who cling to law and 'order' are vulnerable to acquiescing in and thereby sanctioning the status quo. One's positionality in the world does not provide an alibi for ignoring the cries of our neighbour, wherever and whoever they are.

'God's Love and the Disintegration of the World'

Recapitulating himself, Bonhoeffer argues, 'The first task of Christian ethics is to supersede that knowledge' of good and evil which 'appears to be the goal of all ethical reflection' (*DBWE* 6, p. 299). Referencing Genesis 3, Bonhoeffer claims that our orientation is distorted. 'Instead of seeing God, human beings see themselves' (*DBWE* 6, p. 303). Notions of good and evil are self-derived and self-absorbed. A person's conscience emerges as 'the sign of human beings' disunion within themselves … Conscience is the voice of fallen life that seeks to preserve unity at least within itself … Conscience is thus not concerned with a person's relationship to God and other people, but with the relationship to one's own self' (*DBWE* 6, p. 307). Conscience in this sense is a form of 'self-knowledge' that grasps at God and others, colonizing them within the disunion of one's isolated and disordered individuality (*DBWE* 6, pp. 308–9). Even 'love' can be enslaved to this modality (*DBWE* 6, p. 332). For example, the Pharisees 'subject their entire lives to the knowledge of good and evil' (*DBWE* 6, p. 310). Their interactions with Jesus attempt to pull him into this disunity between good and evil, to which Jesus responds from a different plane, simply because he is not in a state of disunion (*DBWE* 6, p. 311). His answers and actions are irritating and evasive to the Pharisees. However, 'The freedom of Jesus is not the arbitrary choice of one among countless possibilities ... He lives and acts not out of a knowledge of good and evil, but out of the will of God' (*DBWE* 6, p. 313). Jesus is not preoccupied with himself, but is free to act contingently in accordance with God's will. Bonhoeffer refers to Matthew 25, suggesting 'When Jesus sits in judgment, his own will not know that they had given him food, drink, clothing, and had visited him. They will not know their goodness. Jesus will reveal it to them' (*DBWE* 6, p. 319). One cannot discern God's will as an isolated individual (*DBWE* 6, p. 322), for even (and supremely) Christ's life was inseparably bound to others, hence *Christ* is love. Those arrested (or freed) from themselves are preoccupied with the one who *is* love, and so the truly human life is embodied. 'And as whole human beings, thinking and acting, we love God and our brothers and sisters' (*DBWE* 6, p. 338).

'Church and World I'

Bonhoeffer claims that concepts such as humanity, tolerance, reason and justice were sometimes pitted against the Christian domain, but in his time had sought protection from the church. In his mind, this makes sense because they find their ultimate essence in Christ (*DBWE* 6, pp. 341–6). As such, 'Jesus thoroughly rejects the false timidity of those Christians who evade any kind of suffering for a just, good, and true cause because they supposedly could have a clear conscience only if they were to suffer for the explicit confession of faith in Christ' (*DBWE* 6, p. 346). 'Jesus cares for those who suffer for a just cause even if it is not exactly for the confession of his name' (*DBWE* 6, p. 346). The church must uphold all things that find their ultimate origin in Christ, whether they are explicitly 'Christian' or not. Justice, whether 'Christian' or humanist, is ultimately enfolded into Christ.

Bonhoeffer roots this claim by juxtaposing two things Jesus said: 'Whoever is not against us is for us' (Mark 9.40); and 'Whoever is not with me is against me' (Matt. 12.30). Both sayings belong together, 'one as the exclusive claim, and the other as the all-encompassing claim, of Jesus Christ' (*DBWE* 6, p. 344). In isolation, each claim could lead to 'fanaticism and sectarianism' or 'the secularization and capitulation of the church' (*DBWE* 6, p. 344). Taken together, Christ is understood as the absolute Lord of all things. The breadth of his lordship is disclosed through being the one from whom all things find their origin, and for whom all things exist.

That does *not* mean Christ sanctions everything. Christ calls everything back to himself as its ultimate origin, purpose and goal. The church is commissioned to share this news with the world in the way it serves, upholds and sometimes challenges the world.

'On the Possibility of the Church's Message to the World'

Bonhoeffer claims it is too simplistic and dangerous to align Christ unequivocally with a particular worldly cause, like a problem solver. This co-opts God into human machinations of success and 'goodness', which Bonhoeffer has already critiqued. 'Jesus is hardly ever involved in solving worldly problems' (*DBWE* 6, p. 354). Sometimes, the most sincere and pious attempts to 'fix' problems can lead to worse problems in the future (*DBWE* 6, p. 355). For Bonhoeffer, the gospel does not offer an 'ideal' system or structure for a moral society. The gospel calls for obedience to Christ within worldly life. 'God's Word is not concerned with the orders as such, but with the obedience of faith rendered within them' (*DBWE* 6, p. 358). Jesus Christ transcends all particularity, and yet he is revealed within particularity, unbound by worldly structures, active in all circumstances. That said, there are 'certain economic and social conditions that hinder faith in Jesus Christ, which means that they also destroy the essence of human beings and the world' (*DBWE* 6, p. 361). Here, he is gesturing at the last essay to which we will come.

'The "Ethical" and the "Christian" as a Topic'

Clearly, some things happen in life without any consideration of ethics. They are habits, aspects of life that sometimes necessitate no enquiry because they are incidental (*DBWE* 6, pp. 365–6). Bonhoeffer suggests that many aspects of life occur subconsciously. Ethical parameters lie 'dormant' when everything operates in its 'God-given order' (*DBWE* 6, p. 367). However, governments, families and workplaces sometimes encounter contingent situations where the responsible action is not self-evident. This encounter occurs mostly when those on the margins of society disrupt what is considered to be that 'God-given order' because they do not fit the apparent norm. Such an encounter, or confrontation, requires the provisional and fallible spheres of worldly life to engage in a 'competitive struggle' as they navigate the encounters that question the assumptions of the 'God-given order' of things. There is no rule for navigating this, other than to discern how to serve one another respectfully. The church must call the state to be a just state, the state must serve families and workplaces, and these things exist for the flourishing of all within the particularity of each polity and uniqueness of human and worldly life. There is always the possibility of redressing assumptions of the 'God-given order' of things.

'The Concrete Commandment and the Divine Mandates'

Bonhoeffer offers a provisional and fallible 'structure' for worldly life within Christ by identifying four interconnecting 'spheres' that are operant within the penultimate:

> God's commandment is to be found not wherever there are historical forces, strong ideals, or convincing insights, but only where there are divine mandates that are grounded in the revelation of Christ. We are dealing with such mandates in the church, in marriage and family, in culture [and work], and in government. (*DBWE* 6, p. 388)

A divine mandate is 'the concrete divine commission grounded in the revelation of Christ and the testimony of scripture; it is the authorization and legitimization to declare a particular divine commandment, the conferring of divine authority on an earthly institution' (*DBWE* 6, p. 389). These are *not* infallible or divinely sanctioned because they can be sinful, but this does not mean they should be abolished (*DBWE* 6, p. 70). Brian Brock explains: 'The mandates have no salvific value, or even ultimate conceptual worth, but they pedagogically indicate basic aspects of creaturely existence that scripture suggests are necessary for the continued existence of all creation, including the unregenerate' (Brock, 2005, p. 26).

Because the world constantly seeks deification, the church is responsible to act in a way that proclaims *Christ's* lordship over it (*DBWE* 6, p. 401), which entails reminding the state of the limits of its responsibility. Bonhoeffer is referencing the totalitarianism of the Nazis, and narrates a space for the church without advocating Christian imperialism, or a radical, religious sectarianism.

In 'The Church and the Jewish Question', which is an earlier essay, Bonhoeffer suggests three ways the church is mandated to act in relation to the state. *First*, it questions the state's legitimacy to act or not act. This includes acting as advocates for those who suffer (see *DBWE* 4, p. 237; *DBWE* 13, p. 217; *DBWE* 14, p. 433). Bonhoeffer himself did this through his radio address in January 1933, challenging Hitler and National Socialism (Green, 2019, p. 355).

Second, the church has an 'unconditional obligation towards the victims of any societal order, even if they do not belong to the Christian community' (*DBWE* 12, p. 365). Bonhoeffer's participation in 'Operation 7' is such an example, where he assisted his brother in-law, Hans von Dohnanyi, in smuggling 14 (originally seven) Berlin Jews out of Germany (Marsh, 2014, pp. 317–18). Andreas Pangritz explains, 'church membership is irrelevant when solidarity with the victims of state policies is required' (Pangritz, 2019, p. 95).

Third, if the church perceives the state to be failing in its responsibility, such as depriving people of their rights, it must take direct political action, 'not just to bind up the wounds of the victims beneath the wheel but to seize the wheel itself' (*DBWE* 6, p. 365). This is only possible because the state is a provisional and fallible entity, endowed by God's command, but preserved only for Christ's sake and subject to his lordship (Green, 2002, pp. 124–35).

The church discerns its responsibility ever anew regarding how to serve the state. The church is free from the state, so it can freely serve the state by limiting its power, even if that involves standing against it for its own sake through Christ (*DBWE* 6, p. 393).

Conclusion

For Bonhoeffer, the devastating and abhorrent evils that had occurred in an 'enlightened' nation such as Germany required not just rigorous intellectual and socio-political rethinking, but tentative self-reflection and repentance regarding the reality of Christ in the world. The ethical frameworks upon which much of Europe had been built were manoeuvred or distorted to deceive and destroy life. Bonhoeffer's extreme context brings our own sensibilities into sharp focus.

Bonhoeffer is most probably writing for readers who are educated and in positions of influence to a certain extent. This makes sense of his plumb-line argument, that faithful disciples of Jesus Christ may be required to act in ways that contravene the status quo and societal flow of the day. One cannot make a principle of this of course, but allegiance to Christ entails acting obediently through free responsibility *with* and *for* others, even and maybe especially when that involves incurring guilt upon ourselves for others' sakes. Bonhoeffer was no revolutionary in the radical sense because he valued obedience. 'The smallest offence against order shocked him. For the sake of the order that had been destroyed on a grand scale, he became a revolutionary' (Dudzus, 1973, p. 82). At its heart, Bonhoeffer's concern was for disciples to be free from their preoccupation with ethical self-justification. This is a challenging vision for the Christian imagination, particularly for those in positions of power and authority who may be tempted to focus on vindicating themselves for their decisions.

The poem 'Jonah' offers a coded testimony where Bonhoeffer conveys the guilt vicariously borne by himself and other conspirators for the sake of all people (Plant, 2009, pp. 207–9).

Jonah

They screamed in the face of death, their frightened bodies clawing
at sodden rigging, tattered by the storm,
and horror-stricken gazes saw with dread
the sea now raging with abruptly unleashed powers.

'Ye gods, immortal, gracious, now severely angered,
help us, or give a sign, to mark for us
the one whose secret sin has roused your wrath,
the murderer, the perjurer, or vile blasphemer,

who's bringing doom on us by hiding his misdeed
to save some paltry morsel of his pride!'
This was their plea. And Jonah spoke: ''Tis I!
In God's eyes I have sinned. Forfeited is my life.

'Away with me! The guilt is mine. God's wrath's for me.
The pious shall not perish with the sinner!'
They trembled much. But then, with their strong hands,
they cast the guilty one away. The sea stood still.

(*DBWE* 8, pp. 547–8)

11

Letters and Papers from Prison

Christiane Tietz informs us that 'The Reich Central Security Office had been concerned for some time by the independence of the military secret service [the *Abwehr*] and wanted to put an end to this' (Tietz, 2016, p. 93). Ahead of his arrest in 1943, Bonhoeffer and his cousin Hans von Dohnanyi did their best to cover their tracks and camouflage their involvement in the conspiracy against Hitler. However, currency violations in the *Abwehr* led the Nazi head office to investigate the all-too-independent Military Intelligence Agency. On 5 April 1943, not long after two attempts on Hitler's life, Bonhoeffer was arrested along with Hans von Dohnanyi and Dohnanyi's wife, Christine (Bonhoeffer's sister). The failure to put 'a spoke in the wheel' (Wind, 2012) of Nazi tyranny must have flooded Bonhoeffer with numerous thoughts regarding the complex reality of faithfulness, freedom and failure. As soon as he was able, Bonhoeffer started spending his time in prison writing extensively while simultaneously being bombarded with questions and claims through Nazi interrogation (Schlingensiepen, 2010, p. 317).

Who actually is Jesus Christ?

Bonhoeffer's prison letters present a stream of consciousness reflecting on Christ, church, Scripture and what eternal life entails. For Ferdinand Schlingensiepen, the main theme that arises in these writings is revealed in a letter to Eberhard Bethge written on 30 April 1944: 'What keeps gnawing at me is the question, what is Christianity, or who is Christ actually for us today?' (*DBWE* 8, p. 362; Schlingensiepen, 2010, p. 351). The language Bonhoeffer used earlier described God and Christ 'for *me*', but this development of God and Christ being 'for *us*' signifies the 'full expression' of Bonhoeffer's theological sociality in Christ (Feil, 1985, p. 75).

In exploring his burning question, Bonhoeffer suggests that Christianity has historically operated with a 'religious *a priori*' of 'God' as a 'working hypothesis' or *deus ex machina*. What he means is that the notion of 'God' has provided a conceptual basis for religious belief and the consequential resources for human self-understanding in the world. 'God' has been regarded as the 'one' who solves the problems humans cannot answer or overcome in themselves. If there has been a question or a problem, 'God' is the answer. Bonhoeffer proposes that the modern world has now 'come of age' through becoming increasingly autonomous and self-sufficient since the Enlightenment. Therefore, modern humanity simply does not need this 'God' any more (*DBWE* 8, pp. 362–4, 366–7, 405–7, 425–6, 455, 478). 'God' is 'being pushed further and further out of our life, losing ground' (*DBWE* 8, p. 426). However, Bonhoeffer seems relieved at this, suggesting that this 'God of the gaps' should indeed be abandoned, because such a paradigm only recognizes a space for 'God' within the confinement and continually diminishing frontiers of human epistemology. Such a God is therefore a 'God' of human constitution, subject to the fleeting needs and ultimate dominion of people. Instead, Bonhoeffer suggests, 'God is beyond in the midst of our lives' (*DBWE* 8, p. 367). Jesus Christ reveals the God who is at the very centre of all things, and not reducible merely to be present in those situations or problems that need solving (*DBWE* 8, pp. 406–7).

This may seem a bit confusing. In what way is the real, biblical God at the centre of life, while the 'God of religion' is at the periphery? The explanation is something of a 'paradox' (Van Buren, 1967, pp. 45–59). 'Before God, and with God, we live without God. God consents to be pushed out of the world and onto the cross; God is weak and powerless in the world and in precisely this way, and only so, is at our side and helps us' (*DBWE* 8, p. 479). For Bonhoeffer, 'This is the crucial distinction between Christianity and all religions' (*DBWE* 8, p. 479). Whereas religion seeks a 'God' to fulfil human needs, the Bible 'directs people toward the powerlessness and the suffering of God; only the suffering God can help' (*DBWE* 8, p. 479). Bonhoeffer embraces the 'world come of age' in anticipation that 'eliminating a false notion of God' actually 'frees us to see the God of the Bible, who gains ground and power in the world by being powerless' (*DBWE* 8, pp. 479–80).

Josiah Ulysses Young III helpfully highlights that Bonhoeffer's assessment is not an accurate analysis of faith expression and socio-political life globally (Young, 1998, pp. 3–4). Bonhoeffer is speaking from within his context as though it is the case for everyone everywhere. Though it may be a bit unfair to level criticism at him for not caveating his reflections as a White European it is worth recognizing that he perhaps assumes too easily that his thinking is universally valid across cultural and even denominational backgrounds. It is too easy to speak for everyone without realizing that not everyone shares the same perspective and narrative. Certain assumptions about what is normal, what is human, how the world looks, and who God or 'God' is, can be answered too quickly by some on behalf of others. I share Young's critique while recognizing that Bonhoeffer's reading of the gospel story gives a fresh way of understanding Christian discipleship in the White Western world, much of which has increasingly pushed God to the edges. Bonhoeffer creatively envisions the centrality of Christ in a world that, despite tremendous human progress, continues to experience and cause tremendous suffering.

Faith in the God who is present in the world through being rejected by it means that 'human suffering and forsakenness is qualified anew', as it now finds its place in God, so there is 'no longer any real forsakenness by God' in the world (Tietz, 2019, p. 165). Suffering is not somehow good, but its presence is no longer devoid of the God who gives meaning amid, and sometimes despite, suffering. Those who suffer and are afflicted or oppressed can be strengthened to know that God is for them and suffers with them.

However, there is a further challenge for those who are themselves not suffering. 'The human being is called upon to share in God's suffering at the hands of a godless world ... It is not a religious act that makes someone a Christian, but rather sharing in God's suffering in the worldly life' (*DBWE* 8, p. 480). Faith entails 'not thinking first of one's own needs, questions, sins, and fears but allowing oneself to be pulled into walking the path that Jesus walks' (*DBWE* 8, p. 480). Christ reveals the God whose power is demonstrated in powerlessness, rejection and crucifixion. Christ reveals God 'in need' and 'poor, reviled, without shelter or bread ... devoured by sin, weakness, and death', and who asks humanity to 'stand by God in God's own pain' (*DBWE* 8, p. 480).

Bernd Wannenwetsch highlights that the religious 'God' has long served as a domesticated functionary to fulfil human needs and questions. Religion has sought to restrain the true God within the confines of an 'existence' that remains devoid of any genuine reality through revelation (Wannenwetsch, 2009, p. 183). 'What brings women and men to acknowledge the suffering God whom they encounter as *their* God is precisely their existential sharing in his very life' (Wannenwetsch, 2009, p. 183). In Christ, God transfigures suffering to himself, and invites humanity to participate. This does not negate any personal outcrying to God over suffering. Quite the opposite! But we may not receive 'theological' answers on our own terms, certainly not in a philosophically coherent theodicy. Instead, suffering becomes a profoundly intimate communing with Christ, a sharing in the suffering of God in the world, which requires renouncing any desire for a counterfeit 'God' who provides theoretical, religious answers (Wannenwetsch, 2009, p. 190). Wannenwetsch summarizes, 'trusting in Christ, living in Christ, and suffering with Christ ... will initiate us into ways of crying for help without reducing God to a problem solver' (Wannenwetsch, 2009, p. 191).

In prison, Bonhoeffer remarks that Christ reveals

> a reversal of all human existence, in the very fact that Jesus only 'is there for others.' Jesus's 'being-for-others' is the experience of transcendence! Only through this liberation from self, through this 'being-for-others' unto death, do omnipotence, omniscience, and omnipresence come into being. (*DBWE* 8, p. 501)

Christ's 'being-for-others' frees humanity to live for God and others in this suffering world. Transcendence, therefore, 'is not the infinite, unattainable tasks, but the neighbor within reach in any given situation. God in human form ... the Crucified One' (*DBWE* 8, p. 501). Sharing in God's suffering in the world means sharing in the suffering of the concrete neighbour, within whom and through whom Christ reveals himself.

The dangers of Christ 'for others'

The 'for others' motif is a plumb line in Bonhoeffer's thought. However, and it may be apparent already, it carries inherent problems and risks. The dangers have been highlighted by others, specifically in how they can reinforce systems of oppression through imposing sexist and patriarchal societal orders (e.g. McBride, 2019; Dahill, 2009; Muers, 2004; Kyung, 1997). In her biography of Simone de Beauvoir, Kate Kirkpatrick shows the issues of imposing a supposedly 'normative' concept or idea upon others, as though there is no particularity and limitation to that concept or idea itself. One's opinion should not be dismissed because of its particularity and socio-political narrative, but validated as something contextually grounded. Disregarding or operating with no awareness or recognition of one's own particularity (such as being a man, for example) ostracizes others precisely because it juxtaposes the 'other' against the perceived 'norm' (Kirkpatrick, 2019, pp. 249–50). We remember Jesus' claim that truth is no universal idea, but a person embodied in flesh, blood, time and space (John 14.6). While Bonhoeffer did not participate in conduct that actively sought to dehumanize or oppress women (Bethge,

1991, p. 198), he nevertheless claimed that patriarchy was a 'good and necessary' arrangement within the divine order (*DBWE* 1, p. 97) that upheld the recognition of difference concretely (McBride, 2019, p. 367). Inequality is not necessarily always evil in his mind, though communist uniformity is (*DBWE* 1, p. 205).

In a sermon that Bonhoeffer wrote for the wedding of Eberhard Bethge and Renate (Bonhoeffer's niece), he writes: 'The place to which God has assigned the wife is the home of the husband ... It is the wife's vocation and happiness to build this world within the world for her husband and to be active there' (*DBWE* 8, p. 85). To be a woman is to be a wife, which is to be *for* her husband, with anticipation/expectation that she will be bearing his children. There is an order assumed here, one that is not equal because Bonhoeffer considers their abilities and social roles to be different. However, this is a concrete arrangement around 'vast differences of ability and social status among human beings' (McBride, 2019, p. 367). Women are considered less able, which is why they are afforded lower status. Women are expected to live 'for others' with the *others* being their husbands, and men in general, with little reciprocity or consideration of how men/husbands should live *for* them. Social roles and perceived abilities are as such because of the arrangements made by men, projected theologically as a divine ordering, exacerbating women's 'inferior situation in society' which 'does not mean that they *are* inferior innately' (Kirkpatrick, 2019, p. 251).

Here, Bonhoeffer's Christology offers a challenge to his own sociopolitical ignorance, particularly his participation in the subjugation of women. The importance of recognizing the call of Christ, who suffers in the transcendent 'other', engenders a broadening of the social imaginative horizons that would otherwise limit one's perspective. Bonhoeffer's pressing focus was the suffering and silencing of Jews. However, McBride argues that there is an embedded sexism within his thinking to 'lock women into predetermined social roles and to the support and maintenance of patriarchal practices and conditions that, intentional or not, restrict the agency, power, authority, and full potential of women' (McBride, 2019, p. 366).

While acknowledging Bonhoeffer's rich Christological thinking, Lisa Dahill argues that he does not perceive how female submission inadvertently becomes a coercive and binding relationship of immediacy, rather than one within which Christ is acknowledged as the mediator between women and men. He clearly notes the potential for abuse of the self over others, but does not adequately distil the difference between the *cor curvum in se* in an oppressor and the oppressed. In other words, he would regard female resistance to submission as a problem of the dominant, female self (Dahill, 2009, p. 171). One of the key ways that horizons can be broadened theologically is holding space for stories and experiences of suffering and marginalization that can prompt deeper reflection on the contextual apparatus within which theological work is active. By giving voice to those who suffer within the penultimate, believers witness to the ultimate hope of Christ's kingdom that will come in fullness when he returns (Billings, 2015, pp. 75–7), so that assumed norms can be reconsidered and, if necessary, redressed in response to Christ's concrete call over and against dominant norms that might serve injustice.

Rather than attempting to co-opt feminist voices into this project, I raise this issue to highlight the fallibility and risk of deifying Bonhoeffer's own thinking, which he would hate, and to humbly applaud voices of Christian resistance that offer a necessary corrective. Bonhoeffer's own Christology informs a view of personhood that is inextricably relational. Within the finitude of his own freedom, his limits of what that entails (given his male individuality) is given cause for reframing, and his own Christology finds its broadening and critique through female persons. This affirms Bonhoeffer's Christological trajectory, but does so by Christologically critiquing his assumptions in the matter using his own motif.

Womanist theologians such as Kelly Brown Douglas have sought to redress issues of patriarchy in Black theology and experience, while maintaining the particular (inter-sectional) experience of being *Black* and *woman*. I had the privilege of meeting Professor Douglas in December 2022 at a symposium on the legacies of Karl Barth and James H. Cone, where she was one of the keynote speakers (though I imagine she will not remember me). I asked her if she might sign a copy of my fiftieth anniversary edition of Cone's *A Black Liberation of Theology*, for which she wrote the Afterword. She most graciously complied, and wrote:

Tim,
Do the work of
God's justice.
Kelly Brown Douglas
9 Dec '22

After hearing Professor Douglas speak at this symposium, I realized myself that, in my zeal for *racial* justice, I had overlooked the multifaceted problem of injustice as it pertains to *sexism*. In hindsight, I wonder whether asking her to sign my copy of Cone's book would have felt patronizing, and for that I am deeply sorry. On the train home from Cambridge, I ordered myself a copy of her book, *The Black Christ*, which I then read in one sitting. I felt as if I was holding my breath the whole time as I sat at the feet of this African American woman of such theological stature, hearing her story alongside some profound critical observations of world history and present theological sensibilities.

Douglas offers the view that chattel slavery was justified by the White Western world 'with claims that they were introducing the "African heathens" to Jesus Christ' (Douglas, 2019, p. 5). This remit was grounded in a bestowal of 'cheap grace' upon themselves, so they could sleep comfortably at night with a 'clear conscience' as 'religious' Christians. 'Apparently, to the minds of many slaveholders, enslavement was the only means Africans had for learning anything about Jesus' (Douglas, 2019, p. 7). Yet this Jesus who was preached to Black slaves was a Jesus who had little interest in their plight as dehumanized commodities, whose salvation was abstracted and severed from history (Douglas, 2019, p. 10). This White Christian 'religion' would cost Black slaves everything, but would demand nothing from the Whites who enslaved them. 'The religion of the white Christ places few demands on persons concerning how they should live their life in relation to others' (Douglas, 2019, p. 13). Douglas challenges the zeitgeist that pervades evangelicalism in the White Western world, arguing, 'In order for Christians to receive salvation, they must engage in liberating acts, not enslaving acts' (p. 26). The challenge is palpable and hot: my salvation as a White man is wrapped up in the liberation, dignity, flourishing and wholeness of sisters such as Kelly Brown Douglas, as well as those who have no platform upon which to be seen or heard.

I regularly recall the keynote presentation that Professor Douglas gave back in December 2022. She was powerful, lucid, confident, real, present, passionate, sharp, prophetic, angry, kind, gracious, sorrowful yet rejoicing (2 Cor. 6.10), critical and clever, honouring and honest. For me, it was an experience of transcendence, of being arrested from my own epistemological, geographical and social/academic horizons and bodily comportment to the world, confronted by Christ who was speaking to me through the body and blood of a Black sister, in a space that subtly engendered a particular mode and posture, but within which she would not shy away from being Black, brave and beautiful (in an eschatological sense). It was a moment where I experienced viscerally that 'Epistemological transcendence has nothing to do with God's transcendence' (*DBWE* 8, p. 367). In her stories, her social analysis and her theological critique, Douglas was performing a transcendent reality, which was a gift for me, since it illuminated in my mind that to live genuinely 'for others' *requires attention to the perspectives of others*. 'The transcendent is not the infinite, unattainable tasks, but the neighbor within reach in any given situation' (*DBWE* 8, p. 501). That is the only way one can faithfully and non-violently say that 'Jesus's "being-for-others" is the experience of transcendence' (*DBWE* 8, p. 501).

Without recognizing the agency of others, without surrendering our epistemological dominion over others, without being willing to live 'for others' *at their behest*, the life for others that Christ calls us to can become distorted, myopic and even demonic. If we preach a Jesus and a discipleship to him that is 'for others', we must be careful to qualify that the ways and means by which we live 'for others' are mutually agreeable and constantly open to being reformed in their social constitution based on the contingencies of individuals in community life. Otherwise, Whiteness prevails as the mode of engagement and Christian communities suffer because 'White participants' who are 'really positive and kind people' continue to make 'racist [or sexist] assumptions' that impact on 'intercultural relationships within the church' (Marsh, 2023, p. 194).

Alongside other womanist thinkers, Douglas raises a critique of Black theology from within the Black space. She claims that the optic of affirming Black bodies unconditionally as per Black male thinkers, 'did not sufficiently specify what it was that Christ affirmed in affirming blackness. Not everything that is black is sustaining or liberating for the black community' (Douglas, 2019, p. 96). For her, the desire for Black liberation fails to address oppression in its various insidious forms within Black communities. Honing the need for recognizing particularity, she refers to class as another factor (Douglas, 2019, p. 97), but primarily foregrounds the silencing of women, who have 'suffered under the yoke of gender exploitation as well as racial oppression' (Douglas, 2019, p. 101) She argues that 'myopic visions' (Douglas, 2019, p. 104) within Black theology are redressed by Black women through their 'belief in a Jesus Christ who is liberator of the oppressed, yet oppresses its own membership' (Douglas, 2019, p. 107).

James H. Cone, often referred to as the father of Black theology, may not have fully satisfied the critiques of womanist theologians, but his later work sought to make space for the oftentimes silenced narratives of Black women within his writing (Cone, 2013, pp. 120–51). Cone's response to female suffering contrasts with societies in Western antiquity, which attempted to suppress female mourning. Greek tragedies attempted to present lament as a 'threat to male political hierarchies, potentially disruptive to the public order and harmony; and the control of female lamentation was possible because Greek tragedy portrayed it as nonrational, foreign, and magical' (Hughes, 2004, p. 18). Cone's later work sought to allow challenges against the stigmatization (with its inherent silencing) of women who lament in ways that challenge the status quo. It would be wrong for *me* to try and use womanist voices to critique Black theology. They can critique it on their own terms with their own more than adequate resources. I merely highlight this to acknowledge that the subject of race can become abstract in our (White people's) attempt to make a principle out of it by ignoring its complexity.

Church for others

In our current moment in world history, one wonders what it means for Christian communities to live 'for others' today in a manner that does not fall into the trappings and surreptitious violence of a pseudo life together. Bonhoeffer's observations and experience reveal that the church is not pure and innocent in relation to the evil and suffering that occurs in the world due to racialization. The Body of Christ is implicated in and, more critically, called to participate in the world's misery and suffering. Trying to monopolize on people's pain or questions by 'winning them for Christ' is a short-sighted and potentially harmful way to live as Christians in the light of world history. The pious and sincere inclination to spiritually seize moments of profound vulnerability with the (often abstract) 'truth' of the gospel is to overlook the gross ignorance of Western Christendom's complex, multifaceted history regarding issues of injustice and evil, with race being a particularly pertinent one for this author, and for many people who are Black. Christians who would identify as 'evangelical' may at times regard situations of suffering or evil – whether it be a global pandemic or the murder of an African American witnessed on social media – as a God-given opportunity to 'jump on a few unfortunates in their hour of weakness and commit, so to speak, religious rape' (*DBWE* 8, p. 363). Some of us in the Western church lament the reality that many people are walking away from Christianity as an organized religion, equating this directly with a decline in Christian faith and discipleship. Of course, the growing secularization of the UK does force us to ponder the extent to which people today are living as faith-filled disciples of Christ. However, this diagnosis seems a little narrow-minded in its outlook.

One perspective regarding the decline of many streams of church is to regard this shift in culture as a Western rejection of the 'God of religion', something that Bonhoeffer encourages. People in the world are perceiving that the 'God of the gaps' has finally died, and, moreover, never existed in the first place. The death of 'God' coincides with the exposure in contemporary society that our self-sufficient and highly prized security that we have sought so desperately is a myth, and comes at a cost for others. It would seem futile (not to mention unprofitable) to disagree with those for whom the church of 'God' is a 'poor, feeble, boring, petty, and bourgeois institution' (Bethge, 2000, p. 36). Maybe it is all these things. Maybe the church's introspective un-freedom and its anxiety for self-preservation has been the very thing that is killing it. Maybe, therefore, we are sometimes lamenting the very things we should embrace, and inadvertently evading what Christ calls us to be and do. I would propose that we must consider again what the church (and indeed the world) really *is*, and what it means to be truly human before God and others here and now, together.

Communities that embrace the God revealed and witnessed in Jesus Christ will have to embrace death. What I mean is that the true church will effectively forsake its own, political, religious or economic self-preservation as either an end or an entitled privilege in itself, effecting its own demise on a worldly register. A church seeking to assert its own existence and credibility by offering a marketable invitation into itself on a level amenable to systems of power, prestige and popularity, turns the church's purpose away from the gospel towards its Whiteness. Measuring 'success' as a mark of 'faithfulness' means that any attempt to be the church 'for others' will risk collusion with stories of human flourishing that are crucified with Christ. The church exists for the sake of others; those who are 'in' it are precisely the ones whom Christ calls out to new life through death (*DBWE* 8, p. 364). Its life source is the one who is himself life, whose freedom is bestowed on those who, without him, are unfree, whose perfect love is mediated for those whose own love is vulnerable to distortions, whose light continues to illuminate the darkness of people whose being 'for others' can be corrupted or contorted. This gospel is proclaimed ever anew when the church renounces its own *being* the church in and of (or *for*) itself, so that it may be the *church*, which is *for* and *with* others in freedom.

Faithfulness to Christ requires communities of disciples of Jesus living fully in the world, in all its complexities and contingencies, joys and sorrows, clarity and confusion, as those who are allegiant to a fundamentally different *Führer*, who leads with a cross, a stumbling block to Jews and foolishness to Gentiles (1 Cor. 1.18–31). If Hitler represents the coercion, dominance, idealism and sovereignty of the self, Jesus represents the grace, service, reality and freedom of God for others. Christ's life, death and resurrection are a radically new way to be human, a breaking of patterns and postures that both deify humanness, on the one hand, and anthropomorphize divinity on the other. In Christ, we encounter our God, our saviour, our brother, our friend, as well as our neighbour. Those who understand their humanity *in Christ* will encounter him in their neighbour by the Spirit's work, not as a given but as a gift. As such, it is in living a life that is not primarily constituted by or oriented towards the self, that a person encounters Christ, precisely because he is 'the man for others', encountered and experienced in the dynamic of a life *for* and *with* others, which especially includes those who suffer in this wonderful yet wounded world, that we might all find healing together in him.

Conclusion

In 2021, I was asked to be involved in a consultation process for Baptists Together, exploring the challenges of equality and diversity in our union of churches in the UK. We wanted to produce a resource to help facilitate conversations around this subject, and to help raise awareness for ministers. A range of people were present, representing those in our churches who sometimes experience marginalization and the sort of inequality that can cause harm. There were women and men, Black, Brown and White, able-bodied, disabled, neuro-diverse, rich and poor, as well as people who represented the LGBTQI+ community. I was a little edgy in that space as I was conscious that my perspective would probably not match up with everyone else's. However, I needed to enter it humbly, with a willingness to listen to others' perspectives.

Many people, particularly those who are of Global Majority Heritage, are exhausted and demoralized by being put in positions where they are asked to share their story, only for people to ignore them and for no lasting change to occur. It was suggested by Wale Hudson-Roberts, our racial justice enabler, that what may be appropriate for this resource would be to give opportunities for people to share their experience of marginalizing others, and to reflect on how redressing one's own inadvertent sensibilities has enabled them to live more genuinely 'for others' in church. Wale's view was that it seemed unfair for those people who experience suffering at the hands of others to have to be the ones who speak up and make themselves vulnerable. The final resource, entitled 'I am because you are', can be accessed on the Baptists Together website, and provides opportunities for people to reflect on their own prejudices and postures that have caused harm to others. I learnt a lot from being involved in producing this resource.

If my life is primarily about discipleship to Christ, that can never be abstracted away from the particularities of time and space, and of the body, story and context within which I live. To say otherwise is, as I have hopefully shown, to undermine much of the life of faith that Jesus invites us to. By renouncing the innate temptation to diagnose what others need from within myself (like I'm fixing a patient), we open ourselves up for a genuine encounter with our neighbour as they truly are. In so doing, we open ourselves up for a genuine encounter with Christ himself, who comes to us through the agency of other people. We may seek God for direction and understanding in the midst of life, but God also comes to us in need, as a God who bears suffering for our sake, and who offers salvation to those who will bear him, who will live for him, and who will be transformed through the encounter. Bonhoeffer's poem 'Christians and Heathens' is one of my most favourite poems, and it gestures at the implications of living a life that is, in Christ, genuinely and holistically 'for others'.

Christians and Heathens

1. People go to God when they're in need,
   plead for help, pray for blessing and bread,
   for rescue from their sickness, guilt, and death.
   So do they all, all of them, Christians and heathens.

2. People go to God when God's in need,
   find God poor, reviled, without shelter or bread,
   see God devoured by sin, weakness, and death.
   Christians stand by God in God's own pain.

3. God goes to all people in their need,
   fills body and soul with God's own bread,
   goes for Christians and heathens to Calvary's death
   and forgives them both.

(*DBWE* 8, pp. 460–1)

Conclusion

At this point of the book, the reader may have formulated their own reflections regarding the pilgrimage we have taken. For experienced Bonhoeffer scholars, there may be a concern that I have not foregrounded certain aspects of Bonhoeffer's thinking or parts of his life that were important to mention. On pilgrimage, there is only so much we can see and notice. I am sure I have not achieved, nor have I sought to develop, a full, systematic survey of Bonhoeffer. The resources on Bonhoeffer are increasingly plentiful and erudite. Anyone who takes the time to read him for themselves will notice things that I have not perceived. This book is most definitely not a definitive summary of Bonhoeffer's life and thought as it pertains to race and White Western Christianity.

There may also be some readers who do not feel I have gone far enough in relation to the work of postcolonialism. To an extent, this was always going to be the case. Part of my ongoing pilgrimage as a Christian theologian involves practising the sometimes humiliating repentance that beckons me to be redirected where I have become lost, which picks up where I have fallen, and which rebukes me where I have trodden upon others unfaithfully. I cannot (and do not want to) totally dismiss where I have come from. To attempt this would, in my view, be naive, as well as problematic, given that much of the damage done requires owning our history, retracing our steps and seeking redemptive paths that have hitherto been unexplored, allowing others to point out other tracks that are less well travelled. I hope this book will prompt others like me to consider a postcolonial pilgrimage, whether that is with Bonhoeffer or with others, and I hope the book will represent an active welcoming of and a need for those who might shape our gaze and gait along the way. In conclusion, let me share one more story, one that gestures at the connection between America and Britain, and which sharpens the situation of race and colonialism for me as someone who is White and, to be specific, British.

On 15 September 1963, the American Civil Rights Movement was in full swing. A fortnight beforehand, Martin Luther King Jr had delivered his impassioned 'I have a dream' speech, which had prompted the Governor of Alabama, George Wallace, to declare that the state needed a 'few first-class funerals' in order to stop racial integration from happening. Many White Christians supported Wallace's zeal for segregated spaces. In Alabama State, the city of Birmingham represented the heart of White supremacy and racism in America, having been dubbed 'Bombingham' due to the common practice of Whites regularly constructing, planting and detonating explosive devices in Black homes and Black churches. Bonhoeffer had obviously been dead for over nearly two decades, having been hanged in Flossenburg concentration camp on 9 April 1945. Yet his observations still resonated for this period, which was also 'deeply distressing. Here one gets to see something of the real face of America, something that is hidden behind the veil of words in the American constitution saying that "all men are created free and equal"' (*DBWE* 10, p. 321).

On Sunday 15 September, in 16th Street Baptist Church, the children of that congregation were participating in their Sunday school as they usually did, ahead of the main church service which would begin at 11.00 a.m. The church had become a key base for the Civil Rights Movement, both organizationally and spiritually. At 10.22 a.m., the Ku Klux Klan set off a bomb that exploded and destroyed part of the building. Four young Black girls were killed. Their names were Addie Mae Collins, Denise McNair, Carole Robertson and Cynthia Wesley. Addie Mae's sister, Sarah Collins, lost one of her eyes in the destruction, and several other people were injured. As if this was not awful enough, the explosion coincided with the subsequent murder of two other Black children, at the hands of both police and 'hate-filled white youths' (King, 2000, pp. 229–30). Many White Christians in America did not consider this to be contrary to their faith, given the imaginative impressions written generationally into their story of the gospel, and of what it means to be human. Many more moderate Christians (including those from other nations like Britain) found it concerning, though we perhaps consoled ourselves as Bonhoeffer did by thinking that 'we don't really have an analogous situation in [Europe]' (*DBWE* 10, p. 293). As an aside, David Olusoga highlights that acts of racial violence also occurred in Britain, spurred in part because of the aversion among many Whites regarding interracial relationships (Olusoga, 2021, pp. 509–10). It was also five years later, on 20 April 1968, when Enoch Powell delivered his famous 'Rivers of Blood' speech which exposed the White supremacist impulse behind at least some of the White British population.

As I ponder the horror of these young Black girls' murder, much of me wants to pause and to sit in silence with the evil reality before me. It is easy to dismiss the horror as something that just happens in America, but I have seen a more subtle and much more British means of terror and racism in shocking and surprising places. Racism in Britain is present, both in the form of the gang confronting my wife and me in the Kentish village I mentioned at the beginning of the book, but also in those who 'aren't racist' but who refuse to afford status, value or any power and redemptive agency to those who are not White. There are many who, like Wilberforce and his gradualist peers, would be firmly against extreme harm against 'non-White' people, but who would also want to manage those people and not afford them the autonomy and voice that requires renouncing ultimate control over them. I think that this was what made Bonhoeffer worthy of respect from James Cone and other Black theologians, as he was willing to learn from his non-White sisters and brothers, and sat under their leadership, which many liberal Whites struggled (and still struggle) to do. What is perhaps more grounding and helpful at this moment is to reflect on the responses of other, more sympathetic and moderate Whites to the congregation in the 16th Street Baptist Church of 1963.

In reflecting on the media fallout from the killings in Birmingham, Martin Luther King observed a notable contrast between the rhetoric and postures within public discourse, and the reflexes that were not on display for the world to see. For example, the mayor of Birmingham 'had wept on television [but] had not even had the common decency to come or to send an emissary to the funerals of these murdered innocents' (King, 2000, p. 233). King laments that 'no white faces could be seen save for a pathetically few courageous ministers' (King, 2000, p. 230). The words and 'crocodile-weeping' of many Whites does not appear to have entailed any communion alongside those who suffered. Perhaps entering into the sorrow and anger of their Black space would have been too discomforting or confronting for many Whites to 'cope' with. It is all to easy to think we understand the perspectives of those who are not White, and to voyeuristically assess them and respond to them at our own behest. We Whites sometimes respond to suffering with an objective poise that seeks a theodicy rather than a Christlike body.

We have explored how Bonhoeffer's approach to Scripture enabled him to recognize and pray for the Jews who suffered the barbaric evil of *Kristallnacht*, where the Nazis 'burned all the meeting places of God in the land', and next to the verse, he wrote: '9.11.38' (Ps. 74.86; see Bethge, 2000, p. 607). Bonhoeffer's infuriation even extended to the Confessing Church, who claimed to put Christ first, but who were more concerned for the self-preservation of their movement than the justice of God, the plight of the suffering, and any gospel that was genuinely good news for the poor. Rather than blaming others or worldly influences, in prison he laments that 'This is our own fault. Our church has been fighting during these years only for its self-preservation, as if that were an end in itself' (*DBWE* 8, p. 389). So many conversations within the White Western church today, whether conservative evangelical or progressive liberal, are about self-preservation, maintaining what often feels like a 'poor, feeble, boring, petty, and bourgeois institution' (Bethge, 2000, p. 36). Shaking our heads with pious grief over the evil in the world is sometimes not enough, but requires prayerful action and active prayer. To take our discipleship seriously means that 'we are to take part in Christ's greatness of heart, in the responsible action that in freedom lays hold of the hour and faces the danger, and in the true sympathy that springs forth not from fear but from Christ's freeing and redeeming love for all who suffer' (*DBWE* 8, p. 49).

King believed that the lack of White bodies at the Birmingham funeral drove the Black community even further towards 'breaking point' (King, 2000, p. 233). In some ways it may have been *even more painful* to witness sympathetic White moderates expressing compassion to a point, but failing to enflesh Christ with them where it would cost something.

During this time, across the Atlantic Ocean, word had spread of the event. John Petts, a stained-glass artist from Llansteffan, a village in Carmarthenshire, Wales, was deeply appalled and wondered whether something could be done as a 'gesture of Christian sympathy in the face of destructive evil, and, as a token, put back at least one of those windows'. A fuller account of the story can be found on The National Library of Wales website (2024), which shows the initial sketches Petts had designed to offer a potential replacement for a stained-glass window that had been destroyed in the church blast. Jessica McCasland and Eva Parker clarify that, 'While the window was inspired by the damage to the church, it did not replace a damaged window. Those were restored. Instead it was installed as a third image of Jesus in the sanctuary' (McCasland and Parker, 2020). This is a digression but worth clarifying for historical accuracy.

John Petts contacted David Cole, the editor of the *Western Mail*, which launched a fundraising campaign towards a stained-glass window for the people of Birmingham. People were not allowed to give more than half a crown (12 and a half pence), because 'We don't want some rich man ... paying for the whole window. We want it to be given by the people of Wales' (The National Library of Wales, 2004). The Welsh were very familiar with the plight of African Americans, due in part to the relationship the nation had with Paul Robeson. Robeson had advocated for their unemployed miners and shared with them the situation of racism in America. Meeting a real person makes an issue real, and suffering becomes a reality rather than just an idea. Furthermore, a strong tradition of Sunday school in Wales meant that the particular timing and subsequent horror of the explosion resonated with many churches and schools.

Wales also carried its own story of marginalization and oppression, having been colonized by the English to the extent that many had suffered domination through language, culture and societal governance (Ellis, 2023). Their suffering no doubt engendered compassion and solidarity with others who suffered. This hopefully highlights that while racism and colonialism are related, colonialism is not necessarily reducible to race in its most obvious sense. This prompts deeper reflection on what needs to be interrogated in the history and thought of White Western colonialism and its relationship with theology. There were people with white skin who wanted to stand spiritually alongside their darker-skinned sisters and brothers. I wonder if this is what James Cone meant when he suggested that people needed to become Black, that is, to become people who seek the liberation of their fellow human beings in the name of Jesus.

Petts' original design for the window was stunning, with images of doves ascending and descending amid bright colours, with the Beatitudes embedded over a rainbow and a deep blue background, sparkling with tiny white crosses. The National Library of Wales reports:

> A telegram was sent to the Rev. John Cross: 'The people of Wales offer to recreate and erect a stained glass window to replace the one shattered in the bombing of your church. They do this as a gesture of comfort and support.' A reply accepting the offer was received and stating that 'Wales was the only country to offer such direct and material assistance'. The window became a symbol that people around the world cared about their suffering and sacrifice, whilst those geographically closest saw them as alien and inferior. 'It was clear that the window in its context of violence must make a statement and an impact both simple and strong – as positive and simple as Christ's message.' Petts felt that his original design avoided the real issues, and was 'too soft'. The Church did not want a provocative statement at such a crucial stage in the Civil Rights movement, and John Petts stressed that he did not want to do anything that might cause further strife. But 'all that I saw and heard there ... strengthened my conviction that to make merely

a lovely window in coloured glass would not be enough'. (The National Library of Wales, 2024)

One can sense the anxiety to get this right, to respond faithfully. Petts wanted to be prophetic, but not at the expense of the safety and agency of the already devastated congregation in Birmingham. His correspondence with Cross would have informed him and shaped his imagination along the way regarding how he responded. If we are familiar with suffering, it is easy to presume to know how others feel, and to think we are well placed to respond on their behalf. While there was a clear sense of solidarity, that solidarity was not dissolved into the imagination of this Welsh artist. I think this is a helpful example of where White folks have been allies and neighbours (cf. Luke 10.29–37). He had a natural compassion that did not claim or presume mastery over those for whom his compassion was directed. As a fallible human being, his freedom for others did not impose upon them, and they embraced his gesture, giving him direction as to how he could craft some comfort. At the behest of the African American Christians, Petts subsequently designed a different image, one of a distinctly Black Jesus. I could describe the image here, but would encourage the reader to find it online, or even visit it in the flesh if they are able, to gaze at it for a while, and to consider the radical word crafted into this window depicting Christ as a Black man. Under this crucified figure of the Black Christ, the following words are stained:

You do it to me

My colleague Anthony Clarke introduced me to this image of the 'Wales Window' when I began teaching at Regent's Park College in the University of Oxford, and it continues to prompt me to reflect on who Jesus Christ is for us today. I recall earlier in 2024 when Anthony was preaching in our chapel service. He shared this image with us all and asked people to reflect on what they see. I remember vividly what people pointed out: the face of Christ being lowered; the way his hands were framed in different ways; the light (or water?) showering Christ in the shape of a cross; the brightness of the colours. No one said what I thought was really obvious, and the main statement of the image. 'Jesus is Black!' I said. Maybe that was a given, or maybe it was so obvious to everyone else that it did not need highlighting. It was possible that the others in our overwhelmingly White congregation were unsure whether it was appropriate to point this out. Is it racist to highlight someone's skin colour, or should we not identify (or 'judge') people based on the colour of their skin? Was

CONCLUSION

I perpetuating racialized horizons that derive from my White Western imagination if I described this person as Black?

There are some who claim we are going too far in the wrong direction these days, suggesting that focusing too much on race politics perpetuates the problems that arise because of race (for example, Hughes, 2024). This is a valid point that needs further consideration. I suppose a significant factor in my perspective has been that we live in a racialized world, and acting as though this is not the case risks evading the problems caused by it. We are all made in God's image. We are all equally loved and valued. But some are considered more equal than others, and our theology needs to reckon with this if we genuinely want to care for all members of Christ's body and God's world.

We can of course make the subject of race abstract in the other direction, deriving ethical ideals based on anti-racism, and I understand the reasons behind this, though such a response arguably risks furthering the isolation people experience from othering and being othered. In an ideal world all people will be treated with mutual respect and equity. However, as Bonhoeffer reminds us, the world, and by extension the church, is not remotely ideal, but real. In society, in the theological academy and in the church, people experience unjust obstacles and oppressive constraints that inhibit their flourishing, and this occurs in part because they are not White. I have witnessed this both in myself and within the institutions I serve. Alongside my White sisters and brothers, I need liberating from the White Christian imagination that turns me away from God and others towards myself. Thus, while he will for ever be a precious companion along the way, I need to look beyond Bonhoeffer in my discipleship and, given his own thinking and experience, I am absolutely sure he would want me to do so. Like Bonhoeffer, I would encourage any White readers to consider that the Jesus we seek to follow looks remarkably like the one whose blood stained the window on 16th Street Baptist Church in Birmingham, Alabama, whose image is borne through the bodies of Black and Brown people, and whose 'darkness' reveals the glory of God in our midst, if we dare to tarry awhile with him along the way. Do White people need to be saved? Yes! We all do, but White folks have a particular journey to make if we are going to inherit the kingdom of heaven. At least, that's what I believe the Black Christ is saying to us, and I believe in him. Bonhoeffer did too.

Bibliography

Primary sources

Bonhoeffer, Dietrich, *Dietrich Bonhoeffer Works* (1996–2014), edited by Victoria J. Barnett, Wayne Whitson Floyd Jr and Barbara Wojhoski, 17 volumes, Minneapolis: Fortress:

Sanctorum Communio: A Theological Study of the Sociology of the Church, Dietrich Bonhoeffer Works, Volume 1, edited by Clifford J. Green, translated by Reinhard Kraus and Nancy Lukens, 1998.

Act and Being: Transcendental Philosophy and Ontology in Systematic Theology, Dietrich Bonhoeffer Works, Volume 2, edited by Wayne Whitson Floyd Jr., translated by H. Martin Rumscheidt, 1996.

Creation and Fall, Dietrich Bonhoeffer Works, Volume 3, edited by John W. de Gruchy, translated by Douglas Stephen Bax, 1997.

Discipleship, Dietrich Bonhoeffer Works, Volume 4, edited by Geffrey G. Kelly and John D. Godsey, translated by Barbara Green and Reinhard Krauss, 2001.

Life Together and Prayerbook of the Bible, Dietrich Bonhoeffer Works, Volume 5, edited by Geffrey B. Kelly, translated by Daniel W. Bloesch and James H. Burtness, 1996.

Ethics, Dietrich Bonhoeffer Works, Volume 6, edited by Clifford J. Green, translated by Reinhard Krauss, Charles C. West and Douglas W. Stott, 2005.

Fiction from Tegel Prison, Dietrich Bonhoeffer Works, Volume 7, edited by Clifford J. Green, translated by Nancy Lukens, 2000.

Letters and Papers from Prison, Dietrich Bonhoeffer Works, Volume 8, edited by John W. de Gruchy, translated by Isabel Best, Lisa Dahill, Reinhard Krauss, Nancy Lukens, H. Martin Rumscheidt and Douglas W. Stott, 2010.

The Young Bonhoeffer: 1918–1927, Dietrich Bonhoeffer Works, Volume 9, edited by Paul Duane Matheny, Clifford J. Green and Marshal D. Johnson, translated by Mary C. Nebelsick and Douglas W. Stott, 2003.

Barcelona, Berlin, New York: 1928–1931, Dietrich Bonhoeffer Works, Volume 10, edited by Clifford J. Green, translated by Douglas W. Stott, 2008.

Ecumenical, Academic, and Pastoral Work: 1931–32, Dietrich Bonhoeffer Works, Volume 11, edited by Victoria J. Barnett, Mark S. Brocker and Michael Lukens, translated by Anne Schmidt-Lange, Isabel Best, Nicolas Humphrey, Marion Pauck and Douglas W. Stott, 2012.

Berlin: 1932–33, Dietrich Bonhoeffer Works, Volume 12, edited by Larry L. Rasmussen, translated by Isabel Best, David Higgins and Douglas W. Stott, 2009.

London: 1933–35, Dietrich Bonhoeffer Works, Volume 13, edited by Keith Clements, translated by Isabel Best, 2007.

Theological Education at Finkenwalde: 1935–37, Dietrich Bonhoeffer Works, Volume 14, edited by H. Gaylon Barker and Mark S. Brocker, translated by Douglas W. Stott, 2013.
Theological Education Underground: 1937–1940, Dietrich Bonhoeffer Works, Volume 15, edited by Victoria J. Barnett, translated by Victoria Barnett, Claudia D. German, Peter Frick, Scott A. Moore and Douglas Stott, 2012.
Conspiracy and Imprisonment: 1940–45, Dietrich Bonhoeffer Works, Volume 16, edited by Mark S. Brocker, translated by Lisa E. Dahill and Douglas W. Stott, 2006.
Indexes and Supplementary Materials, Dietrich Bonhoeffer Works, Volume 17, edited by Victoria Barnett, Barbara Wojhoski and Mark S. Brocker, translated by Victoria Barnett, 2014.

Bonhoeffer, Dietrich, 1995, *Love Letters from Cell 92: The correspondence between Dietrich Bonhoeffer and Maria von Wedemeyer 1943–45*, edited by Ruth Alice von Bismarck and Ulrich Kabitz, translated by John Brownjohn, Abingdon: Nashville.

Other sources

Akinyemi, Aaron, 2022, 'Nigerian student in Ukraine: "They said black people should walk"', BBC, www.bbc.co.uk/news/av/world-africa-60573719 (accessed 30.08.2024).
Alexander, Valentina, 2014, 'Onesimus's Letter to Philemon', in Michael N. Jagessar and Anthony G. Reddie (eds), *Black Theology in Britain: A Reader*, Abingdon: Routledge, pp. 187–90.
Appiah, Kwame Anthony, 2020, 'The Case for Capitalizing the B in Black', *The Atlantic*, www.theatlantic.com/ideas/archive/2020/06/time-to-capitalize-blackand-white/613159/ (accessed 30.08.2024).
Aquinas, Thomas, 1948, *Summa Theologica*, translated by Fathers of the English Dominican Province, New York: Benzinger Bros.
Arora, Arun, 2023, *Stick with Love: Rejoicing in Every Tongue, Every Tribe, Every Nation*, London: SPCK.
Atkinson, David and Eric Laurier, 1998, 'A sanitised city? Social exclusion at Bristol's 1996 *international festival of the sea*', Geoforum 29, no. 2: pp. 199–206.
Banman, Joel, 2021, *Reading in the Presence of Christ: A Study of Dietrich Bonhoeffer's Bibliology and Exegesis*, London: T&T Clark.
Baptists Together, 'I Am Because You Are', www.baptist.org.uk/Groups/379594/Equality_and_Diversity.aspx (accessed 30.08.2024).
Barth, Karl, 1995, *Church Dogmatics I: The Doctrine of the Word of God 2*, edited by G. W. Bromiley and T. F. Torrance, translated by G. W. Bromiley, Edinburgh: T&T Clark.
Barth, Karl, 1994a, *Church Dogmatics II: The Doctrine of God 2*, edited by G. W. Bromiley and T. F. Torrance, translated by G. W. Bromiley et al., Edinburgh: T&T Clark.
Barth, Karl, 1994b, *Church Dogmatics IV: The Doctrine of Reconciliation 1*, edited by G. W. Bromiley and T. F. Torrance, translated by G. W. Bromiley, Edinburgh: T&T Clark.

Bayoumi, Moustafa, 'They are "civilised" and "look like us": The racist coverage of Ukraine', *The Guardian*, www.theguardian.com/commentisfree/2022/mar/02/civilised-european-look-like-us-racist-coverage-ukraine (accessed 30.08.2024).

Bergen, Doris L., 1996, *Twisted Cross: The German Christian Movement in the Third Reich*, Chapel Hill: University of North Carolina Press.

Bethge, Eberhard, 2000, *Dietrich Bonhoeffer: A Biography, Revised and Edited by Victoria J. Barnett*, translated by Eric Mosbacher et al., Minneapolis: Fortress.

Bethge, Renate, 1991, 'Bonhoeffer's Picture of Women', in Guy Carter, René van Eyden, Hans-Dirk van Hoogstraten and Jurjen Wiersma (eds), *Bonhoeffer's Ethics: Old Europe and New Frontiers*, Kampen: Kok Pharos, pp. 194–9.

Biggar, Nigel, 2023, *Colonialism: A Moral Reckoning*, London: William Collins.

Billings, J. Todd, 2015, *Rejoicing in Lament: Wrestling with Incurable Cancer & Life in Christ*, Grand Rapids: Brazos.

Bleby, Henry, 1853, *Death Struggles of Slavery*, London: Hamilton, Adams & Co.

Bosanquet, Mary, 1968, *The Life and Death of Dietrich Bonhoeffer*, New York: Harper & Row.

Braithwaite, Edward, 1977, *Wars of Respect: Nanny and Sharpe*, Kingston: Agency for Public Information.

Brock, Brian, 2019, *Wondrously Wounded: Theology, Disability, and the Body of Christ*, Waco: Baylor University Press.

Brock, Brian, 2007, *Singing the Ethos of God: On the Place of Christian Ethics in Scripture*, Grand Rapids: Eerdmans.

Brock, Brian, 2005, 'Bonhoeffer and the Bible in Christian Ethics: Psalm 119, the Mandates and Ethics as a "Way"', *Studies in Christian Ethics* 18, no. 3: pp. 7–29.

Brueggemann, Walter, 1986, *Genesis*, Minnetonka: Westminster John Knox.

Brueggemann, Walter, 1982, *Genesis*, Interpretation series, Louisville: Westminster John Knox.

Carter, J. Kameron, 2020, 'Bonhoeffer Otherwise: Dietrich Bonhoeffer and the Religion of Whiteness Part 2: Beyond the Religion of Whiteness', www.youtube.com/watch?v=1OBf8ERPD8s (accessed 30.08.2024).

Clough, David, 2023, 'The Implications of James Cone's Critique of Barth and Barthians for the Practice of Academic Christian Theology', *Black Theology: An International Journal* 21, no. 2: pp. 88–97.

Colwell, John E., 2007, *The Rhythm of Doctrine: A Liturgical Sketch of Christian Faith and Faithfulness*, Milton Keynes: Paternoster.

Cone, James H., 2013, *The Cross and the Lynching Tree*, Maryknoll: Orbis.

Cone, James H., 2004, 'Theology's Great Sin: Silence in the Face of White Supremacy', *Black Theology: An International Journal* 2, no. 2: pp. 139–52.

Dahill, Lisa E., 2009, *Reading from the Underside of Selfhood: Bonhoeffer and Spiritual Formation*, Eugene: Pickwick.

Danker, Frederick William (ed.), 2000, *A Greek–English Lexicon of the New Testament and Other Early Christian Literature*, 3rd edn, Chicago: University of Chicago Press.

DeCort, Andrew D., 2018, *Bonhoeffer's New Beginning: Ethics after Devastation*, Lanham: Lexington Fortress.

De Gruchy, John W., 2021, *This Monastic Moment: The War of the Spirit & the Rule of Love*, Eugene: Cascade.

BIBLIOGRAPHY

De Gruchy, John W., 2005, *Daring, Trusting Spirit: Bonhoeffer's Friend Eberhard Bethge*, Minneapolis: Fortress.

Douglas, Kelly Brown, 2019, *The Black Christ*, 25th anniversary edition, Maryknoll: Orbis.

Du Bois, W. E. B., 1989, *The Souls of Black Folk*, New York: Penguin.

Dudzus, Otto, 1973, 'Arresting the Wheel', in Wolf-Dieter Zimmermann and Ronald Gregor Smith (eds), *I Knew Dietrich Bonhoeffer*, translated by Käthe Gregor Smith, London: Collins, pp. 82–90.

Eig, Jonathan, 2023, *King: The Life of Martin Luther King*, London: Simon & Schuster UK.

Ellis, Kevin, 2023, 'See, Judge, Act: Wrestling with the Effects of Colonialism as an English Priest in Wales', in Anthony G. Reddie and Carol Troupe (eds), *Deconstructing Whiteness, Empire and Mission*, London: SCM Press, pp. 208–21.

Emerton, David, 2020, *God's Church-Community: The Ecclesiology of Dietrich Bonhoeffer*, London: T&T Clark.

Evans, Malcolm, 2024, 'Statement from the Principal', *Regent's Park College*, www.rpc.ox.ac.uk/statement-from-the-principal/?fbclid=IwAR0QexZnWN-jM7Ib8FSMHP6NPF6BXRiRXs2zmNhJz4Y6bEPpHPaLYjKLHLjQ (accessed 30.08.2024).

Fabrycky, Laura M., 2020, *Keys to Bonhoeffer's Haus: Exploring the World and Wisdom of Dietrich Bonhoeffer*, Minneapolis: Fortress.

Feil, Ernst, 1985, *The Theology of Dietrich Bonhoeffer*, translated by Martin Rumscheidt, Minneapolis: Fortress.

Forbes, Tony, 1999, 'Sold Down the River', *Art UK*, www.artuk.org/discover/artists/forbes-tony-19642019 (accessed 30.08.2024).

Gardiner, Craig, 2018, *Melodies of a New Monasticism: Bonhoeffer's Vision, Iona's Witness*, Eugene: Cascade.

Green, Clifford, J., 2019, 'Bonhoeffer's Christian Peace Ethic, Conditional Pacifism, and Resistance', in Michael Mawson and Philip G. Ziegler (eds), *The Oxford Handbook of Dietrich Bonhoeffer*, Oxford: Oxford University Press, pp. 344–62.

Green, Clifford J., 2002, 'Human Sociality and Christian Community', in John W. de Gruchy (ed.), *The Cambridge Companion to Dietrich Bonhoeffer*, Cambridge: Cambridge University Press, pp. 113–33.

Greggs, Tom, 2016, 'Bearing Sin in the Church: The Ecclesial Hamartiology of Bonhoeffer', in Michael Mawson and Philip G. Ziegler (eds), *Christ, Church and World: New Studies in Bonhoeffer's Theology and Ethics*, London: Bloomsbury T&T Clark, pp. 77–99.

Halbach, Ross E., 2020, *Bonhoeffer and the Racialized Church*, Waco: Baylor University Press.

Hall, Delroy, 2021, *A Redemption Song: Illuminations on Black British Pastoral Theology and Culture*, London: SCM Press.

Havea, Jione, 2016, 'We're moving from missionary thinking into a pilgrimage culture', *World Council of Churches*, www.youtube.com/watch?v=PdbJIPHykak (accessed 30.08.2024).

Haynes, Stephen, 2006, *The Bonhoeffer Legacy: Post-Holocaust Perspectives*, Minneapolis: Fortress.

Higman, B. W., 1998, *Montpelier Jamaica: A Plantation Community in Slavery and Freedom 1739–1912*, Kingston: The Press.
Higton, Mike, 2023, 'Beyond Theological Self-Possession', in Anthony G. Reddie and Carol Troupe (eds), *Deconstructing Whiteness, Empire and Mission*, London: SCM Press, pp. 13–26.
Holland, Tom, 2020, *Dominion: The Making of the Western Mind*, London: Abacus.
Hughes, Coleman, 2024, *The End of Race Politics: Arguments for a Colorblind America*, New York: Penguin.
Hughes, Richard A., 2004, *Lament, Death, and Destiny*, New York: Peter Lang.
Jennings, Willie James, 2018, 'Can "White" People be Saved: Reflections on Missions and Whiteness', *Fuller Studio*, www.youtube.com/watch?v=SRLjWZxLıIE (accessed 30.08.2024).
Jennings, Willie James, 2010, *The Christian Imagination: Theology and the Origins of Race*, New Haven: Yale University Press.
Jinkins, Michael, 1999, *The Church Faces Death: Ecclesiology in a Post-modern Context*, Oxford: Oxford University Press.
Jinkins, Michael, 1998, *In the House of the Lord: Inhabiting the Psalms of Lament*, Collegeville: Liturgical Press.
Joerstad, Mari, 2021, *The Hebrew Bible and Environmental Ethics: Humans, Non-Humans, and the Living Landscape*, Cambridge: Cambridge University Press.
Judson, Tim, 2024, *Dark Weeping and Light Sleeping: Whiteness as a Doctrine of De-Formation*, Oxford: Whitley.
Judson, Tim, 2023, *Awake in Gethsemane: Bonhoeffer and the Witness of Christian Lament*, Waco: Baylor University Press.
Kavanagh, Aidan, 1992, *On Liturgical Theology*, Collegeville: Liturgical Press.
Kerr, Nathan, R., 2009, *Christ, History and Apocalyptic: The Politics of Christian Mission*, Eugene: Cascade.
King Jr, Martin Luther, 2000, *The Autobiography of Martin Luther King, Jr*, edited by Clayborne Carson, London: Abacus.
Kirk-Duggan, Cheryl A., 1997, *Exorcising Evil: A Womanist Perspective on the Spirituals*, Maryknoll: Orbis.
Kirkpatrick, Kate, 2019, *Becoming Beauvoir: A Life*, London: Bloomsbury.
Kirkpatrick, Matthew, 2024, *Bonhoeffer for the Church: An Introduction*, Minneapolis: Fortress.
Knight, Mark, 2019, 'Sin and Salvation', in Michael Mawson and Philip G. Ziegler (eds), *The Oxford Handbook of Dietrich Bonhoeffer*, Oxford: Oxford University Press, pp. 210–24.
Koonz, Claudia, 2005, *The Nazi Conscience*, Cambridge: Harvard University Press.
Krötke, Wolf, 2019, *Karl Barth and Dietrich Bonhoeffer: Theologians for a Post-Christian World*, translated by John P. Burgess, Grand Rapids: Baker Academic.
Kuske, Martin, 1976, *The Old Testament as the Book of Christ: An Appraisal of Bonhoeffer's Interpretation*, translated by S. T. Kimbrough Jr, Philadelphia: Westminster.
Kyung, Chung Hyun, 1997, 'Dear Dietrich Bonhoeffer: A Letter', in John W. de Gruchy (ed.), *Bonhoeffer for a New Day: Theology in a Time of Transition*, Grand Rapids: Eerdmans, pp. 9–19.
Laville, Sandra, 2024, '"We can't engineer our way out of this": How to protect

flood-hit Severn Valley', *The Guardian*, www.theguardian.com/environment/2024/jan/27/we-cant-engineer-our-way-out-of-this-how-to-protect-flood-hit-severn-valley (accessed 30.08.2024).

Lawrence, Joel, 2013, 'Death Together: Dietrich Bonhoeffer on Becoming the Church for Others', in Keith L. Johnson and Timothy Larsen (eds), *Bonhoeffer, Christ and Culture*, Nottingham: Apollos, pp. 113–29.

Lawrence, Joel, 2010, *Bonhoeffer: A Guide for the Perplexed*, London: T&T Clark.

Leibholz-Bonhoeffer, Sabine, 1971, *The Bonhoeffers: Portrait of a Family*, London: Sidgwick & Jackson.

Levine, Amy-Jill, 2020, *Sermon on the Mount: A Beginner's Guide to the Kingdom of Heaven*, Nashville: Abingdon.

Levine, Amy-Jill, 2015, *Short Stories by Jesus: The Enigmatic Parables of a Controversial Rabbi*, New York: HarperOne.

Marsh, Charles, 2014, *Strange Glory: A Life of Dietrich Bonhoeffer*, London: SPCK.

Marsh, Jill, 2023, '"I Know Where You're Coming From": Exploring Intercultural Assumptions', in Anthony G. Reddie and Carol Troupe (eds), *Deconstructing Whiteness, Empire and Mission*, London: SCM Press, pp. 193–207.

Mawson, Michael, 2019, 'Scripture', in Michael Mawson and Philip G. Ziegler (eds), *The Oxford Handbook of Dietrich Bonhoeffer*, Oxford: Oxford University Press, pp. 123–36.

Mawson, Michael, 2018, *Christ Existing as Community: Bonhoeffer's Ecclesiology*, Oxford: Oxford University Press.

Mayer, Rainer, 1981, 'Christology: The Genuine Form of Transcendence', in A. J. Klassen (ed.), *A Bonhoeffer Legacy: Essays in Understanding*, Grand Rapids: Eerdmans, pp. 179–92.

McBride, Jennifer, M., 2019, 'Bonhoeffer and Feminist Theologies', in Michael Mawson and Philip G. Ziegler (eds) *The Oxford Handbook of Dietrich Bonhoeffer*, Oxford: Oxford University Press, 2019, pp. 365–82.

McCasland, Jessica and Eva Parker, 2020, 'Breaking the Window of Racism', https://magiccityreligion.org/2020/04/01/wales-window-for-alabama/ (accessed 30.08.2024).

McKeown, James, 2008, *Genesis*, The Two Horizons Old Testament Commentary, Grand Rapids: Eerdmans.

McLaughlin, Eleanor, 2024, 'Response' at book launch for Matthew Kirkpatrick, *Bonhoeffer for the Church: An Introduction*, presented on 13 May at Wycliffe Hall, University of Oxford.

Middleton, Timothy A., 2022, 'Christic Witnessing: A Practical Response to Ecological Trauma', *Practical Theology* 15, no. 5: pp. 420–31.

Muers, Rachel, 2019, 'Anthropology', in Michael Mawson and Philip G. Ziegler (eds), *The Oxford Handbook of Dietrich Bonhoeffer*, Oxford: Oxford University Press, pp. 196–209.

Muers, Rachel, 2004, *Keeping God's Silence: Towards a Theological Ethics of Communication*, Oxford: Blackwell.

Na'amod, 2024a, naamod.org.uk/ (accessed 30.08.2024).

Na'amod, 2024b, naamod.org.uk/campaigns/racism-not-kosher/ (accessed 30.08.2024).

Nation, Mark Thiessen, 2022, *Discipleship in a World Full of Nazis: Recovering the True Legacy of Dietrich Bonhoeffer*, Eugene: Cascade.

Nietzsche, Friedrich, 1907, *Beyond Good and Evil*, translated by Helen Zimmern, London: T. N. Foulis.

Olivieri, Vincent, 2023, 'The Word for the Church and the World: Dietrich Bonhoeffer's Pastoral Theology of the Word of God', PhD thesis presented to the University of Aberdeen.

Olusoga, David, 2021, *Black and British: A Forgotten History*, London: Picador.

Pangritz, Andreas, 2019, 'Bonhoeffer and the Jews', in Michael Mawson and Philip G. Ziegler (eds), *The Oxford Handbook of Dietrich Bonhoeffer*, Oxford: Oxford University Press, pp. 91–107.

Parrot-Sheffer, Chelsey, '16th Street Baptist Church bombing', *Britannica*, www.britannica.com/event/16th-Street-Baptist-Church-bombing (accessed 30.08.2024).

Pejsa, Jane, 1991, *Matriarch of Conspiracy: Ruth Von Kleist, 1867–1945*, Minneapolis: Fortress.

Picard, Andrew and A. D. Clark-Howard, 2022, 'The Christian Settler Imaginary: Repentant remembrances of Christianity's entanglement with settler colonialism in Aotearoa New Zealand', *Practical Theology* 15:1–2, pp. 78–91, doi: 10.1080/1756073X.2021.2023948.

Pierce, Yolanda, Fourth Church AV/IT, 'Race, Theology, and the Church – Part 1: Keynote', www.youtube.com/watch?v=-McT1ZqWubY (accessed 27.10.2016) (no longer available).

Pietromarchi, Virginia, 2022, 'More African students decry racism at Ukrainian borders', *Al Jazeera*, www.aljazeera.com/news/2022/3/2/more-racism-at-ukrainian-borders (accessed 30.08.2024).

Plant, Stephen, 2009, '"Jonah": Guilt and Promise', in Bernd Wannenwetsch (ed.), *Who Am I? Bonhoeffer's Theology Through His Poetry*, London: T&T Clark, pp. 197–212.

Poling, James, 1991, *The Abuse of Power: A Theological Problem*, Nashville: Abingdon.

Połońska-Kimunguyi, Eva, 2022, 'War, Resistance and Refuge: Racism and double standards in Western media coverage of Ukraine', *London School of Economics*, blogs.lse.ac.uk/medialse/2022/05/10/war-resistance-and-refuge-racism-and-double-standards-in-western-media-coverage-of-ukraine/ (accessed 30.08.2024).

Pribbenow, Brad, 2018, *Prayerbook of Christ: Dietrich Bonhoeffer's Christological Interpretation of the Psalms*, Lanham: Lexington.

Ragad, Abdelali, Richard Irvine-Brown, Benedict Garman and Sean Seddon, 2023, 'How Hamas built a force to attack Israel on 7 October', *BBC*, www.bbc.co.uk/news/world-middle-east-67480680 (accessed 30.08.2024).

Rah, Soong-Chan, 2015, *Prophetic Lament: A Call for Justice in Troubled Times*, Downers Grove: InterVarsity Press.

Rasmussen, Larry L., 1999, 'The Ethics of Responsible Action', in John de Gruchy (ed.), *The Cambridge Companion to Dietrich Bonhoeffer*, Cambridge: Cambridge University Press, pp. 206–25.

Ray, Stephen G., 2023, *Do No Harm: Social Sin and Christian Responsibility*, Minneapolis: Fortress.

Rayson, Dianne, 2021, *Bonhoeffer and Climate Change: Theology and Ethics for the Anthropocene*, Lanham, Lexington/Fortress.

Reddie, Anthony G., 2023, 'Dealing with the Two Deadly Ds: Deconstructing Whiteness and Decolonizing the Curriculum of Theological Education', in

Anthony G. Reddie and Carol Troupe (eds), *Deconstructing Whiteness, Empire and Mission*, London: SCM Press, pp. 52–71.

Reddie, Anthony G., 2022, *Introducing James H. Cone*, London: SCM Press.

Reddie, Anthony G., 2019, *Theologising Brexit: A Liberationist and Postcolonial Critique*, London: Routledge.

Reddie, Anthony G., 2009, *Is God Colour-Blind? Insights from Black Theology for Christian Ministry*, London: SPCK.

Reddie, Anthony G., 2008, *Working Against the Grain: Re-imagining Black Theology in the 21st Century*, London: Equinox.

Reddie, Anthony G., 2006, *Dramatizing Theologies: A Participatory Approach to God-Talk*, London: Equinox.

Reed, Esther D., 2018, *The Limit of Responsibility: Dietrich Bonhoeffer's Ethics for a Globalizing Era*, London: T&T Clark.

Reid, C. S., 1988, *Samuel Sharpe: From Slave to National Hero*, Kingston: The Bustamante Institute of Public and International Affairs.

Reid-Salmon, Delroy A., 2012, *Burning for Freedom: A Theology of the Black Atlantic Struggle for Liberation*, Kingston: Ian Randle.

Reynolds, Diane, *The Doubled Life of Dietrich Bonhoeffer: Women, Sexuality, and Nazi Germany*, Eugene: Cascade.

Roberts, J. Deotis, 2005, *Bonhoeffer and King*, Louisville: Westminster John Knox Press.

Ross, Jameson E., 2023, *Bonhoeffer as Biblical Interpreter: Reading Scripture in 1930s Germany*, London: T&T Clark.

Rott, Willhelm, 1973, 'Something Always Occurred to Him', in Wolf-Dieter Zimmerman and Ronald Gregor Smith (eds), *I Knew Dietrich Bonhoeffer*, translated by Käthe Gregor Smith, London: Collins, pp. 130–7.

Salamon, Hagar, 2003, 'Blackness in Transition: Decoding Racial Constructs through Stories of Ethiopian Jews', *Journal of Folklore Research* 40, no. 1: pp. 3–32.

Schliesser, Christine, 2008, *Everyone Who Acts Responsibly Becomes Guilty: Bonhoeffer's concept of accepting guilt*, Louisville: Westminster John Knox Press.

Schlingensiepen, Ferdinand, 2010, *Dietrich Bonhoeffer 1906–1945: Martyr, Thinker, Man of Resistance*, translated by Isabel Best, London: T&T Clark.

Scott, Shalmon, 2018, 'The British Monarchy's Involvement in Slavery', *The Jamaica Observer*, www.jamaicaobserver.com/2018/03/24/the-british-monarchys-involvement-in-slavery/#google_vignette (accessed 30.08.2024).

Snyman, Kevin, 2023, '"Come we go chant down Babylon": How Black Liberation Theology Subverts White Privilege and Dismantles the Economics of Empire to Save the Planet', in Anthony G. Reddie and Carol Troupe (eds), *Deconstructing Whiteness, Empire and Mission*, London: SCM Press, pp. 265–80.

Sonderegger, Katherine, 2015, *Systematic Theology: Volume 1, The Doctrine of God*, Minneapolis: Fortress.

Stone, Selina, 2024, *Tarry Awhile: Wisdom from Black Spirituality for People of Faith*, London: SPCK.

Swinton, John, 2018, *Raging with Compassion: Pastoral Responses to the Problem of Evil*, London: SCM Press.

Szasz, Thomas S., 1997, *The Manufacture of Madness: A Comparative Study of the Inquisition and the Mental Health Movement*, Syracuse: Syracuse University Press.

Tarassenko, Joanna, 2024, *The Spirit of Polyphony: Dietrich Bonhoeffer's Musical Pneumatology*, London: T&T Clark.

Taylor, Derek W., 2020, *Reading Scripture as the Church: Dietrich Bonhoeffer's Hermeneutic of Discipleship*, Downers Grove: InterVarsity Press.

The National Library of Wales, 2024, 'The Wales window in Birmingham Alabama', www.library.wales/discover-learn/digital-exhibitions/pictures/the-wales-window-in-birmingham-alabama (accessed 30.08.2024).

Thurman, Howard, 1996, *Jesus and the Disinherited*, Boston: Beacon Press.

Tietz, Christiane, 2021, *Karl Barth: A Life in Conflict*, translated Victoria J. Barnett, Oxford: Oxford University Press.

Tietz, Christiane, 2019, 'Christology', in Michael Mawson and Philip G. Ziegler (eds), *The Oxford Handbook of Dietrich Bonhoeffer*, Oxford: Oxford University Press, pp. 150–67.

Tietz, Christiane, 2016, *Theologian of Resistance: The Life and Thought of Dietrich Bonhoeffer*, translated by Victoria J. Barnett, Minneapolis: Fortress.

Turner, Carlton, 2024, *Caribbean Contextual Theology: An Introduction*, London: SCM Press.

Tuttle, Corey, 2022, '"Now It's All Over!" Church Dogmatics 2.2, Lake Geneva, and Dietrich Bonhoeffer's Universalism', paper presented at the Society for the Study of Theology Annual Conference.

Van Buren, Paul M., 1967, 'Bonhoeffer's Paradox: Living with God without God', *Union Seminary Quarterly Review* 21, no. 1: pp. 45–59.

Waddell, Hope, 1863, *Twenty-Nine Years in the West Indies and Central Africa: A Review of Missionary Life and Adventure*, London: Nelson & Son.

Wannenwetsch, Bernd, 2009, '"Christians and Pagans": Towards a Trans-Religious Second Naïveté or How to be a Christological Creature', in Bernd Wannenwetsch (ed.), *Who Am I? Bonhoeffer's Theology Through His Poetry*, London: T&T Clark, pp. 175–96.

Webb, Simon, 2021, *The Forgotten Slave Trade: The White European Slaves of Islam*, Barnsley: Pen and Sword.

Webster, John, 2015, *God Without Measure: Working Papers in Christian Theology: Vol. 1: God and the Works of God*, London: Bloomsbury T&T Clark, pp. 143–58.

White, Josh, 'Swastikas found carved into toilet doors at Oxford college: Principal slams "deeply shocking" anti-Semitic graffiti found amid pro-Palestinian protests at university', *Daily Mail*, www.dailymail.co.uk/news/article-13455099/Swastikas-carved-toilets-Oxford-college.html (accessed 30.08.2024).

Williams, Reggie L., 2023, 'The Problem of Christianity's Failure in Nazi Germany', paper presented at the *Understanding Bonhoeffer Today* symposium on 15 May at Regent's Park College, University of Oxford.

Williams, Reggie L., 2021, *Bonhoeffer's Black Jesus: Harlem Renaissance Theology and an Ethic of Resistance*, rev. edn, Waco: Baylor University Press.

Williams, Reggie L., 2019, 'Bonhoeffer and Race', in Michael Mawson and Philip G. Ziegler (eds), *The Oxford Handbook of Dietrich Bonhoeffer*, pp. 383–96, Oxford: Oxford University Press.

Wilmore, Gayraud S., 2004, *Pragmatic Spirituality: The Christian Faith through and Africentric Lens*, New York: New York University Press.

BIBLIOGRAPHY

Wind, Renate, 2012, *A Spoke in the Wheel: The Life of Dietrich Bonhoeffer*, London: SCM Press.

Wink, Walter, 2003, *Jesus and Nonviolence: A Third Way*, Minneapolis: Fortress.

Young III, Josiah Ulysses, 1998, *No Difference in the Fare: Dietrich Bonhoeffer and the Problem of Racism*, Grand Rapids: Eerdmans.

Ziegler, Philip G., 2013, 'Dietrich Bonhoeffer: A Theologian of the Word of God', in Keith L. Johnson and Timothy Larsen (eds), *Bonhoeffer, Christ and Culture*, Downers Grove: InterVarsity Press, pp. 17–37.

Zimmermann, Wolf-Dieter, 1973, 'Finkenwalde', in Wolf-Dieter Zimmermann and Ronald Gregor Smith (eds), *I Knew Dietrich Bonhoeffer*, translated by Käthe Gregor Smith, London: Collins, pp. 107–11.

Zoellner, Tom, 2020, *Island on Fire: The Revolt that Ended Slavery in the British Empire*, Cambridge: Harvard University Press.

Index

Abuse xii, 25, 54, 115, 116, 149
Abwehr 42, 145
Abyssinian Baptist Church 7–9, 111, 130
Act and Being 86–8
Adam
 in Genesis 24, 36, 100–3
 humanity in 52, 84
Africa 11, 19–20, 57, 61, 66, 95, 151
African American 7–8, 10, 66, 75, 88, 92, 98, 151, 153, 161–2
Anger xii, 115–16, 144, 159
Anxiety xx, xxi, 14–15, 32, 35, 41, 49–50, 67, 72, 85, 119, 121, 123, 125, 135, 154, 162
America 6–10, 13–16, 18–20, 32, 39, 58, 66–7, 70, 95, 157–62
Aotearoa/New Zealand 19–20
Apostasy 26, 57, 136
Aquinas, Thomas 47, 72–3
Aryan 12, 28, 30, 124
Arora, Arun 33–4
Augustine 41

Baptism 39, 73
Baptists Together 155
Berlin 26, 67, 86, 96, 143
Bethge, Eberhard 12–13, 26, 36–7, 42–3, 65, 66, 86, 88, 96–7, 99, 109, 127, 145, 148–9, 154, 159–60
Bethge, Renate 12, 42, 149

Barth, Karl xiv, 50, 55, 101–2, 150
Bible 3–17, 39, 51, 72, 76, 96, 120, 130, 146
Birmingham (Alabama, USA) 158–63
Birmingham (Handsworth, Great Britain) 21
Blasphemy 126, 144
Black
 Britain 21, 39, 61
 Christ 6–9
 Church 6–9, 21, 34, 66, 70–1, 88, 97, 131, 158–61
 Experience 42–3, 59, 67, 77, 90, 92, 130, 155
 Liberation 10, 62, 64, 72–3, 118, 161
 Self-understanding 32–3, 75–6, 85–6, 123, 129–30, 137
 Slaves 58, 59–60, 72–3, 98, 117, 125, 151–3
 Spirituals 8, 10, 57, 70–1, 98
 Suffering 11, 70, 74, 77, 104, 111, 139, 158–60
 Theology 35, 93, 105, 150
 See also African American, Caribbean, Africa
Bleby, Henry 117
Bonhoeffer, Julie 67–8, 75
Bonhoeffer, Karl 26, 66
Bonhoeffer, Karl Friedrich 15
Bonhoeffer, Paula 66

Bonhoeffer, Sabine, *see* Leibholz-Bonhoeffer
Bonhoeffer, Walter 65
Brock, Brian 116, 124–5, 142
Brown 32, 34, 42, 43, 59, 77, 123, 155, 163

Caribbean 18–20, 40, 92, 116–18
Carter, J. Kameron 27–8
Christendom 27, 153
Christology 3–17, 28, 47–8, 83–5, 87–9, 91, 93, 96, 104, 108, 113, 120, 124, 136, 138, 149–50
Civil Rights Movement 10, 157, 158, 161
Clarke, Anthony 162
Clark-Howard A. D. 19–20
Colonialism 20, 22, 25, 28–9, 46, 58, 95, 125, 157, 161
Colwell, John 23, 27, 125
Cone, James H. xv, 32, 66–7, 150, 152–3, 159, 161
Confession
  Of sin 39, 91, 103, 125, 127–31, 135–6
  Of faith 9, 34, 53, 70, 140
Confessing Church 1, 37–9, 112, 120, 159
Conflict 53, 63, 68, 70, 73–4, 77, 85–6, 114, 131
Cor curvum in se 35–6, 41–2, 51, 86–7, 89, 91, 102, 149
Creation 13, 18–31, 34, 36–7, 41, 50, 52, 55, 62, 88, 95ff., 125–6, 129, 134, 142
Creation and Fall 36–7, 95–107
Creatureliness 4, 21–8, 34, 36–7, 62, 64, 72, 98–105, 126, 137–8
Cross 7, 39, 50, 52–3, 55, 57, 62–3, 84–5, 105, 112–13, 129–30, 136, 146, 148, 154, 161–2

Dahill, Lisa E. 148–50
Death 4, 7, 11, 17, 31, 33–4, 41, 50, 52–3, 58, 66, 89, 96, 103, 112, 114, 118–19, 123–4, 126, 144, 147–8, 154, 156
DeCort, Andrew 52, 97
De Gruchy, John W. 42
Disciple 5, 9–10, 22, 34, 39, 47, 49–50, 57, 63, 65, 71, 73–6, 108–16, 118, 120, 124, 127–8, 144, 147, 152–4, 16, 163
Discipleship 34, 38, 49, 73–6, 108–19
Douglas, Kelly Brown xxii, 10, 150–2
Dualism 20, 133–4
Du Bois, W. E. B. 130
Dudzus, Otto 144

Enemy 38, 42, 44, 61, 65, 75–6, 92, 113–16, 125–6, 128–30
Epistemology 20, 24, 28–9, 40, 85, 86–9, 91, 103, 105, 123, 134, 146, 151–2
Ethics 28, 37, 114, 133–44
Europe 19, 40, 46–7, 77–8, 91, 95, 143, 158
Evil 10, 13, 19, 24, 29, 32, 36, 40, 44, 69, 71–2, 76, 94, 100–1, 104–5, 110, 113–16, 127, 129, 134, 136, 139–40, 143, 147, 149, 153, 156, 160

Fabrycky, Laura, M. 14–15
Feil, Ernst 145
Finitude 99, 103, 137, 148, 150, 152
Finkenwalde 112, 120

INDEX

First World War 65, 91, 97
Fisher, Albert Franklin 7–8
Flesh 8, 17, 22, 24, 30, 35, 62, 73–4, 85, 89–91, 104, 115, 148, 160, 162
Floyd, George xii, 32–4, 130
Forgiveness 4, 7, 38–9, 43–4, 111–12, 127–9, 135, 156
Formation 9, 11, 28, 66–7, 76, 88, 115, 119–20, 134
Freedom 5, 24–7, 29, 31, 36–7, 39, 42, 50, 71, 74, 76, 78, 87, 91, 93, 96, 98–105, 117–19, 122–3, 125, 134–5, 138–40, 15, 150, 154, 160, 162

Gardiner, Craig 66
Grace 5–6, 8, 14–17, 24, 35, 38–9, 49, 55, 64–5, 70, 80, 92–3, 97, 100–3, 111, 118, 121, 126, 130, 144, 151, 154
Green, Clifford J. 66, 143
Greggs, Tom 36, 102
Guilt 52, 57, 72, 103–4, 111–13, 115, 124–9, 135–6, 144, 156

Halbach, Ross E. 64
Hall, Delroy 58
Harlem 7, 64, 70, 88, 111
Havea, Jione xvi, xviii,
Hawkins, John 57–8
Haynes, Stephen 11
Hibbert, George 61
Higman, B. W. 117
Higton, Mike 121
Hildebrandt, Franz 42
Hitler, Adolf 26, 28, 42, 68, 96, 109, 112, 124, 143, 145, 154
Holy Spirit 5–6, 10–11, 16, 23, 39, 50, 76, 88, 155
Hudson-Roberts, Wale 155

Incarnation 8–10, 23, 25, 38–9, 50, 57, 62–3, 87, 122, 124, 134, 137

Jennings, Willie James 20–1, 29, 95, 104, 125
Jews 11–13, 28–9, 37–8, 40, 42–3, 49, 53, 59, 73–4, 97, 124, 128, 135, 137, 143, 149, 154, 159
Jinkins, Michael 89, 130
Justice 11, 27, 49, 60, 62–3, 65, 69–72, 90–1, 104, 113, 115, 117, 129–30, 134–6, 140, 150, 153, 155, 160

King, Martin Luther Jr. 10, 114, 158
Kirk-Duggan, Cheryl A. 70–1
Kirkpatrick, Kate 148–9
Kirkpatrick, Matthew 40, 50, 52, 62, 67, 69
Knight, Mark 48, 50
Kristallnacht 13, 159
Krötke, Wolf 5, 124
Kuske, Martin 5
Kyung, Chun Hyun 148

Lasserre, Jean 7
Lawrence, Joel 24, 83, 89, 100, 109, 112
Leadership 93, 117, 121, 130, 159
Lehman, Paul 7
Leibholz-Bonhoeffer, Sabine 37, 43, 66
Leibholz, Gerhard 37, 43
Letters and Papers from Prison 3, 12, 36, 69, 83, 145–56
Levine, Amy-Jill 11
Life Together 120–3, 130–1

Livingstone, David xvii
London 12, 41, 61, 120
Loneliness 66, 132
Lord's supper 39, 47, 92
Love 3, 8, 11–12, 20–1, 25, 32, 34, 38, 40, 48, 50, 54, 56–7, 61–2, 65, 70–2, 78–80, 94–5, 99, 04, 107, 111, 114–16, 121–3, 129, 133, 137, 139–40, 154, 160, 163
Lynching 76

Marsh, Charles 143
Marsh, Jill 152
Mawson, Michael 4, 84, 126
McBride, Jennifer M. 148–9
McLaughlin, Eleanor 68
Muers, Rachel 84, 148

Nationalism 28, 65, 69, 77, 91
National socialism 22, 42, 97, 124, 143
Nation, Mark Thiessen 114
New York 6–7, 14, 68
Niebuhr, Reinhold 67

Obedience 10, 32, 39–40, 49–50, 76, 98, 100–2, 105, 111, 113, 115, 119, 128, 141, 144
Olusoga, David 39, 57, 61, 158
Oppression 8–9, 24, 33, 44, 54, 69, 71, 73, 76, 100, 102, 104, 108, 111, 114, 116–17, 127, 129, 130–1, 147, 148–9, 152, 161, 163

Pangritz, Andreas 26, 143
Pastor 3–4, 18, 67, 92, 120, 130
Peace 13, 30, 44, 79, 112, 114, 126, 136
Pejsa, Jane 111

Penitence 69, 90, 103–4, 111, 128
Penultimate 55, 62–6, 70–6, 113–16, 136, 142, 150
Petts, John 160–2
Picard, Andrew 19–20
Pierce, Yolanda 33
Plant, Stephen 144
Poling, James 116
Polyphony 23, 70–1, 131
Powell, Adam Clayton Sr. 9
Powell, Enoch 158
Power 6, 8–10, 17, 19, 23, 27, 50, 64, 68–9, 72, 74, 76, 89, 94, 97, 101, 104, 106, 113, 119, 127, 130–1, 135, 143–4, 146–7, 149, 151, 154, 159
Prayer 3, 13–15, 23, 34, 49, 53, 57, 74, 92, 113, 115, 121, 123–32, 135, 159, 160
Prayerbook of the Bible 123–32
Preaching 3, 5–9, 12, 31, 39, 64, 67, 76, 93, 117, 151–2, 162
Pribbenow, Brad 124, 129
Providence 72, 104–5
Poems 94, 105–7, 119, 131–2, 144, 156
Prison 3, 5, 12, 33, 36, 60, 68, 83, 105, 109–10, 118, 145, 147–54, 160
Psalms 12, 13, 66, 115, 124–31

Rah, Soong-Chan 69, 111
Rasmussen, Larry L. 134
Ray, Stephen G. 28
Rayson, Dianne 25
Reid-Salmon, Delroy A. 127
Reynolds, Diane 12, 151
Reddie, Anthony G. 27, 32–3, 93, 121
Reformation 14, 35, 55, 135

INDEX

Reparations 54, 64
Repentance 10, 39, 44, 49, 93, 111, 127–8, 143, 157, 170
Responsibility 26, 40, 49, 54, 56, 58, 78, 101, 104, 114, 120, 136, 138–9, 142, 144, 160
Resurrection 50, 52, 63, 89, 91, 96, 126, 136, 154
Revelation 3–5, 11, 16–17, 36, 45, 48, 50–2, 59, 68–9, 86–9, 96–7, 103, 120, 125, 128–9, 133, 135, 140, 142, 146–8, 154, 163
Roberts, J. Deotis 114
Robeson, Paul 161
Rott, Willhelm 6

Salvation 13–14, 34, 36–9, 41–2, 46–59, 73, 94, 121, 125, 142, 151, 156
Sanctorum Communio 56, 83–5, 88
Schliesser, Christine 114
Schlingensiepen, Ferdinand 13, 145
Scripture 3–17, 75, 93, 96–8, 108–9, 142, 145, 159
Sermon on the Mount 3, 75, 108, 110–15
Sharpe, Sam 116–18
Silence 30, 61, 88, 115, 135–7, 149, 152–3, 159
Slavery 10–11, 16, 30–1, 39–41, 49, 51, 53, 57–60
Solidarity 51, 53, 67, 70, 85–6, 143, 161–2
Sonderegger, Katherine 34
State 26, 42, 65, 68, 135, 136, 142–3
Stellvertretung, see vicarious representative action

Stone, Selina 21, 19
Sutz, Erwin 7
Swinton, John 105
Syria 78

Tarassenko, Joanna 70
Temptation 32, 51, 76, 89, 91, 101, 122, 156
Thurman, Howard 75–6
Tietz, Christiane 11, 66, 87, 145, 147
Trauma, *see* oppression
Tripoli 66
Turner, Carlton 18–19
Tuttle, Corey 55–6
Twilight 101, 103

Ukraine 77
Ultimate 5, 8, 10–11, 16, 27, 36, 41, 48, 51, 53, 55, 58, 62, 64–6, 70–6, 87, 89–90, 97, 103, 105, 109–10, 112–16, 125–6, 128–31, 133–4, 136, 140–2, 146, 150, 159

Vicarious representative action 51–2, 57, 115, 127–9, 135–6, 138 144
Von Dohnanyi, Hans 143, 145

Wales 12, 18, 160–2
Wannenwetsch, Bernd 147–8
Webster, John 48
White
  Church 7–9, 47, 97, 111, 116, 121, 125–6, 131, 154, 157
  Defensiveness 42–4, 72, 123, 162
  Ignorance 16, 18–20, 30–1, 66, 69, 71, 85, 95, 134, 146, 152–3, 160

Particularity 21–2, 25, 27, 35, 74, 90–2, 109, 130, 155, 161–2
Religion 34, 41, 47, 49, 59, 61–2, 64, 69, 73, 75–6, 104, 117–18, 124, 147, 151, 158–9
Repentance 59–60, 86, 93, 163
Supremacy 27–8, 29, 32–3, 39–40, 58, 64, 77–9, 121, 139, 159

Wilberforce, William 61
Wilmore, Gayraud S. 47
Williams, Reggie L. 6–9, 28, 66, 114, 122, 134
Wind, Renate 145
Windrush xv
Wink 114
World come of age 145–7

Young, Josiah III 146–7
Youth 10, 64, 91, 158

Ziegler, Philip G. 4–5
Zimmermann, Wolf-Dieter 6
Zoellner, Tom 118

www.ingramcontent.com/pod-product-compliance
Lightning Source LLC
Chambersburg PA
CBHW022056290426
44109CB00014B/1125